ESSAYS ON MODERN SANSKRIT POETRY

ESSAYS ON MODERN SANSKRIT POETRY

Rabindra K. Panda

BKP

BHARATIYA KALA PRAKASHAN

Delhi : : (India)

First Edition : 2009

Published by **C.P. Gautam**
BHARATIYA KALA PRAKASHAN
3421-A, IInd Floor, Narang Colony Tri Nagar,
Delhi-110035. Phone : 27393083, 32967505
E-mail : bkp3421@yahoo.co.in

ISBN : 978-81-8090-215-4

Printed by :
Salasar Imaging Systems
Delhi

Contents

Preface

The present volume contains some of my research papers which were published in the reputed research Journals. They are related to different aspects of Modern Sanskrit literature. The first paper deals with contemporary Sanskrit poetry. In this paper, an attempt has been made to highlight some of the significant aspects of modern Sanskrit poetry literature. Some of the representative poems of contemporary Sanskrit poets who have made valuable contribution to the field of Sanskrit poetry are selected. The paper throws light on how Sanskrit poets of our time have been considerably influenced by regional language and literature. The second paper deals with the new trends that are found in the field Sanskrit poetry of twentieth century.

The third paper describes the nature of some noteworthy epic poems of twentieth century. In the fourth paper attempt has been made to highlight the contribution of Oriya writers to the field of Sanskrit literature. The fifth paper deals with biographical poems in Sanskrit.

The sixth paper is written on modern Sanskrit poets who have written on Russia and Russian leaders. The seventh paper focuses on the figures of speech that are found in the epic poem, Sri Swami Vivekananda-caritam composed by T.A. Bhandarkar. The eighth paper deals with a translated work Bandinah Swedesa Cinta of Pandita Utkal Mani Gopabandhu Dash and the work is translated by Pandita Prabodha Kumar Mishra of Orissa. The ninth paper makes a literary tudy of the *Miralahari* composed by Pandita Ksama Rao. Similarly the tenth paper contains a literary study of the *Vyastaragam* of Digambara Mahapatra. The eleventh paper embodies a critical study of *Sudamacaritm* of Pundarikaksa Mishra of Orissa. The twelfth paper incorporates a study of *Bhinnapulinam* of Professor Kesab Chandra Dash. The thirteenth paper is on Sanskrit translated works. There are two papers in Sanskrit. One deals with politics as depicted by modern Sanskrit poets in their poems. Other introduces some biographical literature.

All the papers are written in simple and easy language keeping in mind the renders of present day. They bring to light new facts for the first time.

I am very much thankful to the editors of the Sanskrit Journals who published those papers and the proprietor of Bharatiya Kala Prakashan, C.P. Gautama who has published them in the book-form

20-2-2009 **Rabindra Kumar Panda**
Baroda

Modern Sanskrit Poetry*

Throughout the ages poetry has been a fascinating field of literary art. As a finest flower in the garden of literature poetry has been attracting the delicate minds of *sahṛdayas.* Poetry is an art of beauty and it gives pleasure of higher kind. Sanskrit has not only the rare distinction of possessing the oldest poetic work of the world in the form of the *Ṛgveda* but also the rare distinction of uninterrupted and continued tradition of poetry for the last five thousand years. The field of poetry is mostly rich and substantial in comparison with other areas of creation in Sanskrit literature. Keeping the tune of time in view the poets of our time have taken some initiative in composing poems in modern style with modern technique under the influence of English and regional literature. Some poets have welcomed change with the confidence—*purāṇamityeva na sādhu sarvam,* as said by the poet Kālidāsa and some with the belief that *purāṇamityeva ca sādhu sarvam* closely following the immortal heritage of Poetics. At present we observe both traditional as well as modern trends of composing Sanskrit poetry. The dictum—old is gold—also holds the hearts of *kāvyarasikas.* Some have also welcomed modernity to bring out new freshness and beauty in the field of poetry.

In this paper I have attempted to highlight some significant aspects of Sanskrit poetry literature. I have therefore selected some of the representative *Kāvya* works of contemporary Sanskrit poets who have made some

---

* Vishveshvaranand Indological Journal, Vols. XXXIII-XXXIV, pts i-iv, Junes-Dec., 1995-1996.

significant contribution to the overflowing field of Sanskrit poetry. The paper will throw some light on how Sanskrit poets of our time have been considerably influenced by regional language and literature. The poets who have made monumental contribution in composing traditional poetry in Sanskrit are Satyavart Sastri, Rajendra Mishra, Radhavallabha Tripathi, Ogeti Parikshita Sharma and others.

Now, we shall discuss about the new trends in the modern Sanskrit literature. I do not know exactly who founded the concept of the modern Sanskrit poem. But they who came forward to create something new in the field of poetry, had visualized in time that the west was making an inevitable impact and that the ways of thinking and modes of expression had to undergo a change. Poems created by modern poets may be called new poems, because they differ from the traditional classical ones. Classical Sanskrit poetry is written in classical Sanskrit, with strict rules and forms, while new poems of modern age are written in living language used in our daily life without strict rules and forms prescribed by poetics. They maybe called free poems. This new style of poems is a product of 20th century and of the Sanskritists who are interested in making Sanskrit popular among the common masses. In its history of more than a hundred years since its conception, the new poems have become the main trend of Sanskrit poetry in 20th century with its strong vitality, liberal spirit and the flesh and blood ties with the practical life.

At present, an open and rich set up has emerged in poetic circles in India. Free poem representing and reflecting reality is the mainstream. A glance at the works shows that there is no lack of men and women poets in India in this century and their outlook is changed, their experience is enriched and they take note of the modern materialistic trends and technological advances. The major themes of modern Sanskrit poetry are love, struggle etc. If modern Sanskrit poetry has acquired a new dimension and sophistication, in terms of vision, technical integrity, and innovative use of the creative medium, it was because of modern poets' contribution. An unusual blending of the sense of beauty and the sense of joy in living and loving makes modern poetry extremely readable and accessible. The passion for the diverse facts of life and existence makes their poetry rhythm that they try to capture in their poetry is very close to the colloquial speech.

Sandhis are not now necessarily adhered to even in poems. Metres used encompass a wider field. Expression is more graphic, more emotional, not merely traditional. Variety of subjects chosen by the poets for their compositions is amazing. Modern Sanskrit poetry is obviously not fettered by any limitations in this respect. It is noticed that the style greatly varies from poet to poet. Some write simple Sanskrit, others ornate. One tries to communicate, and the other exhibits.

Devotional compositions are an old tradition of any poetry Sanskrit or otherwise. This trend dates from Ṛgvedic period, the oldest available literature in the world. Even in the modern technological age, the urge for devotion and its poetic expression continues unabated. There are attempts in them at stylistic graces but devotion is the main theme. Various easy metres as musical modes are adopted.

There are hundreds of poems written on Sanskrit language. Homage to this ancient language is paid even today in poetic form. Some talk of our national flag; some on Himālaya as the standard, some describe the national movement of *Satyāgraha;* some mourn the present conditions in post-independence days and some enumerate great things of our country including Sanskrit language. In Sanskrit we have poets who are representatives of different regions. There is the theme of separation, the messages through non-humans, the beauty of the land, the eagerness for union, etc.

There is no doubt about the fact that modernity has entered to the field of Sanskrit creative literature. It pervades all the parts of its limbs. Modernity finds expression in language, style, forms, in constructing new images, modes, and its compositions in the art of poetry. Modernity is not confined to any one aspect. We must understand the fact that modernity does not mean a particular phase of time or a particular element which exists in creations of our time, but not in the works of our ancient poets. Modernity is above all a relative term, Whatever is known today as traditional that was also modern at some point of time. And now what is known as modern will turn into tradition after some time. It is interesting to say that in the field of Sanskrit literature tradition and modernity go hand in hand. Both are complementary to each other. Both are related and relatively help to enrich the present day literature of Sanskrit language. As the overflowing stream of traditional poetry is continuing similarly the poetry of modern period.

The significant features of modern Sanskrit poetry are :

1. Metreless compositions
2. Adaptation of regional metres
3. Simple Sanskrit
4. Direct expression of realism
5. New style
6. Small size of poem
7. Use of *citrakalpa* and *rūpakalpa*
8. Use of English and regional words
9. Different forms of expressions.

The use of myths of east and west, use of symbols and images, allusive style and global references, new forms, expression of romanticism, surrealism, symbolism, dadaism and realization of deep sensitivity are the main features of contemporary Sanskrit poetry.

In the field of contemporary Sanskrit Professor Keshav Chandra Dash of Orissa is a major figure. Six collections of poems have come so far from his facile pen. His poem collections are : *Praṇayapradīpam, Hṛdayeśvarī, Mahātīrtham, Bhinnapulinam, Alakā* and *Īśā*. Dr. Dash feels happy to compose his poems in metreless style. He displays his great skill in the use of myths and symbols suggesting something hidden and deep. His expression is of special significance. He is a true representative of modernity. He is an expert builder in shaping emotions and construing towers of images and interesting pictures of meaning. Dr. Dash expresses his feelings in simple Sanskrit but his expressions are framed in such a manner that most of his poems are not easily comprehensible. They lead to diverse shades of meanings. Metaphors are frequently found in his compositions which enhance the inner beauty of his poems. Most of his poems are psychological; some are social mainly on love with its two aspects union and separation.

Harshdev Madhav of Gujarat has introduced some new forms such as *Haiku, Tanka, Sijo* and *Mono* image poems. He has depicted various *Mono* images. It is a novel attempt at introducing modern forms of poetry in Sanskrit literature. He has already published fourteen collections of poems.

Professor Rajendra's *Marīcikā,* is a collection of forty-two Sanskrit poems. The avoidance of metres, use of new style, new image, symbols, new subjects, myths, etc. are the distinctive features of his creation. In everchanging relations of love the poet suggests the unsteadiness of reverse love (*viparītarati*). The controversy in *sambhogaśṛṅgāra* brings modernity in the contemporary Sanskrit poetry. The thirst of love, loneliness of a lover, the deep disappointment of a departed heart, the destruction of dreams are expressed with the meaningful images, symbols, and myths. The poet has not given title to the poems.

Dr. Banamali Biswal, has made some important

contributions. He has published six collections of poems. *Saṅgamenābhirāmā* comprising 35 poems is covered by 300 verses. Dr. Biswal depicts the pictures of the contemporary society and surroundings and his observation is very minute in this direction. In almost all of his poems, the contemporary social problems like terrorism in Punjab and Kashmir, the impact of gas tragedy in Bhopal, the communal riots in Ayodhya, the bureaucracy in offices, the generation gap in joint families, superstitions in the day-today life and the fatal diseases like AIDS etc. are well-depicted. Moreover, Dr. Biswal has tremendous faith towards Indian History and culture in general and Orissan in particular and he is very much loyal in handling such sensitive issues. He has attempted to provide the reader an up-to-date research along with unique taste of good poems. He has provided some new facts about Orissan temples and deities in his collection *Saṅgamenābhirāmā*. The chief characteristic of poems is that the *ramaṇīyatā* is thoroughly experienced throughout the book. The poems possess new expressions from top to bottom. The poems are full of manifold sentiments, presented in a simple and lucid manner. Most of the poems are expressed in *Prasāda-guṇa*, the *bimbas* (imageries) found in this collection are innovative and unbiased. The satire and the situations available in this collection are touchy and unique.

The poems of Dr. Biswal in his second collection of poems *Vyathā* are very fine examples of the sensitivity of a modern young Indian who is firmly anchored in his age-old tradition on the one hand; and on the other, feels deeply disenchanted with the present set up of the society and the human world around. The themes of the poems of Dr. Biswal are surprisingly new, his approach to the problems of life is wonderfully fresh, his treatment of the subject is entirely novel and the metrical outfit of the blank verses in which his poetry is couched-which provides higher freedom of expression to the poet and ensures not only facility of expression but also of comprehension is also an outcome of modern times.

In Gujarat some Sanskrit poets have tried to compose *Garvā*-songs in the line of the songs composed in Gujrati language. They are interesting. This is, no doubt, a good step in popularizing Sanskrit among masses. The anthology *Saṁskṛtamaṇḍalagānāni* edited by Parekh Kanchanlal Hiralal, Saṁskruta Vidvatsabha, Vadodara, 1983 includes the *Garvā*-songs of Paṇḍit Pancanan Badrinath Shastri, Vidya Bhaskar Manisankar Upadhyay, Laksmisankar Sukla, Jaynarayan Pathak, Arunoday Jani and Pradyumna Sukla. V.C. Patel has written *Haikuśatakam*, some of which have appeared in the *Saṁvid* published by Bharatiya Vidyabhawan, Bombay. Ghanasyam Trivedi has published *Nūtanagītāñjali* which contains the translation of Gujarati folk-songs, *garvās* and poems in their original forms and rhythm. His two collections of poetry *Nūtanabhaktirasāyanam* and *Nūtanakāvyaspandanam* are awaiting publication. Trivedi's contribution is really remarkable.

When we talk of *Dalit* trend in literature, it is in the context of modern Indian literature. The term *Dalit* acquired respectability after establishing itself as a major trend in modern Marathi literature. Since then, this trend is trying to acquire pan-Indian character, by finding place in the rest of the Indian languages. Yet, after Marathi, it is only in Gujarati, Kannada, Telugu, Hindi and Punjabi it has created a niche for itself.

In modern Sanskrit poetry, *Dalit* trend is visible. Generally Sanskrit poets do not come from *Dalit* background, and so they do not make *Dalit* life as a centre of their creation. In fact some Sanskrit poets are more sensitive to the sufferings of *Dalit*. Some of the poets are focusing more on *Dalit* sufferings in their poems. The existence of *Dalits* in all the parts of India as a downtrodden section of the society, is a natural ground for the emergence of a *Dalit* trend in modern Sanskrit Poetry. Contemporary Sanskrit poetry is not limited to the boundary of our traditional rhetoric. It has been given a new life and a new freshness. Under the new structural framework modern poetry is seeing the new light of the day.

It is small but beautiful, it is simple but attractive. It is without ornaments but arrests the hearts of connoisseurs because its soul is suggestion. It is a flow, so metre cannot bind it. It is a blow, tradition cannot capture it. It has excellent beauty but waiting for connoisseurs to come, to touch and to appreciate.

At present *Gītas* or lyrical poems have developed to a great extent. The poets of our time under the influence of regional literature have tried to create different types of lyrics using traditional as well as modern metres. They can be sung very easily. One has to appreciate their musical value. Since all those songs are composed in simple Sanskrit, they are easily understood and their beauty is heartily enjoyed. Modernity lies in them in their simplicity. They in fact help in popularizing Sanskrit language and making it a living language. Rajendra Mishra, Srinivasa Ratha, Ramakanta Sukla are some of the vateran poets who have experimented with this trend and created a substantial amount of lyrical literature in Sanskrit. An example is given.

मूलं छित्वा पत्रं सिक्त्वा, पुष्पं फलं कथं कामयसे।
आमलकं हस्तस्थमवाप्तुं परितो दृशं कथं भ्रामयसे।।

दृढ़ पिधाय गवाक्षान् सर्वान्
वाञ्छसि किं किरणान् विवस्वतः।
हृदयपुण्डरीकस्य सौरभं
हित्वा धावसि कथमितस्ततः।।

भ्रमर! भ्रान्तो भ्रमसि मुधा किं विपिने परितोषं न किमयसे।
मूलं छित्वा...।। P. 3

Bibliography

Biswal, Banamali, *Vyathā*, Padmaja Prakashnam, Allahabad, 1997.

Biswal, Banamali, *Saṅgamenābhirāmām*, Published by Srimati Padmvati Biswal, Padmaja Prakashanam, Allahabad, 1996.

Dash, Keshav Chandra, *Bhinnapulinam*, Published by Srimati Subhadra Dash, Puri, Orissa, 1995.

Dash, Keshav Chandra, *Alakā*, Lokbhasa Pracara Samiti, Puri, Orissa.

Dikshit, Hari Narayan, *Desho'yam Kurute Pronnatim*, Eastern Book Linkers, Delhi, 1992.

Nanavati, Rajendra, *Marīcikā*, published by the poet, Baroda, 1993.

Sharma, Hari Dutta, *Balagitāli*, Anjaneya Prakashan, Allahabad, 1991

Pandeya, Kapiladeva, *kāvyaprapanikā*, Minakṣi Prakashan, Varanasi, 2003

New Trends in Sanskrit Poetry of Twentieth Century

The twentieth century is an important period in the history of modern Sanskrit literature. It was the period when the great minds were busy with the innovative ideas for bringing out changes and revolutions to establish the humanism in a form required for the country. It was also a time of peace and freedom. Man was completely free from the slavery. The century has accepted many new challenges and has also accommodated a fresh air of revivalism as well as modernism. The creative literature of this century is especially remarkable for its variety and richness of forms. The rich and varied growth of Sanskrit literature of this period discloses some new trends, which are mainly responsible for the growth and development of modern Sanskrit literature. One can easily see the difference between the classical and modern literature of Sanskrit. The new and powerful trends in fact distinguish the modern Sanskrit from the classical one.

It is true that all those trends about which I am going to discuss, have not a beginning in the twentieth century. But, in this important period of history some persons came to this field and they started thinking freely in the context of time and need. It is because of them, the Sanskrit literature of twentieth century grew to a great extent and got a new form. The powerful trends significantly helped in its varied growth and satisfactory development. From a simple survey, what I instantly observe is that in this century Sanskrit poets have kept themselves in close touch with contemporary events and utilised freely the fresh material with which they come in contact. The creative activity in Sanskrit had also received a fresh impetus. New trends in the field of Sanskrit poetry came into being. Because of these trends Sanskrit language and its literature took a fresh breath. A good number of varieties, new forms, the new modes of expression etc., crept into the field of modern Sanskrit. Most important of all these is that a true picture of modernism is seen in the poetry literature of this century. The conducive literary atmosphere, new enthusiasm of Sanskrit creative artists, a strong impact of pan Indian literature, fall of Sanskrit traditional norms and indifference towards traditional pattern of writtings made the modern poets moved in search of creating something new in Sanskrit so that this literature will not be an easy victim of criticism.

There is no doubt that an analysis of these trends will open up new vistas in the field of Sanskrit creative literature.

The present paper makes an analysis of the new trends, which were dominating, in the field of Sanskrit creative literature of twentieth century. The trends that are immediately come to our notice are of simplification, Naturalness, free flow of feelings, creation of new forms, adoption of regional forms, Symbolism, Lyricism etc. Some of the noted poets who have made significant contribution in developing these trends in modern literature of Sanskrit only find a place in the present paper.

Broadly speaking, we come across two trends—traditional and modern in the field of Sanskrit literature. Both the trends are pertaining to external and internal structures of poetry. It is interesting to say that unlike other provincial literature, Sanskrit literature has maintained its unique feature, that is, the traditional trends such as composing of *Mahākāvyas, Khaṇḍakāvyas, stotras* etc. are also continuing along with the new and emerging trends.

First of all, some of the powerful poets tried to make

Sanskrit poetry free from existing formulae. It is due to their realisation that *Rītirātmā Kāvyasya* which was advocated by Vāmana in sixth century A.D. The poets who could have written very good poems in metres rejected it and started composing in free style. In place of verses bounded in feet with strong chain poems were composed in free style. They are known as blank verses. The style was convenient in expressing freely what the poet wants to express in an unsophisticated garb. Though it was due to the influence of western literature and our provincial literature still the Sanskrit poets did not follow it blindly. A poet who understands his role and responsibility in the context of time can clearly see the logic of it though its critics are many. Another reason which is responsible for this kind of change in Sanskrit is that poetry was accepted not to be a source of enjoyment of the so called *sahṛdayas* like the kings, zamindars and therefore the attention for creating *rasa* was shifted to *dhvani*, suggestion which was accepted as the soul of poetry by the great critic Ānandavardhana.

Truly speaking, a casual survey of the poetry-literature of this century makes us aware of the fact that the poets who were trying to create something new and were serious for contributing significantly to the field of modern Sanskrit literature are few. Many of them are just versifiers. Many of them did not understand what a poetry is and they just follow the form like *andhenaiva niyamānā yathāndhāḥ*. Some came under the pressure of tradition and some were very crazy to bring modernism. Some were not ready even to reject the path of tradition and accept modernism wholeheartedly. But anyhow it was strongly felt that literature should not be only for classes; it should now go to masses. It should not be only a source of entertainment of *rasikas* and that too for few erudite Sanskrit Paṇḍits who are though well-trained traditionally lack modern sense of appreciation and not free from the clutches of narrowness and short-sightedness. It was also felt that Sanskrit literary tradition is falling in one hand and the language is attracting only few readers. Keeping in view an average standard of the readers who are mainly the students, the simplification both in structure and style is necessary. So poetry should be free from obscurity and jargon. The great poets like Satyavrat Shastri, Rasik Vihari Joshi, Ogeti Pariksita Sharma. Abhiraja Rajendra Mishra, Radhavallbha Tripathi, tried to follow the existing literary tradition but gave vent to a trend of simple poetry. What I mean by saying simple poetry is the poetry which is written in simple language but completely devoid of *kliṣṭatā* of various kinds such as use of obscure words, obscure expression, use of śleṣa, atiśayokti *alaṁkāras,* use of outdated symbols, irrelevant images, long compounds, indirect way of describing the objects etc.

It was felt that poetry is not just for pleasure and intellectual amusement. Just like armchair philosophy the armchair poetry is of no use. Poetry can be used as a tool for the development of society and individuality. This called for realism in place of idealism, humanism in place of demonism, truth in place of extravagant imaginations, simple narration of facts in place of exaggerations. The poet was more concerned for social, political and cultural realities.

As a part of this simplification process that old ornamental style is sidelined and also with it many a figures of speech lost their importance forever. It is very much realised that the simplicity is the true beauty of poetry and difficulty is like a demon who devours the beauty of our entire Sanskrit literary tradition. It is well-known that we had in past some intellectual giants who had tried to establish a trend of creating difficult poetry in Sanskrit (*Kliṣṭakāvyaparamparā*). For example, the *Bhaṭṭikāvyam, Subhadrāharaṇa, Rāghavapāṇḍavīya, Rāghavanaiṣadhīya, Kaṅkaṇavandha-Rāmāyaṇa,* etc., which were mainly composed to show off scholarship. As a result they are forgotten forever. The result was the serious failure of these poets. They no doubt spoiled their creative genius and did not receive any appreciation from the people in spite of having a great potentiality within themselves. So the modern Sanskritist tried to create *subodhyakavitā* in place of *durbodhyakavitā.*

The poet of twentieth century was practical and he had some genuine concern for society. He therefore tried to use his creative literature as a mirror of society so that he can express his reactions freely against all odds that are standing on the way of its progress. The free style and process of simplification helped in the free expression. Many Sanskrit poems were composed keeping in view the social odds and dirties. We may call them Social poems. The poets like Vagisa Shastri, Prasasyamitra Shastri are the leading poets of this trend.

It is true that in philosophical books disinterested action is all right, but in practical life everybody follows the rule- *Prayojanamanuddiśya na mandopi pravarttate.* The great Ācārya Mammaṭa lays stress on *prayojana* of poetry because unless a man knows what he is going to get he would not proceed to do it. It is rightly said by an unknown thinker also :

Sarvasyaiva hi śāstrasya karmoṇo vāpi kasyacit/
Yāvat prayojanam noktam tāvat tat kena gṛhyate//

The principle of the Bhagavadgītā- *karmaṇyevādhikāraste ma phaleṣu kadācana-* is not applicable to poets for the reason that *apāre kāvyasaṁsāre kavireva prajāpatiḥ yathāsmai rocate viśvam tathā tat parivarttate/* Mammaṭa speaks about six purposes of poetry. Some are for readers and some are for poets. Poetry brings glory; fetches wealth; gives practical knowledge, wards off mishaps, gives instantaneous joy to the readers and imparts advice in a sweet way of a beloved wife. In the context of Sanskrit language all the *prayojanas* seem to be useless. One can easily understand what kind of reputation a poet receives out of composing poetry in Sanskrit. How much wealth a poet receives out of composing poetry, what kind of practical knowledge our poetry gives to people, one wonders how can it wards off mishaps in the age we live in, what kind of instantaneous joy it gives to us, and how does it give advice in a sweet way like a beloved. Time has changed and with it the perceptions of people. So the old ideas however marvellous they seem are now useless. The problem for a modern poet is to save the language from death, decay and decline and to propagate Sanskrit culture in such a form that it will go to public. That is why many poets have composed poetry on the themes related to Sanskrit language, Sanskrit culture and literary heritage. I would like to call them cultural poetry. Instead of describing the mythological episodes like Kumbhakarṇavadha. Meghanādavadha, Subhadrāharaṇa, it is better to highlight the important aspects of our Indian culture and heritage. This will help Sanskrit growing and its poetry would deserve appreciation. So the trend of cultural poetry started. After independence the Sanskrit poets have felt the importance of our motherland and of its heroes who happily sacrificed their lives for the protection of its glory and gave blood for its freedom.

Another dominating trend in the modern poetry literature of twentieth century is of naturalness. Unlike the poets of our classical Sanskrit literature, for instance, Māgha, Śriharṣa, Bāṇabhaṭṭa, *et al.* the modern poets were fond of naturalness. They are not climbing the peaks of artificiality. In Classical Sanskrit there are many *Mahākāvyas, Khaṇḍakāvyas, Śatakas, Muktakas* etc. which contain far reaching imagination, artificial description, unnecessary use of metaphors, fancies and hyperbols, illogical blend of mythological allusions, superfluous symmetry of contexts, and irrelevant word games. Especially the poetry literature, which is known as *citrakāvya* and rightly designed as *adhamakāvyas* by Mammaṭa are of this type. In the *citrakāvya* one can enjoy the pleasure of making some childish exercise. If the exercise is not so painstaking it results ultimately in nothing. If a piece of poetry lacks *ramaṇīyatā* which is accepted to be its soul, then who will come to enjoy and appreciate it. That is the reason why we have little of *citrakāvya* in this century. Instead we have plenty of poetry that is embeded with the quality fo naturalness.

Modern Sanskrit poetry has a special flavour for the reason that it gives vent to free flow of feelings. Nowadays poetry is not only a means of enjoyment. It is used as a means of criticism, a mode of satire, an instrument of expresssing reactions as a social mirror. A poet is a true observer of our social, political and religious gymnastics and is a true seeker of reality and also an active participant of social processes. He has to make his voice reach to larger sections of society with the expectations that it will bring some significant fruit to society. He should have a concern for the society. He attacks and reacts strongly whenever he finds something wrong and something that is against the dignity and disturbance of our society.

In the field of twentieth century literature we have an appreciable trend of lyrical poetry. Though this trend has a beginning from the great poet Śaṅkarācārya, Jayadeva *et. al*, the modern poets have joined their hands with them and this trend perhaps is dominating almost all the trends which are now current in the field of modern Sanskrit literature. The poets have immensely contributed to this tradition and trend. They have composed poems in the tune of movie-songs, in new *rāgas*, in the *rāgas* which are mainly prevalent in Hindi and other regional languages. The poets of Gujarat have made significant contribution to this trend. They have composed *garbā* songs known as *Maṇḍalagānam* in Sanskrit, gītas, *Dhivaragītas*, and many others which are attractive even for the people. The poets like Rajendra Mishra, Ramakanta Shukla, Srinivasa Ratha, Vaikuntha Vihari Nanda, Mulasankara Yagnika, Badrinatha Shastri, Iccharam Dwivedi 'Pranava', Bhaskarachary Tripathi, Om Prakash Thakur, to name few, have excellent poems as the forerunners of this trend in the century.

Another trend which had just made its mark in modern

poetry literature is the adoption of new forms of poetry namely Haiku, Tanka, Sujo, Dohā, Garbā, Caupāhi, Saya, Sonnets, Mono-image poems. The credit of starting such a new trend in Sanskrit goes to a seminal poet Harshadeva Madhava of Gujarat and others who have experimented with these varities and forms. As a result, the tradition of Sanskrit poet was free from its traditional bond and limitations. Poetry got new freshness with this new perspective.

Another noteworthy trend is observed in the modern literature of twentieth century. That is the minor poems got a new life because of the impact of westerners as well as pan Indian literature. We know that Classical Sankrit has the tradition of composing *Muktakas, Śatakas, Dūtakāvyas, Laharīkāvyas,* but after the model of the western minor poems, which deal with specific ideas and subjects within the compass of a limited number of verses, the modern Sanskrit writer produced a volume of poetry, which is the most common form in which Sanskrit poets are today expressing themselves. In the last century many poets have published their collections of minor poems. I give here the titles of some of the best collections of the century. The *Suṣamā* of Prof. G.C. Jhala is a short collection which includes satires, elegies and descriptive verses. The *puspahāsa* and *Kāvyakusumāñjali* etc. are the important works.

It is interesting to note that the general scholastic atmosphere has also given rise to the trend of personal poems. It is observed that many poets of this century have given expression to their personal sorrows, sufferings, frustrations, problems and reactions. They have tried to convey the readers the *atyācāra* through their poems. But it is interesting to note that all those poets have sung the story of their pains as the representatives of a class of people who always suffer but they do not raise their voice because of fear. We may call them Reactory poems (*Pratikriyātmaka kavitā*). I think, this tradition has a beginning from the great poet Bhartṛhari who has composed many a reactory poems which go by the name of *anyoktis*. Jagannatha Paṇḍita has greatly enriched this tradition. But a serious reader will not miss the significant difference between old and new. Not finding new to write upon and being fed up with old and rotten themes, the poets went ahead with this trend.

Again, satire and light verses are also a line of writing, which has received fresh impetus in the Sanskrit literature of twentieth century. While modern writers have held the traditional type of ridicule, the latter has also returned the compliments, several modern fashions and foibles have come in handy for the latter. The wide varieties of views and quarrels and bickering of diverse parties and leaders have also supplied material for skits and satires. This is a class of writing in which one can see a lively employment of Sanskrit. A few modern poets have used the form *Meghasandeśa* for writing humorous poems. Example of such parody is *Kākadūta* of C.R. Saharsrabuddhe, the *Kākadūta* of C.R. Rajagopala Iyenger, a message sent by a thief in jail and *Śunakadūta* by K.V. Krishnamurti Shastri in which again a thief clapped in jail pleades with a dog as a messenger to his beloved.

The poet of twentieth century has given rise to the trend of symbolism (*Pratīkavāda*). Modern poets have used new symbols, new images, old myths in new contexts so that poetry become reflective instead of descriptive. In Classical poetry the great poets like Bhartṛhari, Jagannatha Paṇḍita, Nīlakaṇṭha Dīkṣita *et. al.* all have created more reflective poetry. The poets like Jagannatha Pathak, Ramkaran Sharma, Rajendra Miśra, Harsadeva Madhava, Kesab Chandra Dash, Rabindra Kumar Panda, Banamali Biswal are the prominent figures who have mainly composed symbolic poetry. They have followed the principle of *vakrokti* mainly advocated by Kuntaka, the author of *Vakroktijīvita*.

Another trend raised its head is of *hāsyakavita*. Many

poets composed parodies, light verses with the only objective that poetry should give instant laughter and make the reader relaxed. Prasasya Mitra Shastri is well-known for this trend.

Another trend which has received much appreciation is of composing poems about the contemporary themes. It creates scope for using fress material and bring newness in literature. Many poets come to our notice who subject their poems to the recent incidents which have relevance and significance. The poets like Haris Candra Renapurkar, Rabindra Kumar Panda, Banamali Biswal *et. al.* have enriched this trend and achieved satisfactory success.

The scope of the paper does not allow me to go into details of minor trends. I focussed only on the major ones for bringing an awareness. *Pratīkavāda, Chāyāvāda, Saralavāda, Muktivāda, Vakroktivāda,* are the major trends of the century.

Some Noteworthy Sanskrit Mahākāvyas of Twentieth Century (1970-2000 A.D.)*

Introduction

The creative genius in Sanskrit has always shown a predilection for the poetic form or *padyarūpa* of *kāvya*. Most of our Sanskrit poets prefer to compose poetry instead of prose though *gadyaṁ kavīnāṁ nikaṣaṁ vadanti* is accepted as a dictum. I understand that the *padya* form of composition has special attractive force for, it contains marvelous beauty, the metrical unity and the rhythmic style, all of which combindly create an inexpressible sense of sweetness loaded with sublime aesthetic rapture. That is why poetry has emerged as one of the best areas of Sanskrit creative literature. The *padya* form has attracted many great minds of past and is also attracting the outstanding poets of present time. In the past, the poetic form has fascinated the scientists, philosophers, religious writers and the general Sanskritists who have preferred to compose the scientific and philosophical treatises like *Carakasaṁhitā, Bṛhatsaṁhitā, Laghujātaka, Kārikāvali, Pramāṇasamuccaya*, etc., to name a few, in the *padya* form. It is well-known that the tradition of poetry begins from the Vedas. The *Ṛgveda*, the first documented literature of human civilization, is written in the poetic form. The *ādikavi* Vālmīki has chosen to compose his *Rāmāyaṇa* in

*. **Journal of The Oriental Institute,** Vol. LII, Nos. 1-2, September-December, 2002 pp.85-111.

this form. Similarly Vedavyāsa, the person of encyclopaedic knowledge, gave us the *Mahābhārata* and the *Purāṇas* in the form of *padya*. It evinces that our creative writers have given importance to poetry and to the poetic form. Being overwhelmed with this, perhaps the great poet Bhartṛhari confidently declares — *sukavitā yadyasti rājyena kim* (what is there more in a kingdom if there is good poetry).

The experiments of Sanskrit poets gave rise to various forms of poetry such as *muktaka, śataka, khaṇḍakāvya* and *mahākāvya*. It is beyond doubt that this poetic culture of past is exerting its profound influence on the minds of the modern poets. After the lapse of several centuries and many significant technological changes, the profound impact of that ingenious culture is paving the way for new horizons. This beautiful form of literature has injected energy and instilled inspiration not only to the poets of Vedic period but even to the great poets like Ratnākara of classical time, who succeeded in composing a magnanimous epic titled *Haravijaya* consisting of fifty cantos in Sanskrit in a very erudite style. Similarly, in the modern period of Sanskrit we have great stalwarts like S.B. Warnekar, the author of the *mahākāvya-Śivarājyodayam* in 68 cantos based on the life of Chatrapati Śivāji and Ogeti Pariksit Sarma, the renowned author of the *mahākāvya, Pratāparāṇāyanam*[1] of 80 cantos based on the life of Rana Pratapa. Therefore, a critic has sufficient reason to be delighted with the fact that the area of Sanskrit poetry has grown to a great extent. Day by day it is also enriched by the marvelous contributions of the visionary writers of modern period rightly deserved to be called the *mahākavis*.

The *Mahākāvyas* (long poems) written in Sanskrit are in fact invaluable gems of Sanskrit literature. They are the best

---

1. Panda, R. K., 'Contemporary Sanskrit Poetry', *Vishveshvaranand Indological Journal*, Hoshiarpur, Vol. XXXIII-XXXIV, Pts. i - iv, June-Dec., 1995-1996, pp. 242-243.

creations of the master — poets who have struggled hard to maintain the glorious literary tradition of India. It is perhaps only in Sanskrit that the tradition of composing *mahākāvya* is continuing till today. But, a cursory look at the huge amount of literature that has been produced so far, gives us the impression that all these *mahākavis* like the old veterans are potent enough in creating the marvelous epics that are no way inferior to the ancient ones. Sanskrit, the language of Indian culture, that has been nurtured by the great visionaries in the land of sages throughout, has maintained its identity even after the fullest development of the regional languages and literature. The Sanskrit poets have tried their best to preserve their sublime thoughts for posterity by putting them in this language in the form of *mahākāvyas.* The Sanskrit writers still continue to produce excellent literature even now.

Moreover, the substantial growth both qualitative and quantitative of *mahākāvyas* (long poems or epic poems) has widened the scope of study and research in Sanskrit. The study of the Sanskrit *mahākāvyas* of modern period is an interesting exercise to understand the human values preached by the poets through their *kāvyas.* The poets of modern period do not maintain the tradition for the sake of tradition. They do feel the literary value of this type of long composition which gives enough scope for displaying one's creative genius and bringing together many interesting things. They have been striving hard to preserve the language which is perishing day by day by making continuous efforts in composing literature in various forms.

They are trying to disseminate the historical truths and to spread the sublime aspects of Indian culture among the students and scholars. They are also endeavouring to set the models of Great Indian heroes by way of presenting their heroic deeds in sweet, sympathetic and convincing manner. All these works reflect social consciousness and are not moving only in the boundary of aesthetic pleasure which has been accepted to be the soul of poetry. Since the poets are mainly contributing to preservation, growth and development of language, culture, and treasure-house of knowledge, it becomes our duty to read their works, to understand their importance and to introduce them to the scholars of Sanskrit. Through this paper I am trying to focus upon some of the noteworthy *mahākāvyas* that are composed during 1976-2000 A.D.

One has to admit the fact that the composition of a *mahākāvya* in Sanskrit is a very arduous task. It requires great mastery over Sanskrit language, profound knowledge of different *śāstras*, erudition in methodology of composition, impenetrable labour and above all poetic potency called *śakti* in the language of Mammaṭa. Therefore, only a few of the aspirants succeed in composing *mahākāvyas* which bring for them eternal reputation and universal recognition.

Before proceeding to introduce the selected *mahākāvyas* of twentieth century, it is necessary to give a definition of the *mahākāvya* for ready reference. Though several works on classical Sanskrit poetics have given some gross definitions focusing the general characteristics of a *mahākāvya*, Viśvanātha's definition given in the *Sāhityadarpaṇa* is accepted to be a standard one and that is given here for the convenience of the readers.

Definition of *Mahākāvya*

A great poem should have a number of cantos (*sargabandha*). The hero should be a deity, or a warrior of a noble family characterized by firmness and generosity of heart or a number of kings belonging to the noble family. Of the Erotic, Heroic, and the Quietist (*Śṛṅgāra, Vīra* and *Śānta*) sentiments, any one should be the principal in it, all others being ancillary thereto. The *mahākāvya* should contain all the dramatic junctures (*sandhis*). The story, pertaining to some virtuous character or characters, must be derived from historical source like the *Mahābhārata* or the *Rāmāyaṇa*. It should have the final objects to be obtained by the hero like all the four *puruṣārthas*, namely, *dharma, artha, kāma* and *mokṣa*, or it should have only one of them. It should begin with a salutation to a deity or a benediction or simply with the mention of a matter leading to the main story of the poem. Sometimes it should begin with a reproach of the malicious or the like, or a eulogy of the God. It should consist of cantos, more than eight in number, neither too short nor too long, each canto comprising of stanzas composed in some particular metre, but ending in those of a different one. A canto may be composed in a variety of metres. At the end of each canto there should be a hint of the subject of the succeeding canto. There should be descriptions of the sun, the moon, day, night, morning, evening, noon, twilight, darkness, ocean, mountain; woods, hunting, the seasons, the enjoyment and separation of lovers, saints, heaven, city, sacrifice, military march, council, marriage, birth of a son etc. These are to be described in a *mahākāvya*, according to the occasion, together with their attendants, incidents and circumstances. The *mahākāvya* is to be named after the poet, the story, the hero or the like, while the designation of a canto is to be made after the principal matter contained therein.[1]

The above given definition gives us the idea that it is not

---

1. सर्गबन्धो महाकाव्यं तत्रैको नायकः सुरः।
सद्वंशः क्षत्रियो वापि धीरोदात्तगुणान्वितः।।
एकवंशभवा भूपाः कुलजा बहवोऽपि वा।
शृङ्गारवीरशान्तानामेकोऽङ्गी रस इष्यते।।
अङ्गानि सर्वेऽपि रसाः सर्वे नाटकसन्धयः।
इतिहासोद्भवं वृत्तमन्यद् वा सज्जनाश्रयम्।।
चत्वारस्तस्य वर्गाः स्युस्तेष्वेकञ्च फलं भवेत्।
आदौ नमस्क्रियाशीर्वा वस्तुनिर्देश एव वा।।
क्वचिन्निन्दा खलादीनां सतां च गुणकीर्तनम्। etc.
Sāhityadarpaṇa, with *Locana* and *Vijñanapriyā*, Bharatiya Book Corporation, New Delhi, 1998, p. 365.

the big bulk alone which makes a poetic composition *mahākāvya*, but the important features prescribed by the rhetoricians, which should be employed in a poetic composition to make it worthy of the name. The rhetoricians hold the view that sentiment is the soul of poetry and the rhetorical figures are only the means to enhance the beauty of the poem. Therefore, the poet should try to present the full and natural development of the sentiment chosen for the epic poem. No epic, bereft of the proper and successful development of its sentiment can be regarded as a fine piece of literary art. In the classical period the poets were selecting the themes of the *mahākāvyas* keeping in view the scope of sentiment. For example, Kālidāsa selected the union of Śiva and Pārvatī for his *Kumārasambhava*, Māgha selected the theme of killing of *Śiśupāla* for his *Śiśupālavadha*, Bhāravi composed the *Kirātārjunīyam* and Kumāradāsa composed *Jānakīharaṇam*. But we come across a significant change in the modern period. For example, the work *Kristubhāgavata* of P.C. Devassia or the work *Nārāyaṇavijaya* of Balarama Panicker. These works are not rich in sentiment. The main objective of these poets is not a delineation of *Rasa*. They are mainly popularising the noble thoughts of the great persons like Christ or Śrī Nārāyaṇa Guru. The themes being completely new become interesting whereas the *mahākāvyas* based on the rotten themes like *Subhadrāharaṇa, Śumbhavadha, Draupadīsvayaṁvara, Karṇārjunīyam, Radhāpariṇayam, Vṛtravadham, Śrīkṛṣṇacaritam, Lavalīpariṇayam*, etc. are monotonous. The *mahākāvyas* which are based on new themes like *Viśvamānavīyam* of Vidyādhara Śāstrī, *Svarājyavijayam* of Dwijendranātha Śāstrī, *Lenināmṛtam* of Padmaśāstrī, deserve special place among the *mahākāvyas* of twentieth century. This shows that the objectives of the modern poets have changed. They have not composed the works in old line being very crazy for name and fame. With this background I now try to introduce some of the outstanding *mahākāvyas* which are carefully selected for this purpose.

Śrīnārāyaṇavijayam

Some of our modern Sanskrit poets have written on the topics which seem to be unusual but are really very interesting. This category appears to be the most important of all. What is worth mentioning and inspiring at the same time is that the turmoil and vicissitudes of the emerging problems of the society affect the Sanskrit poets. The trend of selecting themes from contemporary political, social, and academic scenes and to help people by way of spreading the spiritual messages of the saints and sages is very much promised in this century. In this category falls the *Śrīnārāyaṇavijaya* of K. Balarama Panicker. This *mahākāvya* came to light in 1971. The poem deserves a unique position for its subject-matter. The epic contains the biography, teachings and philosophical thoughts of Nārāyaṇa Guru, a great philosopher and social reformer of modern time. The poet has very nicely described the contributions of this great religious teacher. The epic does not strictly confirm to the rules of the *mahākāvya* as laid down by the rhetoricians like Viśvanātha. It mainly describes the biography of the saint. The hero of the poem is portrayed in all the solemnity and dignity usually associated with such holy personages. Nārāyaṇaguru's teachings, especially on the unity of all religious end, the brotherhood of men, are clearly and emphatically focussed in different cantos. Śrī Nārāyaṇa's oft-quoted message—'One community, one religion and one God for all'— has been ably and thoroughly interpreted in canto XIX. As a measure of relief from the tedious characteristic of didactic and philosophic discourses, the author employs natural descriptions abounding in figures of various kinds, thus enhancing the poetic beauty of the work. The cantos dealing with the consecration of the shrine of the Goddess of learning, the visit of poet Rabindranath Tagore and Mahatma Gandhi and the cemetery of Gurudeva are interesting aspects. Though the epic is pervaded by the sentiment *'śānta'*, the description of lamentations of the people on cemetery of the Gurudeva is full of pathos. Panicker's profound knowledge of Vedānta and logic entitles him to be a true interpreter of the teaching of the Gurudeva. Śrīnārāyaṇa was also an excellent conversationalist whose sense of humour and wit are well-known to his followers. But the poet Panicker has deliberately refrained himself from bringing out this aspect of the Master's character, probably out of his respect for the holy man or because of his feeling that such statements will be out of place in a long poem. The simplicity of language, the lucidity of style and the felicity of expression make the work interesting. It will be easy and pleasant even to the students of low standard in Sanskrit.

It is easily understood that the poet does not strictly follow the classical definition. The hero of the poem does not belong to the category mentioned in the definition. Though *Śānta* may be accepted as the main sentiment of the poem, it is not delineated in the manner it is expected. Nevertheless the *mahākāvya* occupies an important place for its unique theme and its lucid presentation. Some of the verses are given to acquaint the readers with the style of the poet Panicker.[1]

Kristubhāgavatam

The twentieth century has seen many original publications on Christ and Christianity, the latest and the biggest of which is the *Kristubhāgavatam*. The work won the

1. दुरितशतमवाच्यं जातिजन्यं कठोरं
बहुजनपरिहिंसारूपमालोक्य लोके।
अपर इह न दृष्टस्त्वां विना दूयमानो
गुरुमवशजनानां रक्षणे जागरूकः।। XVII. 11 ।।
Śrīnārāyaṇavijayam, pubd. by the Poet., Trivandrum, 1973, Second Part, p. 64.
कामस्य माता कमनीयरूपा
माया महामोहमयी तमिस्रा।
क्रोधादिकैरन्यसुतैरुपेता
तस्यान्तिके तिष्ठति कष्टवृत्ता।। IV.20, ।। *Ibid.*, First Part, p. 110.

poet the coveted Sahitya Academi award in 1980. The *mahākāvya* has many allusions to and illustrations from the Hindu purāṇas and epics. The author ascribes to his growth in an atmosphere of Sanskrit literature which could not but appear even in a work on Christ. Another great influence on the author was of His Eminence Joseph Cardinal Parecattil, the Archbishop of Ernakulam who believes that the Church in India must have its roots in the culture and the tradition of the land. As a Sanskrit scholar he has played an important role in the Indianization of the Church.

The *Kristubhāgavatam* is a noteworthy *mahākāvya* in Sanskrit based on the life of Jesus Christ. The author of this magnanimous epic is P.C. Devassia — a Christian Sanskrit scholar. The *mahākāvya* is written in the accepted form of an epic and can be aptly called the *Kristubhāgavatam.* It embodies the sacred life of the founder of a religion comprising thirty-three cantos corresponding to the years of Christ's life, in 1600 verses. We give here the outline of cantos.

I - The sage meets the Virgin, II - The betrothal, III - The vision of Zacharias, IV - The Annunciation, V - The Visitation, VI - A Journey to Bethlehem, VII - The Birth of Jesus, VIII - The presentation in the temple, IX - The arrival of the Magi, the slaughter of the innocents, X - the childhood of Jesus, XI - The coming of John, the Baptist, XII - The temptation, the call of the disciles, XIII - The marriage feast at Cana and the first miracles. XIV - Jesus and the Samaritan woman. XV - Jesus works many miracles, XVI - More miracles, The selection of the Apostles, XVII - The sermon on the mount I, XVIII - The sermon on the Mount II, XIX - The execution of John, the Baptist, XIX - the story of Mary Magdallene, XXI - The parable of the Good Samaritan, XXII - The prodigal son, XXIII -The woman taken in adultery, XXIV - The raising of Lazarus, XXV - The triumphant entry into Jerusalem, XXVI - The end of the world, XXVII - The last super, XXVIII - The agony in the crucification, XXXII - The Resurrection of Jesus, XXXIII - The ascension.

The present poem is a major achievement in the field of modern creative writing in Sanskrit. It is the first major poem on the whole life of Christ. The author follows all the norms and principles of the epic but does not indulge in too many figures of speech or descriptions of seasons, sun-rise, sunset etc. A few commonly known figures only occur. The common metre employed in this epic is *anuṣṭup* and next to it, is *upajāti*, although the author shows his capacity to handle the other metres as well. The style is simple and clear, endowed with the poetic qualities like *prasāda* and *saukumārya*. In narrating the story of Christ the author relies on the versions of the Gospels and on some reputed biographers of Christ. He has remained faithful to the incidents recorded in the works of reliable biographers. He shows also his freedom and imagination as a poet to introduce some new elements without diluting the authenticity of the narrative. He has followed the *mahākāvya* model and in accordance with the traditional model, the author takes a few episodes mentioned briefly in the Gospels and expatiates on them. The most noteworthy incidents where the poet does this are the love and betrothal of Mary and Joseph, to which he devotes two chapters (I & II), the childhood of Jesus (X), the death of John, the Baptist (XIX) and the suicide of the betrayer Judas (XXIX). Not only the incidents of the miracles are faithfully described but also the famous sayings of Christ are incorporated in an appropriate terms. One of the noteworthy features of the author's treatment is the inclusion of apt analogies and comparisons with personalities and situations that are found in two Sanskrit epics, the *Rāmāyaṇa* and the *Mahābhārata*. Occasional presentations of some well-known happenings in modern India like the assassination of Gandhiji etc. enhance the value of this *mahākāvya*. No effort is spent to make the poem overcoloured or loaded with display of learning or skill. It is simple and straight forward and in the much valued *vaidarbhī* style. There is much *subhāṣita* type of sayings. Prof. Unni rightly remarks : "All the important events in the life of Christ are described here in a chaste and lucid style of classical poets."[1]

The verses in this *mahākāvya* have a natural flow of their own, which cannot but charm a reader. A verse from the canto XVII dealing with the Sermon is given as specimen.[2]

"Do not lay up for yourself treasures on earth, where moths and other insects consume them, and where thieves break in and steal them; but lay up those treasures in heaven where they are not consumed by them, for, where treasure is in that world will your heart also be".[3]

Viśvabhānuḥ

The *Viśvabhānuḥ* (the Universal light) is an interesting epic poem composed on the life history of Swāmi Vivekānanda. P. K. Narayana Pillai of Kerala has composed this *mahākāvya* successfully. This work came to light in 1979. The hero of this poem is Swāmi Vivekānanda. The eminent poet has taken some liberties with the form, but they no way devalue his creative talent. The epic reflects the greatness of the stream of perennial Indian culture beginning from the Vedas under the guise of the description of the noble qualities, character and life of Swāmiji. In addition to this, the course of action advocated by the revered Swāmiji for

---

1. Unni, N. P. "Contribution of Kerala to Modern Sanskrit Literature", *Devavāṇīsuvāsa* (Dr. Ramakanta Shukla Felicitation Volume, Part 11, Devavani Prakashanam, New Delhi, 1993, p. 595.
2. प्रोक्तं तैर्यस्त्यजति दयितां त्यागपत्रं स दत्तां
   तस्यै चेत्थं मुनिभिरधुनाऽहं तु युष्मान् ब्रवीमि।
   यः कश्चित्तां त्यजति परिणीतामृते शीलदोषा-
   द्भर्त्ता सोऽपि व्यभिचरति संत्यक्तभार्यावरश्च ।। XVII. 22 ।।
   Kristubhāgavatam, Jayabharatam, Trivandrum, 1977, p. 192.
3. यूयं मा सञ्चिनुत निधिमात्मार्थमुर्व्यां हि यस्मा-
   त्कीटाद्यास्तं क्षयमुपनयन्त्यत्र मुष्णन्ति चौराः।
   स्वर्गे तान् सञ्चिनुत विभवान् ये हि तैर्न ह्रियन्ते
   वित्तं यस्मिन् भवति भुवने तत्र चित्तं च वः स्यात् ।। XVII. 52 ।। *Ibid.* p. 199

the attainment of greatness would pave the way for future prosperity of India. That is brought out in words full of suggestive significance. This poem which is in every respect a modern one, generates in the mind of the reader an experience of aesthetic pleasure of different shades brought about by sweetness of language and popular metres. Except the 5th canto of this poem which comprises 555 verses in all, all the cantos other than the 16th and 21st contain 25 verses each. The practice of concluding with stanzas in longer metres is not followed in this poem as we find in some of the ancient epic poems. In this poem composed with seven metres namely, *Anuṣṭup, Upajāti, Vasantatilakā, Vaṁśastha, Viyoginī, Pṛthvi,* no hard and fast rule is observed to change the metre in every canto. One verse is given here as specimen.[1]

The significant feature of this *mahākāvya* is that the poet makes a very lucid presentation of the theme. By the proper use of his superb talent he has made the theme interesting. He does not show his depth of knowledge by way of creating artificial descriptions, difficult words, long compounds, unnatural narration and long metres. He is faithful to authentic presentation of the incidents that have happened in the life of the great Swāmiji, one of the great builders of modern India. By way of presenting the character of Swāmi Vivekānanda, the poet has in fact made a commendable work. The poem is having quietude as the main sentiment. Prof. Pillai has composed one more *Mahākāvya - Dharmasāgara* which deals with the life of the great master Śrī Rāmakṛṣṇa Paramahaṁsa in 18 cantos. Prof. Pillai's *mahākāvya* on the

1. ज्ञानात्मनः पशुपतेः प्रियधामरत्नं
वाराणसीमहिततीर्थमुपासनात् सः।
यत्रादिशङ्करगुरुर्निखिलागमज्ञ-
श्चण्डालतः परमुपार्जयदात्मतत्त्वम्।।
Viśvabhānuḥ, printed at V.V. Research Institute Press, Hoshiarpur, 1977. X.20. p. 105.

life history of Vivekānanda is not first of its kind. Many modern poets have written on this theme. The most outstanding one is *Śrīsvāmivivekānandacaritam*[1] written by Tryambaka Bhaskar Bhandarkar of Varanasi.

Keralodayaḥ

Now, we will examine some historical poems of outstanding merit. One of them is *Keralodaya.* It is considered to be one of the best epics of modern period. The poet has set a good model to be followed by the successors. It occupies a special place among the Sanskrit epics for a number of reasons that we will discuss in the following pages. The poem contains 21 cantos and nearly 2300 verses. It deals with the entire history of Kerala - State and its political, social and cultural aspects against the background of South Indian History.

The poem begins from the legendary origin by Paraśurāma up to the reunification of the land in the second half of the 20th century. The balance between poetic imagination and conformity with the available facts has been maintained with great success. Being an authority on Kerala history, culture and literature, the poet has a full command on the field and is at home with all details regarding facts and figures. His poetic imagination helps him to paint graphically the whole picture in keeping with the facts available. As a modern poet with progressive ideas and a literary critic thorough with the rules of the game, Prof. Ezhuthachan attempts not only in composing an excellent *Mahākāvya* following the classical tradition, but also making it accessible from modern standpoint as well. Thus this unique work combines in itself a research thesis on the cultural history of Kerala, a Sanskrit *mahākāvya* of the

1. Panda, R.K. 'A Study of Alaṁkāras in the Swāmī Vivekānandacarita Mahākāvya?, *Journal of Sukṛtīndra Research Institute,* Vol. Vill, 2003, pp. 89-109.

traditional type, and a modern literary work drawn on wide canvas written in the Sanskrit language. In this context the author's statement given in the Author's note is pertinent to note : "This was written in Sanskrit, paradoxically enough, to reach a wider circle of readers, for Sanskrit is both a national and international scholars' language even now, though it is not living language in the modern sense of the term. It is clear that an original work written in any other Indian language has not got that advantage, for translation will definitely minimize its natural beauty. Secondly, I wanted to see how far classical Sanskrit could be used as a vehicle of modern poetry with a serious purpose and progressive outlook. An attempt has been made here to present on a broad canvas the cultural, political and social history of Kerala with a national and international background. But at the same time, care has been taken throughout to see that it is prominently and decidedly a work of art. Though the classical framework is used, the aim has been to present regional life in all its varieties following blindly any old rule, method or set pattern."[1]

The poem is divided into five *mañjarīs* viz. *Svapnamañjarī, Smṛtimañjarī, Aitihyamañjarī, Bodhamañjarī* and *Caritramañjarī.* The theme of the poem is as below :

Paraśurāma at the time of penance becomes lonely and grief-stricken. Brahmā advises him to throw off his axe. He does so. Immediately his heart and the world change. The Arabian sea appears in human form and gives his daughter as a forestchild to the sage. The Paraśurāma story is retained, but relegated to the dream land.

The actual story of the land, which was called Chera in historical times, begins. Patirruppattu and other Sangham works are followed in historical details. King Udayan Cheral and his wife Nalini come first Rule of their son Imaya Verampan and his successors their exploites. The Chera

1. By the Poet, Trivandrum, Kerala, 1978, p. vii.

history is continued. The famous Chenkuttuvan and his conquests the story of Chilappatikaram. The tragedy of Kovalam and Karnaki described. A curse falls on the Southern kingdoms. Chenkuttuvan builds a temple for Karnaki - Kuttuvan's successors - Destruction at the hands of the Cholas. Story of the Eastern branch of the Cheras - Gradual decline of Chenkuttuvan's western line - Cholas destroy Muchiri, their capital - End of the first Chera empire. The Aryan colonization of Kerala - Mayura Sarman of the Kadamba dynasty, Social changes in the land. The second Chera Empire under the Kulaśekharas, Śaṅkarācārya — His deeds and sermons, His critical evaluation of human civilization. Kulaśekhar Alwar and Cheraman Perumal Nayanar-Sthanu Ravi and Tarisapalli Plates, Rama Verma Vikramaditya Varaguna and Paliyam Plates, the Jewish Plates. Bhaskara Ravi accepts the throne. The Chera -Chola war begins. It's various stages - Attacks of Rajendra etc. The Kerala capital destroyed. Rama Verma Kulaśekhara changes his capital. His fresh attempts for freedom. The hundred years war ends and the Cholas routed. The effects of war. Muslims in South India -Malik Kafur-Sangramadira Ravi Verma and his exploits. His mother Uma-gradual rise of the Zamorians. The Zamorians gain power, the help of Muslims. The Mammakam festival came under the control of the Zamorians after the defeat of Walluvanad. The Zamorians become supreme.

Great changes in Europe. Vassco da Gama comes to Calicut. New phase in Kerala history. The Portuguese in Kerala. There is description on wars and treatises, general states of the land, feasts and festivals. The Dutch period. Its end - Martanda Verma of Venad. The British period begins.

The full command of Sanskrit language enables Prof. Ezhuthachan to depict precisely and correctly scenes and situations mirrored in his rich imagination. The ideas contain echoes of the classical thought.

Simple statements are made very attractive and effective. There is originality even in the method of presenting ideas. The author K. N. Ezhuthachan prefers to interpret history from the Marxian point of view. The problems of the labourers shouting for rights and privileges are described very nicely. This *mahākāvya* is a piece of real poetry, which annexed the Sahitya Academi Award. The replay of Śaṅkarācārya in canto ninth when the latter offered him the kingdom shows the poet's sense of propriety. The substance of the Ācārya's teaching is beautifully codified therein. The poet has introduced some alien words[1] into Sanskrit with a view to making the ideas understandable. He has made use of some rare word meanings — which are already fixed on the particular senses. The poet depicts Cinema as the best leader in a satire manner.[2]

The poet has also composed another *mahākāvya*, that is, *Śrīvidyādhirājavijaya* in 19 cantos, which purports to be a biography of Vidyādhirāja *alias* Cattampiswāmi, a modern social reformer of Kerala, who had joined hands with Śrīnārāyaṇaguru. The poet also refers to contemporary dignitaries since they had maintained contacts with the hero of the poem. His other *mahākāvya*, *Nāyakdbharaṇa* or *Aṣṭalayanāyakīya* consisting of 19 cantos deals with the history of the state of Travancore. The 18th century ruler of Travancore, the king Martandavarma and his exploits form the central theme and his conflicts with the chieftains of the

---

1. सदा चरन्ति बत पश्चिमेन
पथा मगल्लस्य ततस्तु नौका।
स्पान्यां पुनः प्राप पिपीलिकेव
नारङ्गिकां भूवलयं भ्रमन्ती।। *Ibid*. XVI. 19 p. 296.

2. शमं दमं च त्यजतः क्रमेण
विगर्हतोऽध्यात्मगुणांश्च सर्वान्।
रराज लोकस्य वरिष्ठनेता
शृङ्गारनेता सिनिमाभिनेता।। *Ibid*. XXI. 194, p. 473.

eight prominent families of the state provide ample scope for the poem.

Yaśodharāmahākāvyam

The *Yaśodharāmahākāvyam* of Ogeti Parikshit Sarma in 20 cantos concentrates on the reactions and emotions of Yaśodharā, the wife of the prince Siddhārtha. It is neither a biographical poem nor a historical poem. It can be called a descriptive poem. The poet has depicted the helpless condition of Yaśodharā when her husband renounced the world suddenly and left her behind with her child Rāhula. The poem has received the Kalidasa Award of the Madhya Pradesh Sanskrit Academy. It is interesting to remind that the subject on the life of Gautam Buddha has received its epic measure of treatment in the hand of the great poet Aśvaghoṣa. But the great classical poet has devoted a small place to Yaśodharā in his *Buddhacarita*. Yaśodharā is a neglected character like Urmilā. It is to the credit of Paṇḍita Sarma that he focuses our attention on this neglected soul and reveals the lonely agony of a devoted wife, whose destiny lifted her to uncommon heights but plunged her also into an abyss of tragedy. The pathos is the main sentiment of this *mahākāvya.* This epic of twenty cantos and of about 1070 verses carries the narrative of Suddhodana, the king of Kapilavastu. The poet has nicely described the events like the marriage of Gautama and Yaśodharā, their revising delights of married life, the birth of Rāhula, the renunciation of Gautama for penance, the tragic sorrow of the royal household, the final visit of Gautama after his enlightenment and the message of Buddha's religious faith. The poem is more an epic of emotion rather than an epic of narration. The tale is woven by descriptions of places, mountain, river, seasons, details of married life and record of important happenings. The emotion-torn mind of Gautama on the eve of his leaving the palace and his young sleeping wife and child in the middle of night, is convincingly presented in canto IX. More central is the picture of grief-stricken Yaśodharā and the people who surround her, which is presented in nearly six cantos. This is a touching picture, though somewhat conventionally drawn. The author does not allow the poem to lose itself in mere pathos and frustration. It is a striking feature of its construction. Yaśodharā emerging from her sorrow with a new awakening and courage, deriving comfort from the lovable pranks and prattle of her beloved Rahula, and the visit of the Buddha which crown her like within understanding and wisdom, are heartening touches making the sadness sweet. The epic is composed on established lines. The poet makes salutations at the outset, and gives an account of his family and personal life followed by a description of Himālaya and the river Rohini, before the thread of the epic narrative is taken in hand. The usual descriptions of the rise and setting of the sun and the moon and of the seasons have their full play in this poem. In the same way, marriage, love-sports, pregnancy, birth of a child, its growing up and other details come to be described in the approved manner of epic composition. Inevitable as the descriptive mode is, it has fortunately escaped staleness and ostentatious conformity to form by two redeeming features. Paṇḍita Sarma is steeped in the poetry of the classical poets. His writing often echoes phrases and ideas from classical Sanskrit poetry. The description of Himālaya (canto I) is full of allusions to the two epics of Kālidāsa. The day-to-day occupations of the separated Yaśodharā remind one of Kālidāsa's Yakṣapatnī (XIX 47-52) and to some extent Bāṇa's Mahāśvetā. The play of Rāhula is reminiscent of Sarvadaman's sport MIX. 31). There are other such reminiscences (see III, 16, IV. 7; V 20, XIV. 15, XV.19). Such allusive mode of descriptions seems to add charm to the new writing. Further, the descriptions, though conventionally arranged, are free from imitation and verbosity. The author himself is a musician and that has helped his descriptive style. The account of vernal sport

(Canto V) is interwoven with the technical names of musical melodies. The poet chooses, with a touch of poetic propriety, the metre *Viyoginī* to paint the picture of separated Yaśodharā (Canto XIII), although most of the epic is written in *upajāti* metre. The sense of music of words and rhythm are sources of pleasure. Occasionally the poet comes out with fresh ideas. Yaśodharā, for example, is described as solidified moonlight in a sustained metaphor (Canto III. 37), the young Gautama and Yaśodharā entwined in love-sport appear as targets of *dvandvārthakāvya* and as *samāsasayyā* (IV 26), the sacred thread on the chest is imagined as the dividing line marking the torn heart of Gautama (IX). Sometimes the author paraphrases well-known ideas (XIV) and introduces the new ones. The poet's eye moving in the old and the new world often brings freshness of perspective.

The poet's diction and style are mature and weighty without being heavy. The poet preserves the dignity of Sanskrit language without sacrificing clarity. Conscious of poetry writing, he does not strain after word-effect, rhetorical display or artificial construction. Occasionally he cannot resist a pun or an oxymoron (I. 1 10, II. 87, IV .54 and VIII. 34). The poet is fond of some words like *yauvat, matalli, bambhara, sayā*, which are repeated. The simplicity and sweetness of his diction, the natural music of his verses and his ability for emotional delineation are sufficiently attractive. The role of *daiva* is nicely described by the poet who has glorified the importance of *gṛhasthadharma*.[1]

It is interesting to say that some of our modern poets have glorified the characters of women. The heroines are depicted as the heroes of the long poems. It is a good trend and it dispels the misconception that male writers are writing

---

1. दैवं यदा यत् कुरुते च कस्मै न कोऽपि जानाति वसुन्धरायाम्।
नावश्च यान्त्येव धरातलेऽपि रसातले हा शकटानि यान्ति।। *Ibid*. X. 38, p. 72
सर्वेषु धर्मेषु गृहस्थधर्मं सुखावहं श्रेष्ठतमं हि मन्ये।
तं तादृशं धर्मगुणं विहाय विरागमार्गे पतितोऽसि राजन्।। *Ibid*. XIV. 35, p 93.

only for the males. The *mahākāvyas* like *Rāṇī Ahalyā Bāi caritam, Victoriacaritam, Sītācaritam, Indirā Gaandhīcaritam, Rādhācaritam* etc. are the best ones of this new trend and all these works glorify the achievements and contributions of women who have proved themselves to be the heroes of India. Prof. Rajendra Mishra brings a pertinent point to light. He observes: "Most of these works do not abide by the principle established by our rhetoricians like Bhāmaha, Daṇḍin and Viśvanātha. *Sītācaritam* and the *Jānakījīvanam,* although based on the traditional *Rāmāyaṇa*-theme, seem upto some extent, free from the archaic-style. Both of these *mahākāvyas* do not accept Rāma as the hero. On the other hand, the heroine of the theme, Sītā seems to be the most dominant character, throughout the poem. Story also differs. According to *Sītācaritam,* for the sake of her husband's honour and royal dignity, she herself chooses the banishment. The composer of the poem Dr. Reva Prasada Dwivedi 'Sanatana' has tried to console the generous readers who feel mentally perturbed to see *devī* Sītā being banished and insulted by her own husband Rāma in public. Abhiraja Rajendra Mishra also in his *Jānakījīvanam,* tries to find the same solution. According to him, the washer-man begs for an excuse in the open assembly of civilians, in the presence of Maharṣi Vasiṣṭha and lord Rāma forgives him for defaming empress of the Kosala empire. Afterwards Sītā goes to the hermitage of Maharṣi Vālmīki only to look after her twin sons Lava and Kuśa for a few days: In these *Mahākāvyas, tatraiko nāyakaḥ surah* etc., fails because of their heroine-dominant theme."[1]

We all know that the great works like the *Rāmāyaṇa* of *Vālmīki,* the *Mahābhārata* of Vedavyāsa, the great Purāṇas and Upaniṣads have been used as the main sources of themes

1. Mishra, Rajendra, Modern Sanskrit Poetry, *in Modern Sanskrit Literature : Tradition & Innovations,* Ed. by S. B. Raghunathacharya, Sahitya Academi, New Delhi, 2002, pp. 117-118.

and their ideas are woven into literary creations by ancient and modern poets. The poems based on the *Rāmāyaṇa* are huge in number. The *Rāmāyaṇa* theme, has in a way exerted a more direct influence on subsequent poets, primarily because of its compactness and ethical basis. The *Mahābhārata* has also significantly helped in composing modern *mahākāvyas.*

Bhīṣmacaritam

The *Bhīṣmacaritam* of Hari Narayan Dīkṣit occupies an important place among the mythological *mahākāvyas* for its aesthetic attributes. As is clear from the title, this epic is based on the character of Devavrata Bhīṣma who possesed a unique personality. Bhīṣma had wonderfully performed an unequalled role for the success of the great battle of the *Mahābhārata* which had taken place between the *Adharma* and *Dharma* and in which the *Dharma* was fighting for its existence. The present epic contains twenty cantos which are well arranged in proper format. The essential elements like plot-construction, characterization, imaginations, descriptions, figures of speech, and appropriate metres deserve our appreciation. The language of Dīkṣit is simple but free from the grammatical errors. As the poet himself is a good scholar of Grammar he has made use of appropriate words those do not confuse the readers rather they facilitate our understanding. The most appreciable thing is that the poet does not make a show of his profound scholarship and proficiency of language. The poem being written in a lucid style and jargon-free language can have an access to all. Since the poet has understood the problems of modern Sanskrit readers he has given a Hindi Translation of the verses. There is no doubt that the pen of Dīkṣit has given birth to an excellent and pleasant epic in a beautiful, impressive and very heart-touching style. The *mahākāvya* is an admirable contribution to modern Sanskrit literature. The work is dedicated to its hero Bhīṣma. The dedicated verses give a glimpse of his noble character. The poet has tried to highlight all the best things that were there in the personality of Bhīṣma. The work is appreciable for its theme and presentation. Though the theme is well-known, it came to light for the first time in the form of a *mahākāvya*. The description of *Mokṣaloka* is given here.[1]

Dhanañjayavijayam

The *Dhanañjayavijayam* of Rama Subrahmaniar is an important *mahākāvya* of 18 cantos. The poet has described the glorious exploits of Arjuna with all his noble qualities in this epic poem. The poem deals with Arjuna's life and achievements up to the stage of the *Bhagavadgītā*. It narrates clearly how Arjuna equipped himself not only for the great war but also for the advice of Kṛṣṇa in the *Gītā*. We find him in his father Indra's court in the heaven shocked by the way of life amongst Gods. He later realizes that their standards and ways of life are different from those of the mortals on earth. We similarly see him as an ascetic praying to God and securing weapons after severe trials. We also see him fulfiling the role of a great householder and husband marrying many princesses who were his admirers. In the *Gītā* the lord says at the time of the Mahābhārata war that he incarnated as Dhanañjaya, the conqueror of wealth. According to the definition a *mahākāvya* must have a theme taken from an epic or history. Firstly, in this poem the theme has been taken from the *Vanaparva* of the *Mahābhārata*. Secondly, the hero should be endowed with many good qualities and noble traits. In this poem Arjuna fulfils all those necessary qualities. Another feature of a *mahākāvya* is the division of the work into various cantos properly and coherently connecting the

1. न जन्मकष्टं न जरा विषण्णता न मृत्युभीतिर्न च कर्णजापता।
विश्वासघातो न न जीविकाभ्रमः स मोक्षलोकः सुतरां मनोरमः।। XIX.19
भाषाविवादो न न भेदभावना न क्षत्रवादो न च जातिभावना।
न वर्गवादो न च संग्रहैषणा च मोक्षलोकः सततं मनोरमः।। XIX. 21
Eastern Book Linkers, New Delhi, 1991.

theme. A canto must deal with a particular idea directly connected with the traits of the hero. Each idea emerges from a consideration of a number of facts. The poem is interesting for its delineation of sentiment, description of natural beauty and sweet language. Though the theme is old yet it seems to be new in the hand of the master poet. An example is given.[1]

Navabhāratam

The *Navabhāratam* of Muttukulu Sridhara is an interesting historical poem. It deals with the story of the modern period of Indian history. The struggle for independence and the story after the historic events form the central theme of this long poem. The roles of the architects of modern India like Motilal Nehru, Jawaharlal Nehru, Mahatma Gandhi, Subhas Chandra Bose and others are well brought out in this epic poem. The work proves that Sanskrit can very well be an effective medium to deal with the modern events of historical importance. There are 18 cantos and 1185 verses. The verses are charming for their melodious rhythm and mellifluous flow. The poet has mainly depicted the situations of modern India. The verses of Sridhara contain beautiful figures of speech. The examples of *Tulyayogitā*,[2] are noted in the footnote. Similarly, it is interesting to note that the poet has employed some rare metres like *Vasantamālikā*[3], *Kusumamañjarī*[4] etc. This attempt is to be highly appreciated

1. पूजापुण्यान्यपि न लभते यो न जयासमेतः स्मारं स्मारं स्मृतिवच इदं शान्तनुश्चिन्ततोऽभूत्।
जायाभावे नहि जगदिदं केवलं सौख्यहीनं लोकोऽन्योऽसावपितु नितरां तेन मेने विपुण्यः।।
Ibid, VIII. 17, p. 109.
2. पार्थे तु पार्थिवमणौ शमनं प्रयाते याते च शान्तिमथ कान्तिचयेऽपि तस्य।
कालः कलिः कलुषतासु ददत्प्रवृत्तिं वृत्तिञ्जगाम तिमिरौघ इव प्रदीपे।। *Navabhāratam*, Devasthali Prakashan, Trivandrum, 1982, III. p. 53.
3. सुखदं कुसुमास्तरं चिरेण स्फुटमालस्यकर्मतां च धत्ते।
क्रमशोऽपचयस्य नान्यहेतुर्विफला शक्तिरनेकधा च लब्धा।। *Ibid*, XVI. 51, p. 269.
4. कर्मचन्द्रकरभासुरं तरुलताविलाससुमसुन्दरं मन्द्रनादपिकगीतिकेकिवरलास्यमेलितमिलातलम्।
सागेरितमुदात्तशैलीशिखरोपराञ्जितपयोधरं क्षेत्रमध्यगनदीतरंगतरलं श्रिये भवतु भारतम्।।
Ibid, VI. 73.

for the reason that the poet contributes to the preservation of the science of metres. It goes without saying that Chandasśāstra or Metrics in Sanskrit is a well-developed discipline. If the poets do not make use of them or if they confine to some selected simple metres then, how can this sophisticated science survive? Furthermore, the poet has well depicted the places and situations of modern India. It is perhaps the most comprehensive work on this theme in Sanskrit.

The poet has given a fine description of the London city in *Pañcacāmara* metre. He has brought out the realistic pictures of the farmers and their misery.[1] Some words are used by the poet in unusual senses.[2]

Pūrvabhāratam

The *mahākāvya Pūrvabhāratam* is undoubtedly an appreciable attempt which shows poet's concern for the true history of India. The work is composed in 21 cantos having 1444 verses written by Kaviratna Prabhudatta Swami of Meerut. It is a unique work in the sense that it deals with the history of India beginning from the mythical Manu and ending with the invasion of Alexander and his encounter with Puru. The author does not follow the history given by the modern historians, instead he depends mainly upon Indian tradition and literary evidences. In the epilogue of the *mahākāvya* the poet says that the pure history of the Aryans has been misinterpreted and stained by the foreign

---

1. अधो युगस्य गच्छन्तौ वृषभौ सीरकर्षिणौ।
   नयतस्तान्मुहुर्वीक्ष्य व्याकुलः पङ्कपावितान्।। *Ibid*, VI. 31
   प्रचण्डतपनाक्रान्तमण्डले क्षेत्रखण्डके।
   म्लानाननसरोजातकान्तयः कृषकाः समे।। *Ibid*, VI. 33.
2. A. स्वप्रमेयप्रयोगार्थं कालीघट्टमवाप सः। *Ibid*, VI. 15.
   B. ऋषिश्रुतायां भरतक्षमायां प्ररूढशालीनतमा कविश्रीः। *Ibid*, VII. 57.
   C. अक्षयैश्चर्यसम्पत्तेर्वाराकरविराजिता। *Ibid*, XI. 70.
   D. यथा काल्ये दिनेशाभा। *Ibid*, 73.

writers. He has therefore written an epic poem to present the real history of the Aryans. The Indian mind that has always been seeking harmony and synthesis instead of harping on differences is aptly picturised in this poem in support of admitting the Buddha as an incarnation by the Hindu society. In diction, choice of words and figures of speech this poem stands remarkably distinct. The poem begins with the beautiful description of magnificent *Himālaya*[1] and the *Āryadeśa*. The verses are full of *mādhuryaguṇa*. They inject the feeling of curiosity and can easily bind the mind of a cultured reader. There are plenty of poetic figures[2] which truly beautify the simple style of Prabhudatta who does not follow that hazardous trend of exaggeration and artificial description. The entire third canto is written in *Anuprāsa-Alaṁkāra*. There is a proper delineation of *vīrarasa* and in some places we find even *karuṇa*. Prabhudatta has composed another historical epic called *Mauryacandrodayam*. The *mahākāvya* contains twenty cantos, and about 1100 verses. The poet has glorified the noble deeds of Candragupta who is the hero of this great poem. The author deserves appreciation for giving us a historical epic, the composition of which is more difficult than the simple biographical poems, most of which just narrate the superficial material in high flown language. We understand that a poet however competent and powerful may be, has to study the life-history of the king and to remember the historical incidents chronologically and to make use of all the names of the persons, places, and incidents etc. in the poem. Among

---

1. अस्त्यद्रिराजाद्दिशि दक्षिणस्यां
   महाहिमोद्भासितभव्यभाल:।
   पयोनिधिक्षालितपादपद्मो
   हरिर्धराभूत इवार्यदेश:।। *Pūrvabhāratam*, Merath, 1974, 1.1.
2. राजन्ति सर्वत्र भुव: प्रदेशा
   भुव: प्रदेशेषु सरस्समूहा:।
   सरस्समूहेषु सरोजलक्ष्म्य:
   सरोजलक्ष्मीष्वलिगुञ्जनानि। *Ibid*, 1. 3.

the biographical poems we have a less number of historical poems which are more important for preserving the history and cultural records.

The epic is published in 1985. The poet deserves appreciation for selecting an untouched historical theme. The hero of this poem is Candragupta Maurya. The poem is having *vīrarasa* as the main sentiment. But the poet has not been so much successful in making appropriate presentation of sentiments. However, the poet has given us a biography of Candragupta (322-289 B.C.) in Sanskrit. A Sanskritist will be more interested to know the details about this king. The poet's concern for preserving the history for posterity is visible from the composition of the poem. So the work has unique importance. The epic possesses some fascinating literary merit.

Conclusion

Now, in the conclusion I have to give my general observations about the *mahākāvyas* I have introduced in the above pages. The epic poems not only give a glimpse of uncommon creative genius of the modern poets but their zeal and enthusiasm for the preservation and propagation of Sanskrit language.

It is found that many of our modern poets have not strictly followed the rules of *mahākāvya* given by the critics like Viśvanātha. They have tried to walk with the time. There is no point in following the trend blindly. All these great poets have made some innovations and in fact enriched the tradition. The most important thing, which I like to appreciate, is that these modern *mahākāvyas* are not burden on readers. They are readable and enjoyable. The simple language and easy way of expression are remarkable and they do not distance the sensitive readers. The feelings have been well depicted without exaggeration. The subjects which have wide appealing, have been selected. Some of them transcend the boundary of the Sanskrit poetic culture.

The metre is an essential ingredient of a *mahākāvya*. The art of the use of proper metres in a *mahākāvya* is an important criterion of the quality of the poem. Early rhetoricians have been very vague on the proper application of the metres in a poem.[1] The change of metre has been emphasized at the end of the canto by Daṇḍin and other later rhetoricians like Viśvanātha.[2] Usually a single metre runs throughout the body of a canto, but Viśvanātha suggests that there can be variety of metres even in a canto.[3] Ramaji Upadhyaya rightly observes : "Metre in poetry serves as a garment of the ideas presented by the poet; just as variety of people use variety of garments for the different occasions, similarly the metres also change in poetry as there is change in the subject-matter. Usually in a *mahākāvya* there is only one subject in a canto; towards the end of the canto, a poet occasionally indicates the subject-matter of the following canto. Looking to this characteristic of a *mahākāvya*, the rhetoricians prescribed that in a *mahākāvya* there should be only one metre in a canto with a change, if necessary, at the end of the canto."[4] It is observed that the poets of modern period are mainly using the popular metres, like *Anuṣṭup, Upajāti, Indravajrā, Upendravajrā, Toṭaka, Mālinī, Vasantatilakā, Mandākrāntā, Sragdharā, Śārdulavikrīḍīta* and *Āryā*. Though the texts on metres enumerate more than 300 metres but only a few of them are found in use. For example, *Paraśurāmavijaya* is a *mahākāvya* written entirely in *Anuṣṭup* metre. It is a sub-standard *mahākāvya* and does not come in the category of the best poems. Some modern poets have left also the

1. प्रवालहस्तैः सुमनःसमूहान्
   विकीर्य रक्ता वयसां वचोभिः।
   गायन्ति सौभाग्यगुणं यदीयं
   नवीननेपथ्यभूतो व्रतत्यः।। *Ibid*. 62.
2. एकवृत्तमयैः पद्यैरवसानेऽन्यवृत्तकैः। *Sāhityadarpaṇa*, op. cit. VI. 320.
3. *Ibid*. p. 321.
4. Upadhyaya, Ramaji, *Sanskrit and Prakrit Mahākāvyas*, Sanskrit Parishad, Sagar, 1978, pp. 106-107.

traditional metres. One innovation is attempted by Paṇḍita Vaikuntha Vihari Nanda of Orissa in his *Kīcakavadha*. The poet has composed the entire epic in different *rāgas*, in *gīta* style. Similarly Dhulipala has composed a *mahākāvya* consisting of ten cantos of 1000 verses in a single *Mandākrāntā* metre. Ogeti Pariksit Sarma has used some deśī metres in his *Pratāparāṇāyanam*. But it compels me to say that our poets should make use of the other metres also otherwise time will come when new generation will not be aware of our rich tradition. It is also not true that other metres do not have beauty. It depends on the writers to find out them and give a shape to their thoughts in the form of those metres so that the rich science of metres will survive for ever.

Similarly, the poets have created only popular figures of speech like simile, metaphor, poetic fancies, concealment, to name a few. The *citra* or picture-type of poetic figure is almost absent in modern compositions. Even the *Śabdālaṁkāras* like *Śleṣa, Mudrā,* etc. have lost their place.

The poets have become comparatively realistic. Many of them do not create any scope for far-reaching imaginations and superfluous descriptions. Generally the poets have avoided the descriptions of the seasons, the sun and the moon, the love-sports, mountains, and feminine beauties. Descriptions have become more natural, sweet and therefore more effective. The poets have also avoided the irrelevant episodes. Furthermore, the modern *mahākāvyas* have not been so serious for the delineation of sentiment which is one of the primary constituents of a *mahākāvya*. Some rhetoricians like Bharata and Viśvanātha consider it as the soul of poetry. Bharata in his *Nāṭyaśāstra* points out that no work can be fully and truly enjoyed without sentiment.[1] According to Bharata, that sentiment which is accorded prominence over the other sentiments presented in a poem is called *Aṅgī* or

---

1. न हि रसादृते कश्चिदप्यर्थः प्रवर्तते। *Nāṭyaśāstra*, VI. 82.

sthāyirasa and the others are called *aṅgas* or *sañcārirasas.*[1] While discussing the characteristics of a *mahākāvya* the rhetoricians like Bhāmaha,[2] Daṇḍin[3] and Rudraṭa[4] remark that the *mahākāvya* should be endowed with all the sentiments not mentioning any specific *rasa*. Viśvanātha clarifies the position and recommend that in a *mahākāvya* out of *śṛṅgāra, vīra* and *śānta* any one should be a principal sentiment, while the rest should be introduced as subsidiaries.[5] But the great poets of twentieth century have not taken that matter seriously and have neglected that aspect to some extent. It must not be said that their poems are completely devoid of sentiment. They are mild but potent enough in arousing interest in the mind of the reader.

We also observe that the language is not becoming a burden like those of the classical epic poems. Keeping in view the practical situation the poets have used the popular, easy and lucid words which enthuse the modern readers. Some of them have made the Sanskritisation of the English words and thereby they have created a new bank of foreign words in the field of Sanskrit and they do contribute to the growth of this dying language.

We all know that *netā* or hero and the other set of character is one of the primary elements of a *mahākāvya*. The poet as a weaver weaves the beautiful web of a plot just with the help of characters. As in the drama the characters are the wheels of the vehicle of a plot, the same is the case with a *mahākāvya*. The characters act always as the mouthpieces of a dramatist or the writer of a *mahākāvya*. Whatever the poet wants to convey or put before the reader, he does it through

---

1. बहूनां समवेतानां रूपं यस्य भवेद् बहु।
   स मन्तव्यो रसः स्थायी शेषा सञ्चारिणो मताः।। *Ibid.* VII. 120.
2. रसैः सकलैः युक्तम्। *Kāvyālaṁkāra*, I. 21.
3. रसभावनिरन्तम्। *Kāvyādarśa*, I. 18.
4. सर्वे रसाः क्रियन्ते काव्यस्थानानि सर्वाणि। *Kāvyālaṁkāra*, XVI. 5.
5. शृंगारवीरशान्तानामेकोऽङ्गी रस इष्यते। *Sāhityadarpaṇa*, Op. cit.p. 365.

his characters. The proper role of characters in a story can make or mar the quality of a poem. So the characters hold a pivotal place in the structure of a *mahākāvya*. Whatever the sentiment or the motive of the composition is, there is always a principal action or the denouement to the core. Whosoever is to enjoy the benefit of the fulfilment of effort is the principal person, for he reaps the real and rich harvest. The motif or the resultant benefit is called the fruit and the enjoyment of the fruit is called the *adhikāra*. One who has the *adhikāra* is no doubt the *adhikārin* and it is he who becomes virtually the principal character, the hero in a composition. He is called the ***netā, nāyaka,*** or the hero because the entire action of a ***mahākāvya*** culminates in his benefit and revolves round him in the main. As we say, our modern poets have tried to make Nārāyaṇaguru, Vivekānanda, Christ as the heroes of their poems. The meritorious poet Ogeti Pariksit Sarma depicted the heroine as the hero. It is a deviation. It is interesting to say that all these poems are not composed with the aim of achievement of the *puruṣārthas* like *Dharma, Artha, Kāma* and *Mokṣa* although the Sanskrit poets have highlighted the importance of all these human values in their works. It is true that no reader will achieve any *puruṣārtha* out of study of the *kāvyas* or *mahākāvyas*. But the study will help him in enlightening his inner being and changing his perspective of life and selecting a proper means for achieving his goal of life.

In this connection it is worth noting that all these Sanskrit poets have made powerful attempts to depict the cultural,, religious, philosophical and spiritual aspects of our Sanskrit culture in fine, logical and convincing manner. They have made commendable efforts to popularise the hidden treasure that has been stocked in the Vedas, Purāṇas, epics like the *Rāmāyaṇa, Mahābhārata,* and in the treatises of religious teachers, philosophers and the founders of religions, who have struggled to make India great with their love, respect and labour.

The poets not only carve the bust of their fable from the popular stories and well-known incidents, but also project the portraits of the contemporary times in their imagination. They carve the idols of conceptions out of the fantasy of their aesthetic perception, giving guide-lines for the future of mankind. Everything in creation is in the continuous and non-stop process of evolving. It is the poet's glory to portray such pictures of life as to inspire the coming generation to evolve on the path of the spiral ascent heaven-wards. Thus, the poets achieve through the projection of transcendental values which become finger-posts on the path of mankind's march to the attainment of ultimate perfection. These are the forms for judging the stature and performance of the great poets, and it is with this yard-stick that posterity measures their height in imagination, breadth of vision and depth in terms of their inspirational projections.

Contribution of Orissa to Post-Independence Sanskrit Literature

Introduction

It is popularly known that Orissa in *Kalākṣetra,* land of Arts. That is why its ancient name is Utkala. From the very beginning, this state has enriched almost all the departments of Arts. The structures of Konarka, the *Gītagovinda* of Jayadeva and the imges of the temple of he Lord Jagannātha etc. speak of its glorious tradition in symbolic language which is intelligible to its lovers. In the delicate lap of Orissa, Sanskrit literature has flourished and it has been cherished properly by dedicated, commited and devoted Sanskrit writers who have struggled with the cruel time to make this language flowing like other regional languages. Needless to say, there are more than a hundred modern writers in the post-independence period, who have worked hard for the growth and development of Sanskrit literature. Unfortunately, many of them are like the flowers of forest. They bloom in corners. They do contain sweetness and fragrance but in the absence of right platform loose everything then and there.

We have to accept the fact that among modern Sanskrit poets of Orissa, few have distinguished themselves and have established their reputation as regular creative writers. They are seriously engaged with this profitless business which gives less but takes more. To create something new in any form or in any way in Sanskrit is really very difficult because the general atmosphere for creative literature is not conducive as very rightly said by the great poet Bhartṛhari in his *Nītiśataka* :

बोद्धारो मत्सरग्रस्ताः प्रभवः स्मयदूषिताः।
अबोधोपहताश्चान्ये जीर्णमङ्गे सुभाषितम्।।

Not only in Orissa, but also in every state, the fate of Sanskrit language is miserable. Accepting this misfortune of Sanskrit literature, those who are, like our devoted soldiers, working for Sanskrit literature and trying to protect it from decline, death and discontinuity, are to be remembered. Their love for this devine language should be respected and must be recorded in the pages of the history of Modern Sanskrit Literature.

With this idea in view, I have included here the name of those creative writers who have contributed in anyway to modern Sanskrit literature. It has been almost a fashion and tradition to look at the big fishes of the ocean and to sing the glory of those who possess some power of position. I do not believe in this idea. Therefore I have tried to bring to light the works which are available to me with the reason that the minor writers should be encouraged. I have, therefore, included the names of the authors who have created something beautiful, something sweet and something good for literature and contributed to this field.

It is not possible here to give a comprehensive survey of all modern Sanskrit writers who have made vital contributions to Sanskrit literature. First of all, the problem, I am confronting with, is the unavailability of published works. It is therefore true that I am preparing a report type of article with the help of insignificant data those are readily available to me.

I. Poems or Padyakāvyas

One department of creative writing in which Orissan writers have achieved significant success is poetry. Poetry has attracted almost all enthusiasts. Though many aspirants have tried their fingers in this area, few only come to our notice, who have carved a niche in the field of modern Sanskrit poetry after independence. Those who shine out in the field of poetry are the following :

Pundarikaksha Mishra

The *Sudāmācarita* a kāvya in Sanskrit has come down from the pen of Paṇḍita Pundarikaksha Mishra who was a well-known scholar of Sanskrit. As the title of the poem indicates, it deals with the story of Sudāmā who had the fortune of having an intimate friendship with Kṛṣṇa, the Lord of the universe. Though the small episode of Sudāmā does not give much scope to compose a *Mahākāvya* on it and there are already many *kāvyas* on this theme, still Paṇḍita Mishra's work distinguishes itself from its counterparts for the reason that he has treated this theme in a beautiful and interesting manner, the manner which is strikingly different from its counterparts. The work is of 101 pages. There are only five cantos having significant titles. These titles which are given at the end of the cantos, give us a good idea about the subject-matter of each canto in an aphoristic manner. There are 500 verses (in the first canto 80 verses, in the second 94, in the third 84, in the forth 112 and in the fifth 130). The theme of the poem is taken from the *Bhāgavata-Mahāpurāṇa*. The poet has made substantial change and has given a good form of poetry to a simple story. He has tried to bring to the notice of the readers the ultimate aim of an ardent devotee of the Lord Kṛṣṇa. People should know about the life of a householder and his great love for the religious activities in spite of his poverty. The poem commences with the prayer of the Lord Jagannātha. Appropriate metres and the judicious use of the figures of speech make the work interesting.

Vaikunthavihari Nanda

Paṇḍita Vaikunthavihari Nanda who is awarded by the Ministry of Human Resource Development on the occasion of Sanskrit year's celibration and also a winner of President's certificate of honour, has distinguished himself from other poets of Orissa by creating some new trends in modern Sanskrit literature. He has composed many *gītas* in Sanskrit in Oriya *rāgas.* His *Kīcakavadha mahākāvya* is a masterpiece. It is composed in Oriya *rāgas,* and a rare composition indeed. It is an important contribution to the tradition of lyrical poetry in Sanskrit literature. He has made many new experiments in the field of Sanskrit literature too. An important feature of his creativity is that he has made *Sanskṛtagītānuvāda* in the same lyrical form of the *kiśoracandrānanacampū* composed in Oriya by the great poet Kavisūrya Baladeva Ratha. He has composed many minor poems for the purpose of Sanskrit Pālās.

खर्वः पार्वणशर्वरीरतिगुरोरापीड्य बिम्बं क्षुधा
मर्त्त्यःकापि सुधाममुत्र वसुधालोके पिबत्यातुरः
व्यर्थं प्रार्थनया कदर्थयसि मां गत्वा दुराशां कथं।
सा किं मद्वशमेति हन्त वियतस्ताराधिकाराधिका।।

केशव! लूतातन्तुवलयवागुराभिः कण्ठीरवराजीव राजीवलोचना साऽस्मादृशी-भिर्वशीकर्त्तुशक्या।

उत्कलभाषयागीतम्-राग-मुखवरी-पेडिपरजावा

झगडिमात्र हेल हे श्याम!

झिमुट हेवाकु सहस्त्रयाम-ध्रुवम्

झाउँलिवा नवतमालरमा, झिङ्किआणि अङ्गे कलणिजमा।१।

झडिव वल कोमल छातिरु झसध्वजपीडाझाञ्जितातिरु।२।

झुमि झुमि लुठि पृष्टे रसार, झुरिवार एका होइव सार।३।

झुलि पाञ्चालीझटकेनाहिंकि, झोला माइला तुम्भुङ्कु काहिंकि?।४।

झुलकि गल कृष्ण अकारणे, जाउ खण्डरसा 'वादसा' भणे।

गीतस्य संस्कृतानुवादः-पण्डितवैकुण्ठविहारीनन्दः

झकटीकृत्य वृथा हे श्याम झटिति भाव्यते सहस्त्रयामः

झावुकायिततमालसुषमामाकृष्य लिप्यते शरीरसीमा

झरिष्यति वलं कोमलहृदः झसध्वजपीडा-वातसुहृदः
झुमंल्लठिष्यसि पृष्टे रसायाः, झुरणमेवसारं सुरसायाः
झलितापाङ्ग ली न शोभते किं झोलायिततनुस्त्वमसि वाकिम्
झलकायितो हे कृष्णाकारणं, झाडखण्डरसावादसाध्यानम्।

Digambara Mahāpātra

Another poet of prominence in Modern Sanskrit Literature is Paṇḍita Digambara Mahāpātra who has made massive contribution to Sanskrit. He has received President's Award for his valuable contribution to modern Sanskrit literature, The following poem-collection have so far come from pen of Paṇḍita Mahāpātra. 1. *Vyastarāgam*, 2. *Surendracarita-Mahākāvyam*, 3. *Mānasasandesa*, 4. *Raṅgaruciram*, 5. *Durnapurāṇam*, 6. *Lalitalavaṅgam*, 7. *Bhavate rocate yathā*.

The *Vyastarāgam* is a collection of fifty Sanskrit poems composed in different metres in lucid style. The work is divided in three parts namely *satya-ucchvāsa*, *Śiva-ucchvāsa* and *Saundarya-ucchvāsa*. This collection embodies the pictures of social realities with excellent stylistic elegance and ideal subtleties. Indian culture, ancient civilization, scientific adventures, importance of Sanskrit, natural beauties of some human character have been aptly portrayed with its natural niceties with a view to make the readers conscious about themselves and their surroundings. Orissan culture and heritage, beauty of nature, art and architecture find good expression in his poetry.

The *Surendracarita mahākāvya*[1] is an epic poem composed in 12 cantos. It seems to me as the best of his works. Surendra Sai, a great freedom fighter of Orissa who had sacrificed his life for the cause of motherland Orissa, has been made the

1. Panda, R.K., *Sudāmācaritam of pundarikakṣa Miśra* : A Study Journal of the Oriental Institute, Vol. 55, Nos. 1-4, 2005-June 2006 Issue, pp. 89-98.

hero of this poem. This *Mahākāvya* highlights his heroic deeds, his love for motherland, his achievements and contributions. Since the poet is a master of poetics, his *Mahākāvya* strictly follows the traditional definition given by the poeticians like Viśvanātha Kivirāja in his *Sāhityadarpaṇa.* Simple language, lucid style, descriptive picturesque, systematic narrative, treatment of nature etc. are the distinctive features of this work.

The *Raṅgaruciram* is a collection of modern Sanskrit poems written in modern *rāgas* mainly prevalent in Orissa and especially used by the Oriya poets of medieval period. This work is a valuable contribution to children literature in Sanskrit. The selection of topics, which can easily create laughter and touch the tender hearts, is a remarkable feature of this work.

His fourth work is *Mānasasandeśa.* It falls in the category of *Sandeśakāvya* or *Dūtakāvya.* In this poem the poet has made his mind as his messanger. The poet explains the futility of our wordly pleasures and consoles the mind not to be deeply involved with this transitory pleasure. It should not be under the illusion and try to realise the highest truth, which in nothing but shelter in the supreme Reality, *Bhagavaddarśana.*

Shrinivas Rath

Prof. Shrinivas Rath is a well-known name in the field of Modern literature of Sanskrit. He has composed many Sanskrit songs, which give a freshness to its reader. His one collection of poems *Tadeva Gaganam Saiva Dharā* published by Rashtriya Sanskrit Sansthana is a valuable contribution to Modern literature. His poems are touching for containing sensitive feelings and their lucid expression. He has now settled at Ujjain.

Keshab Chandra Dash

The impact of change pervades every department of literature. Still the old trend of artificial poetry is continuing.

The poems are written on old subjects out of genuine love for language. But it is important to note that side by side the poets are also becoming conscious of their new responsibilities, duties, their roles in the present situation and the need of the hour. As a result the conventional forms are being avoided and new forms are being created, which give to the poet a larger measure of freedom. Among the poets who have accepted the sense of modernity spontaneously and have played a leading role in creating new trends and new forms, Dr. Keshab Chandra Dash's name comes first. He is a talented and dedicated poet who has been successful in influencing many creative writers of his time. He has enriched the field to a great extent.

Born in 1955, at the village of Hatasahi, Distt. Jajpur, Orissa, Prof. Dash has established himself both as an outstanding scholar and a celebrated creative writer in Sanskrit. As a poet and writer of profound depth Dr. Dash is famous for exploring a new dimension of Sanskrit writings. His literacy works suffuse with deep philosophy of life and aesthetic strength. His following collections of poems have come out: *(1) Praṇayapradīpam, (2) Hṛdayeśvarī, (3) Mahātīrtham, (4) Bhinnapulinam, (5) Alakā, (6) Eṣā* and *(7) Andhasrota.*

Some Sanskrit poets of Orissa have kept themselves in close touch with contemporary events. They have utilised freely the fresh material with which they come in contact. It is one way of creating modernity in Sanskrit literature. It is also an urgent need of the hour. We want to prove that Sanskrit is a living language and the literary activity in Sanskrit is not confined only to the traditional set of compositions and rotten themes which have lost flavour for ever. Our others should take up the current problems as the subject of their compositions. Thereby we can bring some freshness in the field and attract the hearts of the readers. Two well-known poets of Orissa, Rabindra Kumar Panda and Banamali Biswal have mainly composed poems on the contemporary events. The present writer has composed long poems on the Kargil, draught, earthquake, communal riot, Orissa cyclone etc. Dr. Biswal has also composed many small poems on these topics.

Luckily there has been revival of interest in the literary pursuit of Sanskrit and even among Oriya Sanskritists who have received modern education, there has been a growing desire to cultivate the language as a vehicle of their thought and expression. Under the influence and inspiration of Keshab Chandra Dash, a doyen of modern Sanskrit literature, many bright upcoming Sanskritists have taken up pen to enrich Sanskrit literature even though they are well-aware of the fact that there is a limited scope to succeed. The general atmosphere is not encouraging, and the attitude of our Sanskrit Paṇḍits are always pulling them back. Though Sanskrit literature gets few readers to read, appreciate and encourage, yet the lovers of Sanskrit have not closed their eyes for the revival of Sanskrit.

Harekrishna Satapathy

Harekrishna Satapathy has a good name as a poet. He has composed some small poems of Samāsyāpūri type. His long poem on the river Ganges, *Gaṅgājalām dūṣitam* is an important contribution. His *Dharmapada* is also an important contribution. His other works are awaiting publication.

Rabindra Kumar Panda

Rabindra Kumar Panda has made some noteworthy contribution to the field of modern Sanskrit poetry-literature.[1] His nine poem-collections have seen the light of the day. Some are under publication. They are the following :

---

1. Panda, R.K. Biographical Poems in Sanskrit : A Glance, Sri Venkateswara University Oriental Journal, Vol. XLV, 2002, parts 1 & 2. pp. 1-25.

1. *Vanavalli, 1996,* 2. *Partidhvani, 1996,* 3. *Urvee, 1999,* 4. *Nīravajhara 1999,* 5. *Śatadalam, 2000,* 6. *Valākā,* 7. *Kāvyakairavam,* 8. *Kāvyāmṛta-tarangini*

The *Vanavalli* is a collection of 43 poems. Some are very short and some are big in size. Poems are written in simple and sweet language. One can easily find modernity in the structure, style and contents of the poems. The title itself is significant and suggestive.

The *Pratidhvani* is a collection of 97 poems composed in free style. Most of the poems are philosophical and suggestive. New images, new symbols and novelty in approach make the poems interesting.

The *Urvee* is a collection of 130 poems written in easy language and lucid style. It represents the ultra modern trends of modern Sanskrit poetry. Poems are suggestive and bring home poetic sensitivity.

The *Nīravajhara* is a collection of 52 poems. Most of them are composed in the form of *gītas*.

The *Śatadalam* is a collection of 8 *Śatakakāvyas* and 2 *Khaṇḍakāvyas* written in different traditional metres. There are in all 1500 verses.

The *Valākā* is a collection of 50 free style poems on a variety of themes.

The *Kāvyakairavam* is a collection of 21 kāvyas composed in different metres. The work consists of 1000 verses.

Panda's poems are not loaded with jargons which always stand on the way of aesthetic taste. They are free from artificiality and contain a rhythmic flow of feelings.

Banamali Biswal

Banamali Biswal has made important contributions to this field. He has published five collections of poems namely *Saṅgamenābhirāmā, Vyathā, Priyatamā, Dārubrahma* and *Valentine day sandeśa.* The *Saṅgamenābhirāmā* consists of 35 poems and 300 verses. Biswal depicts the pictures of contemporary society and surroundings. His observation is very minute in this direction. In almost all of his poems, the contemporary social problems like terrorism in Punjab and Kashmir, impact of gas-tragedy in Bhopal, the communal riots etc. are nicely depicted.

The poems of Biswal in his second collection of poems *Vyathā* are very fine examples of the sensitivity of a modern young Indian who is firmly anchored in his age-old tradition on the one hand and on the other, feels deeply disenchanted with the set up of the society and the human world around. The themes of the poems of Biswal are new. His approach to the problems of life is fresh. His treatment of the subject is novel and the material outfit of the blank verses in which his poetry is couched is also an outcome of modern times.

The *Ṛtuparṇā* contains 102 free style poems. Because of its thematic variation, the collection is privileged to provide its readers a rare scope to rejoice a variety of poetic tastes in a single substratum.

The *Valentine day Sandeśa* is a small collection of mono-image poems.

The *Priyatamā* is a collection of free-style poems.

The *Dārubrahma* is a collection of Sanskrit lyrics based on Oriya *bhajanas* on the Lord Jagannātha.

Prafulla Kumar Mishra

Prafulla Kumar Mishra has composed two collections of poems namely *Citrakuraṅgī* and *Brahmanābhi.*

Suryamani Ratha

Suryamani Ratha has composed a *Śṛṅgeriśataka.* It is an interesting piece of poem.

Harekrishna Meher

Meher has composed *Mātṛgītāñjali*, a *gītikāvya* in Sanskrit.

Bhubaneswara Kar

Kar has composed *Doṣaśatakam*-a century of verses on the blemishes.

Bharativihari Dash

Another poet of Orissa, Bharativihari Dash has composed some minor poems. One of them is *Vande Mātaram.* It is a *gīta* type of poem.

Harihara Hota

Harihara Hota is a new name in contemporary Sanskrit literature. He has just entered into the field. However, his poems have some inrinsic merit and therefore it must be taken note of. *Utkalamātṛbhūmiḥ* is one of his good poems.

Bhupatibhusana Mishra

Bhupatibhusana Mishra is a familiar name in the field of modern Sanskrit literature. He is a minor poet. He is composing poems occasionally. However, his poems are pregnant with patriotic feelings. He mainly writes on Indian culture, importance of Sanskrit language, Indian values etc. The poet Mishra has earned good name for his sweet, musical and lyrical style of composition. The Sanskrit pracārakas sing one of his best poems, *naumi punyabhārata* in their regular sessions.

Ramanatha Nanda

Older literature on the lives of noteworthy personalities mixed fable and fact and narrated in poetic and eulogistic style the lives of important individuals with descriptive excursions obscuring the few historical data. In the new biographies, the high flown style gave place to a simple narrative prose and such accounts have appeared on a varities of personalities, historical figures of the saints both ancient, medieval and modern scholars, political leaders and public figures of the recent time. Ramanatha Nanda of Jaipura of Orissa has composed a long poem.

From the pages of the Sanskrit magazines I could gather names of some contemporary poets whose works have not appeared in book-form. To mention few names : Gadadhar Dash, Brajkishore Naik, Achyutananda Dash, Subash Chandra Dash, Sadananda Dash, Kishore Chandra Mahapatra, Patitapabana Banarjee, Kamlesh Mishra, Manmohan Acarya, Sugyana Mohanty, Surendranath Mishra *et. al.*[1]

II. Drama Literature

To my knowledge, the most neglected part of Sanskrit writing in Orissa is drama. In other states, poetry and drama have often gone hand in hand. In Orissa while poetry forged ahead drama literature has lagged behind.

Sudarshana pati's *Siṁhalavijaya* (Berhampur, 1951) is a drama on an episode of Orissan history fitted with Orissan songs.

Suryamani Ratha has composed a play name *Paropakarī*. It is a small play based on the theme of the *Mahābhārata*. The work is of 22 pages and has only six scenes. The killing of Vakasura in Ekacakranagarī forms the subject matter of the play. The approach is traditional.

Recently Surendra Nath Sarangi has composed two plays namely *Vandemātaram* and *Abhijñānaśakuntalam*. The first play, as is clear from the title itself, is full of patriotic feelings. The second one is simplified version of the *Abhijñānaśākuntalam* of Kālidāsa.

III. Novels and stories

Keshab Chandra Dash

The novel is the epic in prose of the modern age, though in Sanskrit very few novels rise to that status. On the whole,

1. Prajapati, Sweta, Ādhunika Sanskrita-Kaviyon ki dṛṣṭi meṁ jīvana (life in the eyes of the Modern Sanskrit Poets), Dr.K. Vol. 9, Dr. Bhāratī, Allahabad, pp. 77-78

what is true of the drama and the short story is true in case of novel also. In Orissa, Keshab Chandra Dash is the first person to write novels in Sanskrit. He has already composed 10 novels and has created a significant treasure of literature for which every Sanskritist should be proud of. His creative genius and profound love for labour has given a new colour to modern Sanskrit writing. This class of writing can be definitely called modern. We see again a trasition from a background and theme like that of the *Kāldambarī* to a social millew.

It is perhaps in the short story that one might notice prominently the new developments coming over Sanskrit. The short form as such is not new to Sanskrit but the form in which it is now handled Sanskrit owes to the west. In Orissa, there are some progressive writers who are doing justice to this modern forms. They have composed short stories mainly on social evils like the dowry system, exploitations, curruption, blind beliefs in the name of value sysyem. Prof. Dash has taken a leading role and has influenced his successors who are walking in his line. He has composed the following works : *1. Śītalatṛṣṇā, 2. Pratipad, 3. Nikaṣā, 4. Aruṇā, 5. Añjali, 6. Āvartam, 7. Ṛtam, 8. Madhuyānam, 9. Tilottamā, 10. Śikhā, 11. Visarga, 12. Śaśirekhā, 13. Om Sānti, 14. Nimnapnthivī, 15. Diśavidiśa, 16. Urmicuḍā, 17. Śūnyanābhi, 18. Patāka, 19. Mahān* and *20. Ekadā.*

Banamali Biswal has made a mark in the department of short-story writing. His first collection of story which appeared in 1998 is *Nīravasvana*. The work embodies thirty short stories presented in easy and flowing language. Most of the stories deal with social problems and existing evils, superstitions, exploitations, residential problems in the cities and social customs. The characters are very well sketched and they speak out their own problems. His other work is *Bubhukṣā* which is a collection of 24 short stories.

Narayana Dash is a new name in modern literature of

Sanskrit. He has published one collection of story i.e. *Gaṅge ca yamune Caiva* and also some stories in Sanskrit magazines.

Pramod Nayak has published seventy short stories in the *Lokasuśrī* magazine published by Lokabhāṣā Pracāra Samiti. His stories are too small but create interest. Since the author is budding, nothing more is expected from him.

Sampadananda Mishra, through new in this field, is well-appreciated for composing stories with an intension of creating humor. His work, *Hāsyamañjarī* is a valuable addition to the Kathāsāhitya of modern period.

Rabindra Kumar Panda has written some novels and stories but some of them are awaiting publications. *Chinnacchyā* is his published collection of stories.

Things on the whole appear to be brighter. Orissa has every reason to look forward with hope and confidence to a bright future of modern Sanskrit literature. It is not only on account of her vast potential reserves of natural resources but on account of her high tradition in the field of art and culture, which is growing and expressing itself in new forms. Day by day new writers are coming up with new zeal and commitment not only for maintaining the pristine glory of Sanskrit literature but also to make it a language of common people who struggle for survival but love literature also for making their life worth enjoyable.

As we see, Sanskrit has always kept an intimate relation with the popular tongues and the literature of them. In the modern period, the critical and historical story of Indian Literature has induced many Sanskritists to render into the Sanskrit medium some of the best works from his own regional literature.

IV. Translations.

Prabodha Kumar Mishra has translated Utkalamani Gopabandh's Kāvya into Sanskrit namely *Vandinaḥ Svadeśacintā*.

Ananta Tripathy Sharma has made noteworthy contribution to enrich this important field of literature. He has translated some of the Sanskrit plays of Shakespeare into Sanskrit. The *Dvādaśa ratri* (twelfth night) is one of them.

Recently Govinda Chandra Udgata has made a laudable attempt in this department. He has translated the Oriya work, *Śrīrādhā* of Ramakanta Ratha into Sanskrit.

At the end I have to say with heavy pain in heart that there are plenty of talented young writers in Orissa, who are in need of guidance, training and inspiration. At least lamps are to be kindled if we cannot do anything for them. There is the need of a comprehensive survey and critical study of all these works.

Biographical Poems in Sanskrit A Glance*

Introduction

It is a matter of great pleasure for a lover of Sanskrit to observe that a regular tradition and an appreciable trend of composing *carita-kāvyas* (biographical poems) in Sanskrit has been continuing in full swing. The tradition of writing biographies both in prose and poetry on the life of eminent persons is rooted in antiquity. The earliest works in India, which could be termed biographical, occur in Buddhist literature written in Pāli, and they narrate the life story of Buddha. In fact, great religious teachers, saints and monarchs were practically the only subjects of ancient Indian biographical writing. Furthermore, the art of biography was regarded purely as a branch of the *belles-letters* and generally used verse as its medium of expression. This naturally made the employment of flights of poetic fancy and romantic hyperbole inevitable and the modern idea of biography, as the truthful transmission of personality was evidently not relevant in those circumstances. Again, owing to his stance of reverential admiration for the subject, the ancient Indian biographer could seldom maintain his own freedom of spirit,. which is said to be another duty of the biographer. Nevertheless, though biography as a genre as we understand it today, was, like many other forms of modern writing, the gift of modern education there was a considerable body of

1. The S.V.U. Oriental Journal, Vol. XLV.

biographical writing during the centuries before the British conquest. The tradition of the lives of great religious teachers and saints is as old as the *Buddhacarita* of Aśvaghoṣa in Sanskrit. Ancient Jaina literature, both in, Sanskrit and Prākṛt, abounds in biographies of Mahāvīra and other saints, and the Hindu religious teachers like Śaṅkarācārya, Rāmānujācārya, and others. The tradition of the lives of kings can be traced to Bāṇabhaṭṭa's well-known *Harṣacarita* composed in 7th century A.D. It is known that the earliest attempt is the *Buddha-carita* of Aśvaghoṣa. Sanskrit poets even from the beginning of the classical Sanskrit literature have composed biographies of eminent persons both in verse and prose. But, most of them are composed in verse. The purpose behind such compositions is two-fold. Besides providing aesthetic enjoyment to connoisseurs, the *carita-kāvyas* serve as a record of the activities of those persons who have made something good for the benefit of society or for the country. The *Carita-kāvyas* thus unfold not only the history of those persons but also the conditions of the time, in which they had lived and worked. Further, in those parts of India where the tradition of historical writings did not develop, unlike Kashmir where Kalhaṇa's *Rājataraṅgiṇī* and its subsequent supplements came into being, the type of biographical writing provided a lot of historical facts and information to fill up gaps in Indian history. Bāṇa's *Harṣa-carita*, Bilhaṇa's *Vikramāṅkadeva-carita*, Padmagupta's *Navaśāhasāṅka-carita*, to name only a few, are such works of older period. So some of the *carita-kāvyas* are historical poems. But, all the poems are not historical. Even in some *carita-kāvyas*, history does not find a place. The poet sings only the glory of the person in superficial words and projects the person in such a form that a reader will find something appreciable in him. As Mammaṭa says in his *Kāvyaprakāśa*, one of the purposes of poetry is to give the knowledge of social behaviour. The poet is like a guide. It becomes his responsibility to show the right path to his readers who are to be instructed to follow the path of Rāma, not of Rāvaṇa, the great demon. It is the supreme purpose, which prompts a poet to highlight the qualities, works and contributions of the person, he has subjected for his composition. Others such as *Kṣatrapati-caritam, Indirāgāndhi-caritam* etc., of their stature, combine to perpetuate this tradition. They are primarily intended as poems embellished by all the trappings sanctioned by the theory, with the result, it is the form that dominates the narrative and historiography. Contrary to these versified *carita-kāvyas,* the *Harṣa-carita* of Bāṇa addresses itself to detail the checkered career of Harṣavardhana with the gimmicks that Sanskrit prose admits in ample measure. It, however, concurs with them in making the narrative a handmaid of the flamboyant medium. This is precisely what accounts for the failure of these so-called ancient biographies to meet the purpose they are intended to serve. They are essentially poems, *dṛśya* or *śravya, gadya* or *padya.*

Some Important Carita-kāvyas

This tradition of the *carita-kāvya* has happily percolated down to the present age. Some of the contemporary Sanskritists have been quick to exploit it, with certain modifications to fruitful desirable results. While attempting biographies of the stalwarts like Bālagangādhar Tilak. Mahātma Gāndhi and Jawāharalāl Nehru etc , the modern Sanskritists have been bold of avoiding the pitfalls that stalked his predecessors. He is acutely alive to the requirements of modern time that invariably insists on the measured but elegant presentation of the narrative. Outer trappings are relevant to him to the extent they serve to enliven the otherwise insipid narrative. The cautious effort to strike balance between the form and content has resulted in the emergence of a number of *carita-kāvyas* that come close to the modern concept of biography. They are distinguished by a full-fledged depiction of the *Carita* of the person concerned without over-burdening it with such embellishments as combine to turn history into fiction.

The *Buddha-carita* of Aśvaghoṣa describes the acts of Buddha from his birth to his demise. There is a similar work entitled *Jina-carita* dealing with the life of Buddha less-successfully on the model of Aśvaghoṣa's *Buddha-carita.* It represents a poetic development in Pāli similar to that represented by the *Buddha-carita* in the Sanskrit Buddhist literature. A complete Sanskrit text of the *Buddha-carita* is not available at present. Samuel Beal offers us an English translation of the whole text, which is prepared from its Chinese version. In the Chinese version, the text of the *Buddha-carita* consists of twenty-eight cantos while in the Sanskrit text edited by Cowell and subsequently by Johnston, the first thirteen cantos only can be claimed to be the composition of Aśvaghoṣa together perhaps with some portions of canto XIV. Whatever may be the case, the *Buddha-carita* is an outstanding work. It is, to my knowledge, the first *carita-kāvya* in Sanskrit. The work is so seminal that it could influence many successors who started composing *carita-kāvyas* under the strong influence of Aśvaghoṣa who laid the foundation stone of the tradition of *carita-kāvyas* in Sanskrit.

Similarly the *Vikramāṅkadeva-carita* of Bilhaṇa is an important work of this tradition. This work is historical. It narrates the history of the princes of the Calukya dynasty of Kalyāṇa Someśwara I, Someśwara II and particularly of Vikramāditya VI who ruled from 1076-1127 A.D. As the chief aim of Bilhaṇa is to extol his heroes exuberantly and compose a poem as per the rules of the literary criticism, he cares more for imaginative things, not for the factual presentation of the history of Calukyas. The events narrated by him are historical but what is presented in the poem gives a distorted picture of it. The poem begins with a myth about the origin of the dynasty of this king. The God appears always in this poem when the king does something immoral. Even though the work is a mixed form of both history and myth, its historical importance cannot be neglected.

In this line comes then the *Naiṣadha-carita* of Śrīharṣa who wrote it probably under Vijaycand and Jayacand of Kanauja in the second half of the 12th century A.D. It is a great epic in 22 cantos and narrates the story of Nala in an elaborate style. But, in the twenty-two cantos of the epic, the poet does not succeed in carrying the narrative up to the description of happenings of the newly married couple. The poet ends his poem in a description of the moony night in a conversation between Nala and Damayanti. The work is pedantic and made only for a selected few.

Another important work of this tradition is *Navaśāhasaṅka-carita* of Padmagupta or Parimala. The real theme of this *mahākāvya* is fabulous. The work refers to some historic names and events. Hence, it is considered to be a historical poem. It has 18 cantos and relates the mythical theme of the winning the princess Śaśīprabhā, daughter of the Nāga king. The poet had composed this epic for the glorification of his patron, the Sindhurāja Navaśāhasāṅka of Malwa. Historical essence remains only in the narration of the myth in this epic poem of Parimala.

Worthy of special mention is the *Śrīkaṇṭha-carita* of the Kashmirian poet Maṅkha (1135-1145 A.D.) who handles the myth of the overthrow of Tripurāsura in his poem. The tale, however, has secondary importance. The main goal of the poet is to describe the seasons, the sunset, the court-entertainment etc., according to the rules of Sanskrit poetics.

Haracarita-cintāmaṇi of the Kashmirian poet Rājānaka Jayaratha (1200 A:D.) is an important work. But, it does not fall in this general category. It has some special importance. It is mainly a religious epic and full of Śiva-legends and teachings of Śaivism.

Another important work of this trend is the *Rāmapāla-carita* of Sandhyākaranandi. But, this work has some special features. Each stanza in this poem has two meanings and one of them relates to the hero Rāma and the other to the king Rāmapāla who ruled over Bengal in the eleventh century A.D.

Rāmapālacarita is a unique composition in many respects. It gives a historical account of the successful revolution in Northern Bengal, which cast the Pāla king Mahīpa, his life and throne, and of the restoration of the paternal kingdom' by Rāmapāla, his youngest brother. The great revolution and specially the restoration form the main theme of the work and we know of no other Indian text, which deals with an important contemporary historical episode with such wealth of details.

Vīra-Kamparāya-caritam or the *Madhurāvijayam* is a heroic poem in nine cantos composed by Gaṅgādevi (1367 A.D.), the chief queen of the Kampana of Kānjīvaram. She is the queen of the first son of Bukka I, the hero of the poem. It describes in the manner of a *mahākāvya* the exploits of Kampana resulting in the elimination of the Sambhuvarāya rule in the Toṇḍaimaṇḍalam and the extermination of the Madurai Sultanate. She has described in it the historic deeds of her husband including his march against Campa of Kāñcī and against the Muhamuddan ruler of Madurarājya. It is a poem of high merit and great historical value. It throws much needed light upon the political situation in the south and the position of Vijayanagar *vis-a-vis* the other Southern states.

Vādirāja's poem *Yaśodhara-caritam* has its own individuality and striking features. It possesses an artistic unity; its descriptions are proportionate and its expressions are precise, natural and figurative. The arrangement of plot and the flow of narration are masterly and their moral instructions are effective often shatteringly slashing at contemporary evils. Vādirāja is seen here as a mature poet. In his flow of poetry, not a word is in excess and the figures of speech came at the poet's command. In sheer poetic quality, the *Yaśodhara-carita* is second to none in Sanskrit literature; and as the hottest and a sweetest *mahākāvya* it is entitled to a singular place in the history of Sanskrit poetry. It is short in compass, modern in theme and moralistic in tone. The episodes of rebirths are often looked upon as boring but they supply opportunities to a resourceful author to multiply his characters both human and sub-human. Vādirāja has ably turned them out to his advantage. The animals in this poem not only afford entertainment, but also serve to analyze human motive with unerring discernment on the variety of life.

There are three *Kumārapālacarita-kāvyas* composed by Hemacandra, Jinasiṁhasūri (1265 A.D.) and Cari- (1914) respectively. The epic poem *Kumārapāla-carita* called also *Dvāśrayakāvya* of Hemacandra is written partly in Sanskrit and partly in Prākṛt. Hemacandra proves himself simultaneously a poet, a historian and a grammarian in two languages. The epic has 28 cantos in all; 20 cantos in Sanskrit and 8 cantos in Prākṛt. The first seven cantos are to serve as illustrations to the rules of the first seven sections of his Sanskrit grammar, whilst the eighth canto stands in a similar relation to the author's grammar of Prākṛt. The work contains a history of the Cālukyas of Anhivad (Anahillapura) and particularly of Kumārapāla. In cantos XVI to XX, that are devoted to the latter, this prince is extolled above all as a pious Jaina, who prohibited bloody sacrifices and trading in flesh, got erected Jaina temples etc. The last two cantos contain moral and religious reflections. From the concluding portion of the work it is evident that Kumārapāla was full in life.

Mahākavi Kṣemendra has also contributed to this tradition. He has composed *Daśāvatāra-caritam*. It is a poetical abstract of the stories of Viṣṇu's incarnations. The work cannot be considered as an independent composition. The subject matter of the first nine incarnations is taken from the Purāṇas. The seventh chapter, which represents Viṣṇu's incarnation as Rāma, shows novelty of conception. Here the whole of the *Rāmāyaṇa* is narrated with Rāvaṇa as the central figure. The result is quite happy and the vividness of description adds to the charm. The work, however, has great importance as it contains the earliest known reference to the Buddha being considered as an incarnation of Viṣṇu. The narration of the Buddha's life is an abridgment of the story as told in Buddhist works. The style shows maturity of conception, and is easy and flowing. The work was finished in the 1066 A.D. on the Tripureśa Mountain.

In modern times Śrīpāda Śāstri Hasūrkar of Indore has composed many *carita-kāvyas*: *Buddhadeva-caritam, Vardhamanasvāmi-caritam, Śaṅkarācarya-caritam, Vallabhācārya-caritam, Rāmadasa-caritam, Sikhaguru-caritāmṛtam, Pṛthvīrāja Cahvāṇa-caritam Mahārāṇa Pratāpa Siṁha-caritam, Chatrapati Śivaji mahārāja-caritam.* I think, this great poet has made a special place of his own in the field of poem-composition and there is no other poet who has written so many *carita kāvyas* in Sanskrit like Hasūrkar.

Next to him, Satyavrat Śāstri has composed three *carita-kāvyas* in Sanskrit, namely *Śrībodhisattva-caritam, Indirāgāndhi-caritam,* and *Śrīgurugovinda-siṁha-caritam.* Of these, two are *mahākāvyas* and the last one is a *khaṇḍa-kāvya, Śrībodhisattva-caritam* seeks to offer in fourteen cantos comprising of one thousand verses the Sanskrit version of some of the most elevating and instructive *avadānas* of the Bodhisattva as detailed on the Jātaka stories. The poet has reduced the Bodhisattva's *avadānas* hitherto available in Pāli, to mellifluous verses. The work opens up new vistas in Sanskrit literature that has been rather parsimonious in dealing with the Buddhist themes in poetry. Though somewhat fragmented in nature, the *Bodhisattva-caritam* has a broad canvas, spanning fourteen cantos of uneven size. The main sentiment of the poem is *Śānta*. But, *Śṛṅgāra* in both its aspects also finds impressive expression in this interesting poem. The *Bodhisattva-carita* is not beset with the type of digressive descriptions. The poet is not enamoured of the conventional descriptions of sunset, moonrise etc. His descriptions are invariably brief and are interwoven in the texture of the poem with such finesse that they form pretty patterns that often lend it added charm. The descriptions are effective and powerful. The greatest asset of this *mahākāvya* is its language, which is distinguished by exceptional sweetness and chastity. The language is adorned with a variety of figures of speech and is marked by pleasingly smooth evenness.

Indirāgāndhi-caritam of Dr. Śāstri forms an important link in the long chain of *carita-kāvyas* in Sanskrit. It is a complete biography of the late Prime Minister Indira Gandhi. The work is first of its kind in Sanskrit. There are 25 cantos in this poem. It is composed in facile and mellifluous verses marked by spontaneity and sweetness. This epic poem describes on the basis of authentic records the life history and achievements of one of the greatest women of the world.

Satyavrat Śāstri's *Śrīgurugovindasiṁha-caritam* is the solitary versified biography of Guru Gobind Singh that he had composed on the tercentenary celebration of the birth of the tenth Guru by the Guru Gobind Singh Foundation, Patiala. Divided into four cantos and composed of 366 verses in different metres, this *carita-kāvya* would be rated as a *khaṇḍa-kāvya* technically though in performing the prohibitive task of dealing with the Guru's checkered career in its entirety and not being confined to any of its facets it could be rated as a *Prabandha-kāvya*. But, in the poetician's language the *Śrīgurugovindasiṁha-carita* is a *khaṇḍa-kāvya*. It details, albeit briefly, the Guru's life in its entirety. The eventful career of the Guru marked by an exuberance of vicissitudes, thrilling and elevating, forms a subject for a *Mahākāvya*. It is intended to be a versified biography of the great Guru.

Paṇḍita Kṣamā Rao has carved a niche in the field of creative literature in Sanskrit. She has composed three biographical poems viz. *Tukārāma-caritam*, *Rāmadāsa-caritam* and *Jñaneśwara-caritam*. Her *Mīrālaharī* is also a biographical poem though it is not entitled as such. She has also composed a biography of her father, Śaṅkar Pāṇḍuraṅga Paṇḍit.

Medhāvrata Śāstri has composed some biographical poems viz. *Brahmarṣi Virājananda-carita, Nārāyaṇaswāmi-carita, Jñānendra-carita, Nityānanda-carita,* and *Dayānanda digvijaya mahākāvya.* He has made valuable contribution to this tradition.

From the survey of the biographical poems it is known that the carita of Śrīrāma, Maryādāpuruṣottama has influenced many Sanskrit poets. So there are many *kāvyas* written on the life of Rāma. *Śrīrāma-caritam* is one of the best *Mahākāvyas* produced from Kerala. The poem was originally conceived and partly composed by Godāvarma, Vidvadyuvaraja (1800-1851) who passed away while he was working on the thirteenth canto of this poem. It was his grand nephew Kochnni Rāja (1858-1921 A.D.) who later completed it. Both were princes of the Koḍugnallūr Royal house, which was the foremost centre of learning in Kerala in the last century. Unlike previous poets who have often taken liberties with Vālmīki's tale, the authors of this *Mahākāvya* have scrupulously stuck to the sage's version. The first thirty-two cantos retell the story from Rāma's birth to his installation as the king of Ayodhya and the remaining eight, deal with *Uttara Rāmāyaṇa. Śrīrāma-carita,* however, is not a mere summary of Ādikāvya. Far from it, what Godavarma and following his example, Kochunni Rāja, have done is, so to say, to fill up the gaps left by Vālmīki. Those portions of the story, which Vālmīki has dealt with in detail, have been summarized and the two poets have elaborated those portions, which Vālmīki has skipped over. In this, as in many other aspects, they appear to be following the example set by Kālidāsa. It may be recalled that, of the six cantos in the *Raghuvaṁśa* that deal with the Rāma's story Kālidāsa has devoted to, *Bālakāṇḍa* just a single canto to the rest of the tale until the defeat of Rāvaṇa, a whole canto for Rāma's return's journey to Ayodhya and two cantos for *Uttara Rāmāyaṇa*. A similar patern has been adopted in the *Śrīrāma-caritam*. In this *Mahākāvya* the first two cantos are devoted to a summary of *Bālakāṇḍa*. It is only in the third canto that Godāvarma begins to reveal his poetic gifts. Beginning with the third, he spends five full cantos to give a vivid portrayal of what may be described as the honeymoon of Rāma and Sītā.

The third canto shows how Rāma slowly overcame Sītā's initial shyness and timidity. The eighth canto of the *Kumārasaṁbhava* is the obvious model, but Vidvadyuvaraja displays refreshing flashes, of his imagination in handling the subject. Expanding Vālmīki's many seasons the six seasons from Vasanta to Śiśira are described one after the other in the fourth canto, somewhat in the manner of *Ṛtusaṁhāra*. This canto written in the Drutavilaṁbita metre and embellished with Yamaka through out is a proof of the poet's fantastic mastery over works. The highlight of the fifth canto is a description of the seasons of flowers, while the next two contain description of nightfall, moonrise, night and dawn. The influence of the third and eight cantos of the *Kumārasaṁbhava* are clearly visible here. It should be emphasized that these are not descriptions as they provide the right back ground for the activities of the honeymooning royal couple. In contrast to these five cantos, the eighth canto summarizes the eventful Ayodhyākāṇḍa in some one hundred Anuṣṭubh verses. Against this, the Araṇyakāṇḍa takes seven cantos and the Kiṣkindhākāṇḍa six. These thirteen cantos are mainly given to descriptions. Among them special mention should be made of the elaborate portrait of Sītā that Godāvarma paints. In this *Śrīrāma-carita*, the poet presents Sītā through the eyes of Rāvaṇa when he sees her for the first time in the hermitage. This makes it more natural. The same technique is used to describe Rāma's personality in canto ten. There the poet records Śūrpaṇakhā's reaction in seeing Rāma. Not to be left behind Kochunni Rāja who completed the poem displays his resourcefulness in different ways in later cantos. A good example would be the part where he deals with the dispatch of the Vānara armies in search of Sītā. In the nineteenth canto, Sugrīva gives his followers a detailed description of the areas they have to cover and the routes they should follow and in the twentieth, he gives them Rāma's message for his spouse. Taken together these two cantos, written in the Mandākrāntā metre form a Sandeśa kāvya in the manner of *Megha-sandeśa*. *Sundarakāṇḍa* and *Yuddhakāṇḍa* are condensed into eleven cantos. Highlights include an impressive description of Lanka and word portraits of Rāvaṇa and Mandodarī. In the *Uttara Rāmāyaṇa* which is compressed into eight cantos, the poet gives a detailed description of the royal couple's second honeymoon following their reunion and return to Ayodhyā. *Śrīrāma-caritam* fulfills all the requirements of a *Mahākāvya* as laid down by the rhetoricians like Daṇḍin. Kālidāsa has influenced both uncle and nephew. However, in many respects, they have taken their cue from later parts like Māgha and Śrīharṣa who perhaps saw poetry as an intellectual exercise more than anything else. This is evident from the extravagance of their descriptions and the over elaboration of imagery. The two poets also seem to take pleasure in displaying their vast erudition in various scientific disciplines in Sanskrit.

Some Sanskrit poets have composed biographical poems-on the life Śrīcaitanya who is regarded as an incarnation of Viṣṇu and Śrīkṛṣṇa, his devotees and followers. The earliest work on the life of Caitanya is *Caitanyacaritāmṛta,* a metrical narrative composed in Sanskrit by Murāri Gupta, a resident of Navadvīpa and a contemporary. It consists of four *prakramas,* sections and. remains a valuable record of Caitanya's life although many extraneous and miraculous legends find a place in it. Next came after *Caitanya-caritāmṛta* by Paramānanda Sen, son of Sivananda Sen, a close associate of Caitanya. He was awarded the title of Kavikarṇapūra for his poetic talent by Caitanya himself. His epic poem consists of twenty cantos, depicting all the major events of Caitanya's life and presenting him as a deliverer of mankind, an incarnation of Śrīkṛṣṇa. He also wrote a biographical drama in ten acts: *Caitanya-Candrodaya nāṭaka* at the command of Gajapati Pratāparudra, king of Orissa. He was partly influenced by Śrīkṛṣṇa Mishra's allegorical drama *Prabodha-candrodaya* and introduced some allegorical characters in his work. It is the first biographical drama based on the life of a contemporary religious personality.

Pāṇḍavacarita is a *mahākāvya* produced in Kerala. It has sixteen cantos. It contains an account of the story of the *Pāṇḍavas* based on the *Mahābhārata*. The story of the Pāṇḍavas upto the choice of the bride Pāñcālī is the theme of the first and second cantos. The coronation of Yudhiṣṭhira as the heir apparent, sage Nārada's narration of the story of Sunda and Upasunda, Arjuna's pilgrimage to the secred fords etc., are narrated in the next canto. The burning of the Khāṇḍava forest and Yudhiṣṭhira's performance of the Rājasūya sacrifice, his defeat in the game of gambling, Pāṇḍava's retirement to the forest etc., are subject matter of the forth and fifth cantos. The penance of Arjuna to obtain *Pāsupatāstra*, his fight with Śiva in disguise as a hunter, Śiva's blessing of Arjuna, the story Bhīma fetching the Saugandhika flower and the reunion of Arjuna with his brothers etc., are narrated in canto six to nine. The life of the Pāṇḍavas *incognito* in the Virāṭa country. The slaying of Kīcaka, the cattle-robbery of the Kurus etc., are described in the next two cantos. Kṛṣṇa's role as messenger is the main theme of the twelfth canto. The last four cantos are devoted to narrating the preparations for the Kurukṣetra war and the various stages of it. The author has carefully picked up almost all the incidents, which are directly connected with the heroic deeds of the Pāṇḍavas, from the first canto onwards. Therefore, the sentiments *Vīra* and *Raudra* have been delineated obviously in almost all cantos of this work. The sentiments of heroism can be found in descriptions of Arjuna's fight with the hunter in the

Kurukṣetra war. Śṛṅgāra and Bhakti are also delineated as subordinate sentiments.

Yadunātha-carita or *Bhāgavatasaṅgraha* is a *Mahākāvya* of unknown authorship and date. In ten cantos it narrates the story of Kṛṣṇa. as told in the tenth skandha of the *Bhāgavata.* It is written in simple style. The work derives its name from the theme dealt with by the author. The legend of Yadunātha (Kṛṣṇa) is narrated in the poem, and hence the title Yudunātha is significant. The other title *Bhāgavatasaṅgraha* is suitable to the work as it is an abridged form of the tenth skandha of the *Bhāgavata purāṇa.* There is no direct evidence regarding the authorship and date of the poem. But the verses in the beginning of the poem mention that the poem was written at the instance of the queen of Quilon who was the sister of the king Ādityavarman of fifteenth century A.D. The author probably belongs to Cennannur since mention is made of Śiva of Aruṇācala in the poem.

Titles of Some Carita-Kāvyas

It is not possible here to give the summary of all the biographical poems along with a note of criticism. Here are given the titles of some of the *carita-kāvyas* in Sanskrit. The list is not comprehensive. But the works, which are important and are readily available, are only included here so that a reader will find a glimpse of this tradition and trend. There are many other biographical poems which are not given any *carita* title like *Nehrū Yaśas Saurabham, Indirā Yaśastilakam, Rajīva Saurabham* etc. But we have not included such works here because of the paucity of space. A list of 115 Carita Kāvyas noticed by me are appended at the end of the article in alphabetical order for easy reference.

Conclusion

K.V. Sarma has classed the biographical literature under two headings, namely, the literature produced before the impact of western concepts and the literature from then up to modern times. He rightly remarks: "The writings of the early period were prone to the introduction of legendary accounts, exaggerations and parallelisms characteristic of classical Sanskrit and to be devotional and moralistic rather than objective and balanced. In tune with the thought of the times, the lives portrayed pertained primarily to the saints and the royalty. During the second period, when the norms of western biographical writing began to seep into India, its impact also began to be felt by the Sanskrit writer. For one thing, the vision of the Sanskritists and as a result he began to view men and matters in a more realistic perspective, with a critical eye and an inquiring spirit. For another, the prevailing nationalist movement, too, had its effect on him. Thus, while he took up for portrayal prominent personalities from all walks of life, he also took pains to collect data from diverse sources and set them out in an objective manner, to form authentic biographies. However, it has to be noted that, in spite of these efforts; there still remain, in these works, traces of classical presentation germane to Sanskrit poetic tradition. This aspect apart, the substantial biographical literature produced in Sanskrit during modern times may be taken to represent a welcome diversion from the biographical writings produced during the earlier phase."[1]

He further remarks about the modern trend that though the contents of the works are biographical, the treatment is poetic, with the use of high flown style eulogies and descriptive excursions not germane to the biography proper.[2] The advent of western literature in India and an understanding of the norms and practices followed in modern biographical writings appear, to have wrought a definite change in Sanskrit biographies produced from around the beginning of this century. Stress bean to lay on

1. Sarma K.V., Sanskrit-Coanparative Indian Literature, Section 9, Biographical Writtings, Page 1022-1026.
2. *ibid.*

personalities and the objective recording of events. Poetic effusions began to give way to simple prose or narrative verse. The scope of the biographies was extended to include leading persons in all walks of life, to wit, to historic personalities, old and new, saints and social reformers, political leaders and freedom-fighters, poets and philosophers.

Biographical Literature is an important and significant sector of modern Sanskrit Literature. Internationally significant religious and spiritual figures like Śaṅkarācārya, Vivekānanda, Political personalities like Mahātmā Gāndhī, Paṇḍit Nehru, Lokmānya Tilak, Indirā Gāndhī, Rājiv Gāndhī; popular saints and mystics like Jñāneśvara, Rāmadāsa, Tukārāma and freedom fighters like Vira Surendra Sai, Sardar Patel etc., have become the subject of biographical Poems in Sanskrit.

Actually, writing biographical poems on historical personalities, is undoubtedly a very difficult task. Biographical work should not be a mere history or biography, *i.e.*, an insipid statement of dates and facts nor can it be a mere 'fiction' or 'fantasy' soaring only on the wings of imagination-however, sweet or charming. Thus, an author of biographical poetry-be it either in poetic or in dramatic form; has to steer between two extremes: history and imagination, cautiously but artistically. The proper and perfect synthesis of history and literary art; truth and fiction lies at the root of the success of a biographical poem. But, most of the biographical works only commemorate the good deeds and preaching of the heroes. Being written with the utmost reverence, they are full of exaggeration and cannot be called biography in the strict sense of the term. Also lacking in them are details about the wordly lives of their subjects, the result of an indifference to documentation. The biographers since independence have.written with a view to inspiring the younger generation to develop national character as well as their individuality. The biographer's main interest has been more academic than aesthetic. Hence, an artistic biography is a rarity, with biographers caring more for content than for literary form. These biographers have chosen their heroes mostly from political, spiritual, social and cultural fields. This brief survey of the biographical literature leaves us with a feeling of satisfaction. It is fairly rich not only in quantity but in quality too. All these poems whether small or big not only provide us with close and intimate pictures of the personages about whom they are written but also help us gather some important information about the social, political, cultural and literary life of the age. Rising above the dry historical documents and panegyrics these poems have established themselves as a branch of creative literature which is no way a mean achievement.

APPENDIX

An Alphabetical List of Carita Kāvyas

1. *Abdullā-caritam* of Laksmīpati
2. *Ahalyā-caritam* of Sukharāma Śāstrī
3. *Ananta-caritam* of Vāsudeva Ātmārāma
4. *Anāmaswāmi-carita* of Muniratnasūri
5. *Aṁbarīṣa-caritam* (22 verses) of Mahākavi Gomatidāsa Elattūr Rāmasvāmi Śāstrī
6. *Bhallāla-carita* of unknown author
7. *Bhaktasiṁha-caritam* of Svayaṁprakāśa Śarmā
8. *Bhārata-carita* of Kṛṣṇācārya
9. *Brahmarṣi-Virajānanda-carita* of Medhāvrata Śāstrī
10. *Bhūdeva-caritam* of Maheśacandra Tarkacūḍāmaṇī
11. *Buddha-carita* of Aśvaghoṣa ed., E.B. Cowell, Bibliotheca Indica, Oxford, 1885.
12. *Candracūḍa-caritam* of Umāpatidhara
13. *Candraprabhā-caritam* of Śaṅkaralāl

14. *Candraprabhā-caritam* of Vīranandi
15. *Candraśekhara-caritam* of Dhuvermajana
16. *Cālukya-caritam* of Lakṣmīnārāyaṇa Śāstrī
17. *Cimnī-caritam* of Kavi Nīlakaṇṭha
18. *Caitanya-caritam* of Kavikarṇapūra
19. *Daśāvatāra-caritam* of Śrīradhakṛṣṇa Tiwārī
20. *Daśāvatāra-carita* of Kṣemendra
21. *Dāsa-caritam* of Śrīśailasūri, ed., by Sri T. Ananthanarayana, SV Oriental Series No. 20, Tirupati, 1990.
22. *Dilīpa-carita* of unknown author
23. *Divyasūri-caritam* of Śrīgaruḍavāhana
24. *Dhruva-caritam* of Gaṇapatiśāstrī
25. *Dhruva-caritam* of Jayakaṇṭha
26. *Gajanī Muhammad-caritam* of P.G. Rāmarthakavi
27. *Gajendra-caritam* of unknown author
28. *Gāndhāra-caritam* (50 verses) of Elattūr Rāmāsvāmi Śāstrī
29. *Gāndhī-caritam* of Sādhuśaraṇa Miśrā
30. *Gopāla-caritam* of Padmanābha Bhaṭṭa
31. *Gopāla-carita* of Śrīkṛṣṇacaitanya
32. *Gaurī-caritam* of Veṅkaṭasūri
33. *Gaurī-caritam* of Vṛndāvana Śuklā
34. *Haracarita Cintāmaṇi* of Jayaratha
35. *Hari-carita* of Caturbhuja
36. *Hari-carita* of unknown author
37. *Harivaṁsasāra-carita* of Govindamakhi
38. *Hemakumāra-carita* of Samaprabhācārya
39. *Haihayendra-carita* of Bhānubhaṭṭa
40. *Jagadguru-caritam* of Sarvānanda
41. *Jahāṅgīra-caritam* of Rudrakavi

42. *Jinadatta-carita* of Guṇabhadra
43. *Jīvandhara-carita* of Guṇabhadracārya
44. *Jorjadeva-caritam* of G.P. Padmanābhasāśtrī
45. *Jorjadeva-caritam* of Lakṣaṇasūri
46. *Jñānendra-carita* of Medhāvrata Śāstrī
47. *Kumārapāla-carita* of Hemacandra
48. *Jñāneśvara-caritam* of Kṣamādevī
49. *Kṛṣṇa-carita* of Bilvamaṅgala
50. *Kṛṣṇa-caritam* of Mānadeva
51. *Kṛṣṇa-caritam* of Motīrāma
52. *Kṛṣṇabāla-carita* of Bilvamaṅgaḷa
53. *Kṛṣṇa-carita* of Samudragupta
54. *Kṣatrapati-caritam* of Umāśaṅkara Śarmā Tripāthī
55. *Laghurāma-carita* of Y. Mahāliṅga Śāstri
56. *Lakṣmīnārayaṇa-caritam* of Śrīnivāsaputra
57. *Lāl Bahādur Śāstri-caritam* of Ramesh Chandra Śuklā
58. *Liṅgāikyabhāvikāsa-caritam* of Mahāliṅgakavi
59. *Mahatāb-carita* of unknown author
60. *Mahīpāla-carita* of Caritrasundara
61. *Muni-caritāmṛta* of Dillīpādattopādhyaya
62. *Munisuvrata-carita* of Muniratnasūri
63. *Maithileśa-caritam* of Ratnapāṇi
64. *Nandi-caritam* of Kṛṣṇakavi
65. *Nārāyaṇaswāmi-carita* of Medhāvrata Śāstrī
66. *Naiṣadhīya-carita* of Śrīharṣa
67. *Nityānada-carita* of Medhāvrata Śāstrī
68. *Nehru-caritam* of an unknown author
69. *Padyaharṣa-carita* of Rājagopāla Cakravarti
70. *Patañjali-caritam* of Rāmabhadra Dīkṣita
71. *Pārśvanātha-carita* of Vādirājasūri

72. *Prabhāvaka-carita* of Candraprabhasūri
73. *Prajāpati-caritam* of Kṛṣṇakavi
74. *Pratyekabuddha-carita* of Lakṣmītilaka
75. *Pradyumna-carita* of Mahāsena
76. *Prahlāda-caritam* of Jayakaṇṭha
77. *Raghuvīra-caritam* or *Sukumarslitāna-caritam* Ibburamji
78. *Raghuvīra-carita* edited by T. Ganapati Śāstrī
79. *Raghunātha-carita* of Jagadasāhā
80. *Raghunātha-tārkika-śiromaṇi-caritam* of Raviray
81. *Raghuvīravarya-caritam* of Tirumalakonācārya
82. *Rantideva-caritam* of Laksmi Warrier
83. *Ranatadivya-caritam* of Śrīnivāsa
84. *Rāma-caritam* of Kāśinātha
85. *Rāma-caritam* of Mohanaswami
86. *Rāma-caritam* of Viṣvaksena
87. *Rāma-caritam* of Yuvarāja Rājavarma
88. *Rāma-caritam* of Raghunātha
89. *Rāma-carita* of Abhinanda
90. *Rāmapāla-caritam* of Kavi Sandhyākaranandi
91. *Rāghava-caritam* of Ānandanārāyaṇa
92. *Rāmadāsa-caritam* of Kṣamādevī
93. *Rāmānuja-carita campū* of Śrīrāmānujācārya
94. *Rāmānuja-carita-kulaka* of Anvayācārya
95. *Rāmānujadivya-caritam* of unknown author
96. *Śaṅkarācārya-caritam* of Govindanātha
97. *Śambhu-caritam* of Vṛndāvana Śukla
98. *Śambhurāja-carita* of Harikavi *alias* Bhānubhaṭṭa
99. *Śarabhojī-caritam* of Anantanārāyṇa
100. *Śāntinātha-caritam* of Meghavijayagaṇi
101. *Śāntinātha-carita* of Ajitaprabhācārya

102. *Śikhaguru-caritāmṛtam* of S.S. Hasurkar
103. *Śivakaivalya-carita* of V.M. Kulkarni
104. *Śivakaivalya-caritam* of Veṅkaṭa Rao
105. *Śrīkaṇṭha-caritam* of Mankha
106. *Śrīcālukyarāja Ayaṇavaṁśa-caritam* of Śyāma Bhaṭṭa Bharadvāja
107. *Śrīharicarita Mahākāvyam* of Śrīharipadmanābha Śāstrī, ed., T. Venkatacarya, Adyar Library & Research Centre, Adyar, Chennai, 1960.
108. *Śrīkṛṣṇa-caritam* of Śivadatta Tripāṭhī
109. *Śrīkṛṣṇa-caritam* of Ramesh Candra Śuklā
110. *Śrī Muttusvāmi Dīkṣitacandra-caritam Mahākāvyam* of V. Rāghavan, 'Punarvasu', No.l, Srikrishnapuram Street, Chennai-600 014
111. *Śrībhāṣyakāra-carita* of Kauśika Veṅkateśa
112. *Śrībhubya-caritam* of Ganapati Śāstrī
113. *Śrīpada-caritam* of Sakalakīrti
114. *Śrīrāma-caritam* of Rāmaviśāla Tripāṭhī
115. *Śrī Vallabhācārya-caritam* of S.S. Hasurkar
116. *Śrī Pūrṇānanda-caritam* of an unknown author
117. *Śrī Swāmī Vivekānanda-caritam* of Tryaṁbaka Śarmā Bhāṇḍarkar
118. *Sāvitrī-caritam* of Śaṅkaralāl
119. *Sītā-caritam* of Revā Prasad Dvivedī
120. *Subodharāma-carita* of Bālammāḷ.
121. *Sudāma-caritam* of Puṇḍarīkākṣa Miśrā
122. *Sudāma-caritam* of Śrīnivāsa
123. *Sudarśana-caritam* of Sakalakīrti
124. *Suratha-carita* of unknown author
125. *Surendra-caritam* of Śivarāma
126. *Surendra-carita mahākāvyam* of Digaṁbara Mohapātrā

127. *Sumatīnātha-carita* of Samaprabhācārya
128. *Surjana-caritam* of Gauḍadeva.
129. *Sthavirāvali-carita* of Hemacandra
130. *Tukārāma-caritam* of Kṣamādevī
131. *Tyāgarāja-caritam* of Sundareśa Śarma
132. *Udayavarma-caritam* ed., Sāṁbaśiva Śāstri
133. *Uttararāma-carita kāvyam* ed., Rāmapiṣāroti
134. *Varāṅga-carita* of Jaṭāsiṁhanandi
135. *Vāsudeva-caritam* of Veṇidatta
136. *Victoria-carita-saṁgraha* of Keralavarma
137. *Vidvat-carita-pañcaka* of Nārāyaṇa Śāstrī Kiste
138. *Vighneśvara-carita* of Rāmavadhāni
139. *Vikramāṅkadeva-carita* of Bilhaṇa
140. *Vivekānanda-caritam* of K.S. Nāgarājan
141. *Vīra-kāmparāya-carita* (Madhura Vijayam) of Gaṅgādevi ed., by Potukucci Subrahmanya Sastri with his own commentary in Sanskrit and Telugu translation, Rajahmundry, 1960
142. *Vrajendra-caritam* of Sadānanda
143. *Vṛṣabhānu-caritam* of Sakalakīrti
144. *Veṅkateśa-caritam* of Ghanaśyāma
145. *Yaśodharā-caritam* of Vadirājasūri

Modern Sanskrit Poets on Russia and Russian Leaders*

One of the sublime features of Sanskrit literature is that it propagates universal values which are perishing day by day from the human world. The human beings under the pressure of materialistic culture and technological advancement are not fully realizing the importance of them. The values are required for the fullest growth of humanism and human societies in the world. The oldest literature of Hindus known as Ṛgveda preaches the ideology *vasudhaiva kuṭumbakam* (the entire universe is a family). Almost all the Sanskrit poets highly appreciate this ideology and endeavour to expand it in the best possible way. Even the Sanskrit poets of modern period, not giving any importance to other ordinary things meant for temporary pleasure, strive hard to spread this noble idea through their literature. They make use of literature as a potential instrument of social progress, perennial peace and paramount stability.

To my knowledge, the modern Sanskrit poet fully realises his role and takes it as his duty to work for the people of the whole universe. So he does not get confined to the wall of India and Indian geographical boundary. Interesting thing is that the Sanskrit poet thinks it as his *Dharma* to do

Journal of The Oriental Institute, Vol. 51, Nos. 3-4, March-June, 2002 Issue, pp. 277-289.

*. The paper was presented in the National Golden Jubilee Seminar organised by the Dept. of Russian, on "Russian Language, Literature and Society: The Indian & Russian Experience', March 18-20, 2004.

something good for the universe.[1] It is therefore very rightly said that *Na ṛṣiḥ kurute kāvyam*. It means he who is not a *ṛṣi* (sage) cannot compose poetry. *Ṛṣi* is one who is visionary, far-sighted, has deep insight into various branches of learning, has intuitive perspective and has capacity to develop an universal attachment to the sublime and the beautiful of the entire universe being free from geographical, social and cultural narrowness. Even if a poet comes across something vulgar, trivial or grotesque in nature or in the happenings of the world, he elevates it to a thing of beauty.[2] He plays a very significant role in the field of intellectual extension and contributes profoundly to the continuity of *lokayātrā* as rightly said by *mahākavi* Daṇḍin in his *Kāvyādarśa*.[3] I have pleasure in saying that some of the Sanskrit poets have made valuable contribution in this direction. They are not influenced by the modern literary trends that are

---

1. काव्यनिर्माणचातुर्यं कवीनां धर्म उच्यते।
   किं तया काव्यनिर्मित्या देशजाती न धारयेत्।।
   राष्ट्रोन्निनीषया काव्यं कुर्वन् विज्ञानवर्धनम्।
   तृणाय मन्यते राज्यं कविः सत्याप्तिलिप्सया।।
   Vāsiṣṭha, Satyadeva, *Satyāgrahanītikāvya*, 1939, I. 12.34 and 35; Quoted in *Sanskrita Sahitya : Bīsaviṁ Śatābdī* of Radhavallabha Tripathy, Rastriya Sanskrit Sansthan, Delhi, 1999, p. 25.
2. रम्यं जुगुप्सितमुदारमथापि नीच-
   मुग्रं प्रसादि गहनं विकृतं च वस्तु।
   तद्वाप्यवस्तु कविभावकभाव्यमानं
   तन्नास्ति यन्न रसभावमुपैति लोके।।
   Daśarūpakam of Dhanañjaya with *Avaloka*, (Hindi Edition), Ed. Bholashankar Vyas, Banaras, Chowkhamba Vidya Bhavan, 1955, p. 282
3. इह शिष्टानुशिष्टानां शिष्टानामपि सर्वथा।
   वाचामेव प्रसादेन लोकयात्रा प्रवर्तते।।
   इदमन्धं तमः कृत्स्नं जायेत भुवनत्रयम्।
   यदि शब्दाह्वयं ज्योतिरासंसारान्न दीप्यते।।
   Kāvyādarśa of Daṇḍin, Ed. A.L. Thakur and Upendra Jha, Mithila Institute of Post-graduate Study and Research in Sanskrit Learning, Darabhanga, 1957, pp. 2-3.

prevailing in the contemporary literary scene. They have sung for universal brotherhood, eternal peace and human development. In the present paper I have made an attempt to bring to light some of the noteworthy works of modern Sanskrit writers who have written on Russia and Russian leaders.

It is interesting to say that the creativity in the modern period of Sanskrit has entered a new phase. It has undergone a significant change in the twentieth century. Some of the Sanskrit writers of the modern period have emerged as world citizens. They have imbibed a global perspective. Therefore their poems written in Sanskrit relive the experiences of their air-travel through foreign countries. Consequently travelogue has acquired the status of an established form in modern Sanskrit literature. It is found in the form of epic poem, half-epic poem, *Śataka* and minor poem. These Sanskrit poets who have availed an opportunity to visit foreign countries, have selected the themes related to those countries. This literature is no doubt relevant in the context of social progress.

As is well-known, one of the objectives of poetry is to give proper guidance to the people who are in need of it. The critic Mammaṭa has said in his *Kāvyaprakāśa* that a poet should instruct people to walk in the path of Rāma, not in the path of *Rāvaṇa*. The great sage Vālmīki, therefore, composed the great epic *Rāmāyaṇa* which has been preaching that noble ideal and will do the same as long as the human civilization persists. He influenced and inspired innumerable persons all over the world to follow the footprints of Rāma and firmly established the Rāma-culture in the world. He could be able to do it by way of presenting the sublime character of Rāma, Sītā, Lakṣmaṇa, Hanumān, and through them, the noble thoughts which have universal application. He could convince people through his sweet and charming words. Coming in the line of the great visionary Vālmīki, the modern poets started composing poems on the great heroes of the world. They highlighted their deeds, characters and personalities in artistic manner, a manner which will appeal to the hearts of the connoisseurs. From this perspective literature is serving society and contributing not only to the enjoyment of some happy-go-lucky readers but also to the human development. It will be also an interesting exercise to evaluate some poems of Sanskrit literature from this perspective. One will be happy to know that Sanskrit which was used to function as a vehicle of national consciousness and a lingua franca for the Indian sub-continent, has acquired an international perspective and that is our main goal in understanding the image of Russia and Russian leaders from the study of Sanskrit creative works of the twentieth century.

However, it is not so much known that modern Sanskrit poets have written poems on the countries like Russia, Germany, Thailand, Paris, Holland, Teheran, East Africa, Bangladesh, Nepal, Bali and Java.[1] But, of all the countries on the earth, Russia has been the most attractive country for some Sanskrit poets. Even our ancient writers, the authors of the Purāṇas have referred to Russia. The purāṇic name of Russia is said to be Lakṣadvīpa. Some people interpret the word as Ṛṣīya (the place of Ṛṣis). The love and affection of Sanskrit poets for this country are evidently clear from the number of prose and poetry works written in Sanskrit language. First, I present here a brief survey of the Sanskrit works written on Russia and its prominent leaders who have contributed a lot to the development of Russia and have built an international image in the pages of the world history.

---

1. Raghavan, V., *Sanskrit Literature : Contemporary Indian Literature : A Symposium*, Second Revised and Enlarged Edition, Sahitya Academi, New Delhi, 1959, p. 224.
   Raghavan informs that B.C. Chabbra's *Nyaktarajanapadaśobhā* is a description of Holland. Dr. Kunhan Raja has written poems on Teheran and Ramakrishna Bhatt has written poems on East Africa.

In the beginning of this century, Harridatta Paliwal 'Nirbhaya', an eminent Sanskrit poet and a revolutionary attached to Bhagatsingh's group, wrote some essays and poems on Russian poetry.[1] He depicted very nicely the natural beauty of Russia. To my knowledge, he is the first person to begin a new trend in the field of modern Sanskrit literature. Then, Padmashastri from Jaipur of Rajasthan composed — *Lenināmṛtam*, a *mahākāvya* in Sanskrit.[2] Of all Indian languages, it is perhaps only in Sanskrit that such a voluminous epic containing more than 2000 verses in different classical metres, is composed, describing the life and deeds of the great Russian leader, V.I. Lenin. For this commendable work the farsighted poet Padmashastri was felicitated by the Govt. of Russia. Likewise Nagarjuna (Vaijanatha) composed a marvellous *Khaṇḍakāvya-Leninśatakam* — a century of verses of Lenin.[3] This poem is also known as *Leninstuti*. I came to know about another important epic poem, that is, *Tolstoy-caritam* on the life of the great writer Tolstoy but the name of the author of this *Mahākāvya* is not yet known to me. Professor Rajendra Mishra observes about these two important works :

"*Lenināmṛtam* and *Tolstoyacaritam* are the modern Sanskrit *mahākāvyas*, based on the superb character and deeds of Lenin and Tolstoy, the political and cultural leaders of Russia. It could be possible only in the modern Sanskrit poetry, that the supreme personalities like Lenin and Tolstoy belonging to other country, have been reverentially

---

1. Foreword of Radhavallabh Tripathi to Russiaśatakam of Acharya Digambara Mahapatra, pub. by Umesh Chandra Mahapatra, Rourkela, Orissa, 2003, p. 1.
2. Shastri, Padma, *Lenināmṛtam*, Visweswarananda Vaidika Sodhasamsthana, Sadhu Ashrama, Hoshiarpur, 1976.
   Prof. Rahasavihari Dwivedi has prepared a good study of this work. Since the original work is not available, Sanskrit references are taken from this work.
3. Tripathi, Radhavallabha, *op. cit.* p. 95.

delineated. It confirms the broad outlook of the modern Sanskrit poets."[1]

Professor Dwivedi has dealt with[2] some of the important features of *Lenināmṛtm.* Another poet of outstanding merit, Paṇḍita Sivadatta Sarma Chaturvedi has composed two *Śatakakāvyas* namely *Lenin-śatakam* and *Kālamārka-śatakam.*[3]

In this century a minor poem entitled *Gorbachova-laharī* is composed by Rasik Patel of Navasari of Gujarat. Similarly Paṇḍita Digambara Mahapatra of Orissa has written two interesting works, one in prose, that is, *Pāścātyasaṁskṛtam*[4] and other is *Russia-śatakam*[5] a century of verses only on Russia.

I also came to know that some Sanskrit scholars have attempted the work of translation from Russian into Sanskrit. One of them is Dr. Bhagiratha Prashad Tripathy known as Vāgīśa Śāstrī. This eminent scholar has translated seven stories of Tolstoy from Russian into Sanskrit.[6] The translation is a scholarly work and it is as good as the original composition. Difficult words are also explained under footnotes. The Sampurnananda Sanskrit University, Varanasi, has prescribed this work as a textbook. Dr. Vāgīśa Śāstrī has received a special award by Uttar Pradesh Sanskrit Samsthan for this commendable work.

Besides the independent *Kāvyas*, there are also references to Russia and its important events in some *mahākāvyas*. One

1. Mishra, Rajendra, *"Modern Sanskrit Poetry"*, *Wisdom in Indian Tradition*, Professor K.P. Jog Felicitation Volume, Pratibha Prakashan, Delhi, 2000, p. 118.
2. Dwivedi, Rahasavihari, *Sanskrita-mahākāvyon kā Samālocanātmaka Adhyayana* (from 1961-70 A.D.), New Bharatiya Book Corporation, Delhi, 2001, pp. 382-390.
3. Dwivedi, Rewaprasad, *Modern Sanskrit Poetry in Modern Sanskrit Literature : Tradition and Innovations,* Ed. by S.B. Raghunathacharya, Sạhitya Academy, New Delhi, 2002, p. 59.
4. *Pāścātyasaṁskṛtam*, pub. by Umesh Mahapatra, Rourkela, Orissa, 2003.
5. See Footnote No. 1.
6. *Tolstoy-Kathā*-saptakam, Chowkhamba Vidyabhavan, Varanasi, 1907

of such *mahākāvyas* is *Keralodaya*[1] composed by K.N. Ezhuthachan. The poet writes that the first socialist state under the leadership of the working class was established in Russia by Lenin and his followers after the October revolution in 1917.[2] The poet refers to the sudden change in the policy of the communist when Russia entered the war. The imperialist war became people's war.[3]

In spite of my best efforts I could not collect all published works of these modern Sanskrit writers. I could collect only three of them. So I have prepared a general study of these three works as the subject-matter of the present paper.

First, I present here some of the important features of the great epic *Lenināmṛtam.* The author of the epic poem is Padma Shastri of Rajasthan. The poem is a biographical one composed on the life-history of V.I. Lenin (1870-1924) who was the leader of Bolshevik revolution. The dimension of the poem is confined to 15 cantos, which comprehensively contain the distinctive features of Communism, the biographical details of this great leader, the geography of Russia and also the friendly relations existing between Russia and India. It is a representative work of this century exclusively written on the philosophy of communism in Sanskrit language for the first time. The objective of the poet is very clear in the introductory verse.[4]

---

1. Ezhuthachan, K.N., *Keralodayaḥ*, Pub. Poet himself, Kerala, 1977
2. रष्यामहाराज्यतलेऽतियत्नैर्लेनिन्प्रभृत्युज्ज्वलसत्त्ववद्भिः।
   उद्घाटिता कर्मकराधिकारा लोकादिमा कापि समाजनीतिः।। *Keralodayaḥ*, XXI. 94, p. 450
3. साम्राज्यपापिष्ठरणं प्रशस्तपुण्याध्वरोऽभूत्कथमेकरात्रे।
   विवृण्वते स्माऽऽगमनस्य केचिन्महाद्भतस्तब्धहृदे जनाय।। *Keralodayaī* XXI. 197, p. 474
4. रूसे जारकुशासनप्रमथनेनोन्मत्तभावान्विता।
   वीरा लेनिनदिष्टमार्गपथिका ये तत्यजुः स्वानसून्।
   तेषां क्रान्तिकृतां विमुक्तिमनसां पादार्चनाहेतवे
   सत्काव्याञ्जलिरेष भावसुरभिः प्रस्तूयते सादरम्।। *Lenināmṛtam*, p. 1

The subject-matter is divided into fifteen cantos: 1. Outlines of communism 2. Beauty of Russia 3. Birth of Lenin 4. His Student-life 5. Imprisonment of Lenin in Siberia 6. Birth of the doctrine of Bolshevik 7. People's revolution 8. Victory of Bolshevik group 9. Lenin's inter-group struggle 10. Downfall of Jāratantra 11. Coming of Lenin to Petrogad 12. Failure of July revolution 13. Lenin's Sovernity 14. Lenin's death 15. Russia-India relationship.

The characterization, delineation of sentiment, development of plot, the versified dialogues, the employment of dramatic techniques, development of patriotic spirit as per the need of the hour, poetic form that is given to a dry subject etc. are the sublime features of this *mahākāvya*. The style adopted by the poet is *Vaidarbhī*, which contains soft words, small compounds, lucid presentations and easy language. The poet has made use of appropriate metres necessary for proper expression of various sentiments. The judicious use of the metres along with proper delineation of emotions in an artistic manner no doubt enhances the merit of the poem. The poem has beautifully depicted the characters of all those persons who play a definite role in Russian politics and are associated with the hero of the long poem.

The poet has described the pathetic condition of Lenin's mother Mariya.[1] The lotus like face of Mariya, became brilliant by the rays of the Sun-Lenin, when she came to know about the conception but that luster immediately vanished because of her drinking of the water of poverty-ocean. The poet brings a good imagery of Mariya's miserable condition in the verse. He identifies Lenin with sun and creates a very good metaphor though it is very common in Sanskrit.

Another feature of the poem, which gives me pleasure is that the poet has brought into the real incidents like a

---

1. गर्भगते लेनिनसूर्यरश्मौ प्रफुल्लिताऽभून्मुखपङ्कजश्रीः।
दारिद्र्यदुःखार्णवपानयोगान् मातुस्तदापीतमुखं बभूव।। *Ibid*, II. 3

historian in a natural way. In a verse the poet says that Lenin was a divine person[1] like an incarnation of Viṣṇu. He came down to earth like the lord Kṛṣṇa to help the poor people suffering from severe poverty.

As the main objective of the poet is to depict the noble character of this hero, he has taken care of the main things which have made his character so high, so noble and so outstanding. One of them is his supreme dedication for the country. The poet has depicted the work of his dedication in some verses.

There are very good *subhāṣita* type of sayings in the poem. An example[2] will be sufficient for us to understand our poet's mind. What he says is that a weak man does not achieve anything in this world. He cannot get pure fame. Without power one cannot even imagine of peace. This reminds us the Upaniṣadic words *Uttiṣṭhata, Jāgrata, prāpyavarān nibodhata, kṣurasyadhārā-niśitāduratyayā durgam pathastat kavayo vadanti.*

In this great epic, the poet Padma Shastri depicts systematically and artistically the life and work of the hero Lenin. The main sentiment of the poem is *Vīra* (heroic), that is, *yuddhavīra*,[3] one of the four varieties of *Vīra rasa*. Other sentiments like *karuṇa, śānta*, and *bhakti* are also delineated properly as subordinate ones in their proper contexts. The work fulfills all the requirements of a *mahākāvya*. It is a sublime contribution to modern Sanskrit literature and in need of an analytical study for better understanding of the mind and art of Padma Shastri, a progressive poet of this century.

---

1. गर्भस्थितेनास्य विवर्तनेन संसूचितं जारविवर्तनं च।
   जरायुजातोऽपि जराविमुक्तः स निर्जरत्वं समवाप सद्यः।। *Ibid*, III. 12
2. क्व शक्तिहीनेन जनेन शुभं यशो नृलोके समवाप्यते वै।
   शक्त्या विना शान्तिप्रकल्पनापि सत्यं हि मिथ्या कथिता नृलोके।। *Ibid*, XI. 33
3. यदि मन्मृत्युना रूसे क्रान्तेः संस्फुरणं भवेत्।
   सहस्रधा मरिष्येऽहं ध्रुवं देही विदह्यते।। *Ibid*, IV. 20

Now, I deal with the *Pāścātyasaṁskṛtam* — a prose work composed by Paṇḍitarāja Digambara Mahapatra of Orissa. The travelogue, the Sanskrit one of western counterpart, comprises poet's experiences that he has accumulated carefully while he was in Moscow as a visiting professor of Sanskrit being invited by the Maharṣi Maheśa Yogī Viśvavidyālaya. The poet has described the incidents that had happened and the problems he had faced during his stay in Russia. But he has not made only a simple narration of the tour. He properly expresses his deep concern over the issues of cultural and philosophical elements that flow as the undercurrent and form the basics of life of the people of both the countries. The present travelogue is a fresh design of simple prose in modern Sanskrit. Written in two parts, the book is a pleasant recollection of the sweet and profound experiences of the poet. Sri Mahapatra was invited for four months in 1995-96 by the Vedic Science foundation of Moscow to teach Yoga-Vedānta philosophy as well as Sanskrit to Russians. It is in this background that the work of Sri Mahapatra comprising his close impressions of Russia has an added significance.[1]

In his other work *Russia-śatakam*, the poet Mahapatra recaptures the indescribable beauty and greatness of Russian continent. He makes a fascinating description of all the beautiful things that he had seen in that country during his stay in Russia. The poet has glorified the tradition and culture of that country. He has tried to take the Sanskrit readers to an unknown world of Siberia and Tundra. The poetry of Sri Mahapatra successfully refutes the misconception that Sanskrit paṇḍits are narrow-minded and fail to appreciate the achievements of other cultures. The *Russia-śatakam* is in fact a very appropriate tribute to the philosophy of liberty,

---

1. एते छात्राः संस्कृतस्य महत्त्वमवगच्छन्ति। मयापि पृष्ट्वा ज्ञातं तत्। एतेषामयं विश्वासो यदियं संस्कृतभाषा अतीव प्राचीना। अनया भाषया वेद-पुराण-दर्शनादीनि बहुमूल्यानि भारतीयशास्त्राणि लिखितानि। *Pāścātyasaṁskṛtam*, p. 31.

fraternity, equity and to the glory of proletariat that is cultivated in Russia. Sri Mahapatra mainly aims at describing the greatness of the Russian leaders who have made some prominent mark and had made significant contribution in their respective fields. The poem begins with an auspicious prayer[1] addressed to the country Russia, which bespeaks poet's deep love for this country.

Moreover, the poet has described the dignity of labour that is honoured in that country. According to our poet Russia is a pious land of competent leaders. This is why people shine there in every sphere of life. The great leaders have been successful in extending the glory of their nation. The poet has described the geography of the Soviet nation. Colingard city is adjacent to the frontier of Japan in the east of Russia. In the west, Blodivastov city is adjacent to the frontier of Europe. The vast snow-white Tundra region is located nearer to the northern pole while the famous Amuru river is in the south. In this scenario, the vast continent Russia looks prominently beautiful. The people of Russia are very polished and have maintained their cultural traditions. They are restlessly making efforts for the upliftment of their own motherland. For their own cherished accomplishment, they have been paying respect to the manliness, which is the symbol of power of the people and have been labouring hard for proper development of the nation. India has always established cordial relation with Russia. Not only in the big cities but even in villages and rural areas, life styles of people have developed owing to massive scientific and technological progress. It is understood that people have been the owners of affluence and prosperity by virtue of ceaseless efforts and keen carefulness. It is very astonishing to visit Moscow, one of the great cities of Russia. What a magnificent city it is! It is wearing an inexplicable beauty.

---

1. यत्र श्री राजते भूयो विज्ञानधनसम्पदाम्।
   वन्दे तं रुषियादेशं ससम्मानमहं मुदा।। Russiaśatakam, Verse. 1.

The multi-storied buildings of this city are very high and they look like touching the sky. The pavements are very wide and cleaned. Under this city many metro trains are plying round the clock.

The poet Mahapatra also sings the glory of Lenin. The great leader has got universal recognition as a legend and founder of Russia. He had great love for his countrymen as his own sons and had done very good works for their welfare. He is worshipped in his country as a God and is respected in the world. Irrespective of caste and gender, all people right from the child and old man appear adept in their own duty. The people of Russia are usually very clever and decisive. It is a matter of pleasure that these people through their good behaviour and sweet talks fascinate the hearts of the visitors and appear to be their close relatives. Keeping good relation with the male members in each concern, women achieve also unexpected success. It means, there is no discrimination between women and men. Being impressed with the greatness of Russian Art, the poet has elaborated some features of fine arts and dance arts of Russia that are found on many stages of Art existing at various places of Moscow city. The people of Russia give importance to agriculture than any other thing. They know very well that the prosperity of the nation is dependent on agriculture. For all-round development of the nation, they, realizing the importance of agriculture, pay much more attention to the farmers and their labour. Russians possess interest too in martial arts and they are very skilful in that art.

Russia is very powerful today by virtue of scientific development and by its indigenous power. The scientists of the continent have reached several planets of the cosmic universe. Yuri Gagarin of Russia is the first astronaught to have circled the world on April 12th in 1980, and that incident had stunned the people of the whole world. R. Peregave has received universal reputation as a medical scientist. Ferodiv's name is written in golden letters as a skilled physical scientist.

The history of Russia preserves the name of Mandeliv who was an expert in physical science. A seer of Russia by name Karolov has earned a good name as an expert in space science. Swetlana is considered to be a rare person in the world for her going to the space. Valentina Nikolaya Terescova had been to space and had shown wonderful brilliance in this direction.

The diversified culture of Russia is reflected on the customs, luxuries and dishes of the Russians. Russians have great love for their culture. The eminent poet has depicted various aspects of Russian culture in this work.

The Russian literature has a significant place among its counterparts. In the thick forest of Russian literature Leo Tolstoy has emerged as a powerful lion. The literary works of this great stalwart are highly appreciated by the great intellectuals of the world. Leo Tolstoy is immortal for his great book '*War and peace*'. Similarly Alexander Puskin is remembered by the people of Russia. Notwithstanding the fact that a rival enemy assasinated him, he is still survived in the countless hearts of the readers owing to his timeconquered literature. The Russian Art Gallery named after him is displaying the superiority of his works of literature.

The collected sculptures and paintings in the museums of Russia are extra-ordinary. The picture and statues in the form of art, craft, sculpture, oil-paintings and the portraits of great personalities, handmade wooden sculptures, metal statues on the road-sides, crossroads, and sky-scrappers look lively like the original ones. The poet Mahapatra became overwhelmed while visiting the Art galleries. Karl Briullov (1799-1852) is the most famous artist in the field of Fine Arts and Figure-painting. Another great artist is Alexander Ivanov (1806-1858). Today one of his paintings — the appearance of Christ to the people, the canvas of which is very vast size of (540" x 750") is exhibited in the Moscow museum.

Mikhail Gorbachov who has given message for universal peace, has been remembered by the people of Russia as an honourable president of the Russian Republic.

Doc Vledimeer was a great seer of Russia. The slaves had named him as Kiban Russ. The slaves who were staying in Russia, had been converted into Christians renouncing the practice of worshipping God at the instigation of Kiban Rus. Earlier there was not a bit of odour of Christianism in Russia. The slaves of Russia were worshipping the sun, fire, wind and the nature as god like Hindus. Doc Vledimeer was the ruler of those slaves. He went to Greece and got training about the Christian religion and coming back to Russia propagated Christianism. He became famous by the nick name of Kiban Rus due to his fame as a persuader and propagator of the Christian religion in Russia. By his inspiration and powerful propagation, the slaves relinquished the worship of Lords and become Christians. Andrei Rublev was a talented artist who illustrated the mystery of life through paintings. His fantastic creation is an epitome of time and will be shining for ever as an image of affluent Russian aristocracy.

The poet has spared no pains in making this century poem lovable and enjoyable. The extra-ordinary vision of Sri Mahapatra has not left anything anywhere in Russia which is grand, which is beautiful, which bears some historical significance, which is popular as art and architecture and which is praiseworthy for standing as a token of magnanimous Russian culture.[1] Even the poet has enriched his work by furnishing minor details about the life style of Russian people, their attitude[2], their humanitarian

---

1. किं वर्णयानि महतीं रुषियासुकीर्तिं
मूल्यं कलाकुशलतामथ पौरुषञ्च।
सङ्गीतचित्रमधिकारगदं च सर्वं
वर्वर्त्ति यत्प्रतिपदं रुषियाजनेषु।। *Russiaśatakam,* verse 68, p. 42.
2. शिल्पप्रकल्पकृषिसंस्कृतिवित्त नीति–

spirit, their interests, their socio-cultural traits and dedications for the progress and prosperity of the nation. The poet has not forgotten to picturaise the love and affection of Russian people that he has received during his stay in Russia. The friendliness, naturalness and humanism are well depicted by the poet Mahapatra who is known for his competence and creativity in the field of poetry.

After reading the work carefully I realised that the poet has made pertinent investigation for selecting and collecting necessary material for giving a life to his poem. The presentation of authentic facts collected duly from the original sources have created a special flavour and has enhanced the literary value of the poem more than that is normally expected from such works.

The poet has dealt with the topics namely Russian arts, agriculture, the efforts for world-peace, scientific and technological developments, advancement in war-technology, literature, natural beauty of the rivers, paintings, sculptures, political traditions of Russia, past glory of Russian culture, expertise of Astronauts, social revolution, heroism of Russians, fragrance of Siberia and others on which the poet has composed the verses in mellifluous style. The poem is well-designed and well-divided into various sub-sections. Though it is a small work still it is very much important for the reason that Sanskrit readers will know more from this work about Russia.

The poet has expressed in his preface that he was extremely delighted to see Russia and her inhabitants who are hard working, intelligent, progressive and affectionate. The social, cultural and religious values of Russia have impressed the poet to a great extent. The poet is highly pleased with social manner of Russians who are

---

स्थापत्यवैभवकलाकृतिषु च भूयान्।
नानाप्रयुक्तिगरिमा परिदृश्यतेऽद्य
देशेऽमिता निपुणता वत पुंस्त्वभाजाम्।। *Ibid*, 84; p.51

conscientious and wise and therefore arrest the hearts of the visitors easily by their sweet and soft speeches endowed with natural love and affection. The grandeur of metro-cities like Moscow and Pravidensky has given an everlasting pleasure to the author of the poem. In this poem the poet has voiced for the extension of friendly relations between two countries. He is confident that a healthy relationship will grow further for the well-being of the people of both the countries.

The poet's heart has been overwhelmed with the natural beauty of the river Bolga that has unfolded her god-gifted beauty before him. The fantastic picture of this river gets a proper treatment in the hand of Paṇḍita Mahapatra who, like other eminent poets of classical Sanskrit literature, paints in words the manifold beauty of nature and aptly brings out her subtle nuances.

The poet observes Russia as a land of mufti-colour, where the institutes, offices and business centres are attracting by their grandeur of artistic and architectural designs. The nature is living everywhere. The poet has expressed his pleasure to look at the progress of Russians in all the fields like agriculture, Industry, Culture, Commerce, Sculpture, Art and Architecture. It is a matter of great pleasure for our poet that other countries in the world are trying to follow the footsteps of Russia in that direction. Russia has earned a great name for the substantial efforts it has made for the well-being of the entire World.

Our tradition proclaims that *Śṛṅgārī* cet *kaviḥ*. The poem contains some romantic feelings. The poet Mahapatra has not missed to describe the beauty of Russian women in some beautiful verses which suggest the sense of freedom and liberation of women.[1] They have own the right of selecting their own husbands and that reflects an advanced culture of highly civilized society.

1. केचित्स्वपन्ति सिकताशयनेऽङ्गनाभिः प्रेम्णार्धनग्नतनुभि सह सुन्दरीभिः।
मन्ये विभावसुकवोष्मकरप्रकाशै- रुद्वैजयन्ति मदनस्य मनोरथं ते।। *Ibid*, verse 51; p. 32.

The poem is a product of the present time when the good poets are not trying to exhibit their knowledge by writing highly pedantic poetry. Their main aim is not to please the patrons and to impress the paṇḍits. Therefore the figures of speech which are an easy medium to serve this purpose are not given that much importance as we see in the classical works. The modern poets think that figure of speech is not an essential element of poetry and not an intrinsic requirement for it. The most important thing is sentiment, to which the figures of speech are nearly subservient. It is interesting to see that similes, metaphors, poetic fancies and corroborations are used in this poem.

It is well-known that metre is not only an accessory or conventional requirement of poetry, but it is a part of its perfection, for it provides the poetic spirit with the most natural way for its expression. Ever since man has been, all deep and sustained feeling has tended to express itself in rhythmical language and the deeper the feeling the more characteristic and decided the rhythm. No honest critic can ever deny the importance of the role played by metres in poetry. For it provides the aesthetic pleasure, which is the chief end of a poetic composition. The poet has intelligently used several metres, which help in the enjoyment of the poem. It is an additional quality of the poem. In addition to it, the poem is composed in simple style which can attract even non-Sanskrit readers.

From the above presentation, it is very much clear that Sanskrit poets have depicted the image of Russia and its prominent leaders in an appreciable manner. They have glorified their contributions and have tried to popularize their works and achievements. Starting from the natural beauty of this continent, the Sanskrit poets of modern time have appreciated the attitude of the Russians, their work-culture, their love for the progress of the country, their philosophy of life, and their great heroes. By bringing to light the noble features of the characters of the great leaders like

Lenin, Gorbachove and others our Sanskrit poets have tried to inject those aspects in the minds of our young students who will be inspired and motivated to imitate the footprints of those leaders. The poets have indeed done a commendable job in glorifying the *vasudhaiva-kuṭumbakam* — culture of India, not being confined to the physical boundary of our country. They have proved that Sanskrit language and its literature is not only for India and Indians.

K.V. Sharma has classified the biographical literature under two headings, namely, the literature produced before the impact of western concepts and the literature from then up to modern times. He rightly remarks: "The writings of the early period were prone to the introduction of legendary accounts, exaggerations and parallelisms characteristic of classical Sanskrit and to be devotional and moralistic rather than objective and balanced. In tune with the thought of the times, the lives portrayed pertained primarily to the saints and the royalty. During the second period, when the norms of western biographical writing began to seep into India, its impact also began to be felt by the Sanskrit writer. For one thing, the vision of the Sanskritists and as a result he began to view men and matters in a more realistic perspective with a critical eye and an inquiring spirit. For another, the prevailing nationalist movement, too, had its effect on him. Thus, while he took up for portrayal prominent personalities from all walks of life, he also took pains to collect data in an objective manner, to form authentic biographies.[1] "All these poems whether small or big not only provide us with close and intimate pictures of the personages about whom they are written but also social, political, cultural and literary life of the age. Rising above the dry historical documents and panegyrics these poems have established themselves as a branch of creative literature which is no way a mean

1. Sarma, K.V., *Sanskrit-Comparative Indian Literature, Biographical Writings*, Sahitya Academi, New Delhi, p. 1023.

achievement. We should be proud of our poets-heroes".[1] The promises especially valuable in the context of creating *viśvabandhutva* feeling of universal brotherhood. All these works will be a source of lars of modern Sanskrit literature. I would like to conclude this essay with the following words of Rājaśekhara[2] : "कविवचनायत्ता लोकयात्रा। सा च निःश्रेयसमूलमि" ति महर्षयः। यदाहुः–

काव्यमय्यो गिरो यावच्चरन्ति विशदा भुवि।
तावत्सारस्वतं स्थानं कविरासाद्य मोदते।।

1. Panda, R.K., "Biographical Poems in Sanskrit: A Glance," *Srivenkatesvara University Oriental Journal*, Vol. XIV, Parts I & II, 2002, p. 20.
2. Rajaśekhara, *Kāvyamīmāṁsā*, Ed. C.D. Dalal and R.A. Sastry, Revised and Enlarged, Third ed. Oriental Institute, 1934, pp. 2-3.

Alaṁkāras in Śrī Swāmi-Vivekānanda-Carita-Mahākāvya

Paṇḍita Tryambaka Bhandarkar's *Srī Swāmi Vivekānanda-Carita-Mahākāvya*[1] (SVC) is one of the best epic poems produced by the Sanskrit poets of twentieth century. It is also one of the excellent biographical poems (*Carita-kāvyas*) composed so far in Modern Sanskrit literature. Out of the three great poems that have been composed on the life of Swāmi Vivekānanda, Paṇḍita Bhandarkar's poem occupies a special place. It is for its intrinsic merit, originality, superb presentation, lucid style, fine language and an appropriate construction of poetic elements. As is very clear from the title of this poem, the life and activities of Swāmi Vivekānanda is dealt with in this poem in historical order. It does not contain simply a catalogue of events of what has happened in Swāmiji's life. It does not also glorify the personality of Vivekānanda in superficial words as we commonly find in Sanskrit poems. Here is a fine blending of fact and fiction which brings a true *ramaṇiyatā* to the heart of connoisseur. As far as the size of the poem is concerned, it consists of eighteen cantos which bear the significant titles and give also the essence of each canto in an aphoristic manner. The poem, as per our literary tradition, commences with the respectful salutation[2] to Śrī Rāmakṛṣṇa

1. *Śrī Svāmi-Vivekānandacarita* (an epic poem on the life of Swāmi Vivekānanda with an auto-commentry), The Kashi Sanskrit Series 217, The Chowkhamba Sanskrit Series Office, Varanasi, 1973.
2. श्रीरामकृष्ण-युगमुज्ज्वलमेकसंस्थं
जातं जनेष्वजनि विश्वजनीनमुच्चैः।

Paramahaṁsa who is the preceptor of Swāmi Vivekānanda. There are 1121 verses in all, composed in different appropriate metres which suit their sentiment. The author, who is gifted with both *prajñā* and *pratibhā* and equally equipped in all the technical skills of composing a Sanskrit *kāvya* of high standard in the line of the great stalwarts like Kālidāsa, Bhāravi, Māgha and their successors, has spared no efforts in making the poem beautiful and enjoyable.

It is understood that the poetic figures are originally intended to lend beauty to the expression, but in course of time, the figures exercised fascination for the successive generations of poets to the extent that they ceased to be mere outer trappings and got settled down as an independent discipline.

One should not forget that there was a time when the *alaṁkāras* were thought to be the essence of poetry and they were indispensable to a good poem. The face of a lady, though beautiful, does not look attractive without the employment of proper ornaments, said Bhāmaha[1]. Vāmana also laid great stress on the utility of *alaṁkāras* by asserting boldly that a poem is to be accepted for its embellishments[2]. Mammaṭa paid great importance to the *alaṁkāras* by incorporating them in his definition of poetry[3]. *Alaṁkāra* is identified with beauty itself, not as instruments of beauty. Therefore the good poets have applied their minds in framing their verses in such an embellishment form which will make

---

वन्दे तमन्धतमसावृतजीववृन्दे

प्रज्वालितो जगति येन विवेकदीपः।।

1. रूपकादिरलङ्कारस्तथान्यैर्बहुधोदितः।

न कान्तमपि निर्भूषः विभाति वनिताननम्।।

Bhāmaha, Kāvyālaṁkāra, Bihar Rashtrabhasa Parishad, 1962, I. 13, P. 7

2. सौन्दर्यमलंकारः Kāvyalaṁkāṛasūtravṛtti, 3/2/14;

तददतिशयहेतस्त्वलंकाराः *Ibid* 3.1.2

3. तददोषौ शब्दार्थौ सगुणावनलंकृति पुनः क्वापि।

(K.P.) *Kāvyaprakāśa*, ed. and trans. by Ganganatha Jha, P. 4

the verse beautiful. Though generally viewed as outer trappings, the *alaṁkāras* are natural to the Sanskrit poetry. It is, however, their judicious use, which makes the poem beautiful.

This paper attempts to show how poet Bhandarkar has made this poem beautiful by means of poetic figures.

A study of the SVC reveals that the author of this epic poem was a master of versification and choice expression. A student of literary criticism will not fail to discern in his verses a large number of *alaṁkāras*, both of sound and sense. Many of them leighten the sense implied and rise to the state of *Rasavad alaṁkāra.* In the present paper thirty four figures have been identified, but the ones most commonly met with are Alliteration, Simile, Poetic fancy and Metaphor. All the figures occuring in this work have been identified and arranged and their references indicated. While these *alaṁkāras* have been arranged in an order, their definitions have been supplied from the works of poetics like *Kāvyaprakāśa* of Mammaṭa, *Kuvalayānanda* of Appayadīkṣita, *Kāvyādarśa* of Daṇḍin and *Sāhityadarpaṇa* of Viśvanātha. These difinitions and elucidation thereof, are intended to facilitate the study of the work from the point of view of its *alaṁkāra* content.

A poetic composition has its two aspects: words, which constitute its outer figure, and the connotations of those words *i.e.* meanings. Thus the *alaṁkāras,* which add charm to any poetic piece, can be of two types: decorating the words *i.e.* the *śabdālaṁkāras* and decorating the meaning *i.e.* the *arthālaṁkāras.* Those, which decorate the words, entirely depend upon the words for their existence, for they cease to survive, as soon as another replaces a word. On the other hand, the *alaṁkāras* based on meaning, continue to exist even with the change of letters and words.

Now, I shall deat with the *śabdālaṁkāras* first and then the *arthālaṁkāras.*

1. Anuprāsa (Alliteration)

Alliteration consists in the (consistent) similarity of (consonant) letters[1]. The figure most frequently occurs in this poem. An example is given here—

जीर्णं वस्त्रमिव त्यजामि सुखतस्तूर्णं स्वकीयं वपुः
पूर्णं कर्तमथापि कार्यमवनौ कीर्णं यतिष्ये ध्रुवम्।
यावद् ब्रह्ममयं समग्रमिति न ज्ञानं जगत्यां जनै-
स्तावत् प्रेरयितुं प्रयत्नपरता मन्ये मदीयं तपः।।

SVC. XVIII.54

Other examples are : I. 1, 2, 5, 6, 7, 9, 11, 12, 14, 33, 36, 37 II. 27, XIV. 3, 5, 11, 12, 26 XVII. 3 XVII 54.

2. Yamaka (Chime)

There is Chime when there is the repetition of letters in the same order with a different meaning[2]. We give here only an example of *Padādipadānta-yamaka* from the SVC.

इत्थं यमी रवेन्दुदिनानि लङ्का लंकारवद्बोधरुचिं वितेने।
तेनेदृशं प्रेम नृणाममानं मानश्च तस्मिन्नभवत् समेषाम्।।

SVC. XIV 19

3. Citra

A poetic figure arising from the arrangements of letters which are placed in such a way that either (i) they form an arrow, sword, lotus, drum, wheel, disc, plough etc., or (ii) they can be read vertically, horizontally, crosswise or even in reverse order giving the same or different meaning. Our poet has composed only one *citrālaṁkāra* and that is presented in *Hārabandha.* It is not given in the text but in a separate page before the beginning of the *kāvya* proper. The verse is presented here—

?1. वर्णसाम्यमनुप्रासः। KP. 319

2. अर्थे सत्यर्थभिन्नानां वर्णानां सा पुनः श्रुतिः यमकम्। KP. P. 324

कन्दो नः स्यान्नवीनः कुमतिकृतिततिं नाशयन् मे यदेयः
श्रुत्यन्तप्राप्तसत्तप्रथितमतरतश्चित्रकर्माऽकलंकः ।
कर्ता सर्वसह्यं स स्वसृतिमतिरतिं सद्यतिः कीर्तिमूर्तिः
सप्रोद्यद्रूद्यविद्यः सततशतनतः क्षोणिवित्तो विवेकः।।

After these three *śabdālaṁkāras*, now we take up the *arthālaṁkāras*.

4. Atiśayokti (Hyperbole)

It is Hyperbole when, (i) the object under consideration is described as if submerged in another, (ii) the object is something (more than what it is) when an assumption is introduced by 'if' etc., and (iii) when there is an inversion of cause and effect[1].

An example of Atiśayokti :

प्रासादं नीयमाने यमिनि नरपतिर्मोचयित्वा तुरंगान्
युक्तान् दीप्तांशुमुक्ताफलरुचिरतरं स्यन्दनं राजकीयम्।
कर्षन्स्वाभ्यां कराभ्यां सह जननिवहैः प्रीतियुक्तः पदव्या-
मासीदीर्ष्यालुदेवैर्दिवि गमनपरैः साद्भुतं प्रेक्षणीयः।।

SVC. XIV 26

Some other examples are : XII.II, XIV. 7

5. Ananvaya (Self-Comparison)

A figure of speech[2] in which a thing is compared to itself, the object being to show that it is matchless and can have no other *upamāna*.

रामनादनगरीजनेश्वरः पूजयन्प्रमुदितो यतीश्वरम्।
यत्तदादरसमस्तदादरः क्वापि तस्य तुलना न दृश्यते।।

SVC. XIV 22

---

1. निगीर्याध्यवसानं तु प्रकृतस्य परेण यत्।
प्रस्तुतस्य यदन्यत्वं यद्यर्थोक्तो च कल्पतम्।।
कार्यकारणयोर्यश्च पौर्वापर्यविपर्ययः।
विज्ञेयाऽतिशयोक्तिः सा। KP. 390

2. उपमानोपमेयत्वे एकस्यैवैकवाक्यगे अनन्वयः। KP. 365

6. Apahnuti (Concealment)

It is Concealment when the object under reference is negated and another is affirmed[1].

An example of Apahnuti :

देवैः पुरा जलनिधेर्मथनादवाप्तं
पीयूषमेव रचितः स्थविरैः प्रवादः।
सत्यं त्वनेन विदुषाम्बुनिधिर्जगाहे
बोधामृतं च मथितं जगते प्रदातुम्।।

SVC. XIV 10

Here the object of comparison or the object to be described is negative and the standard of comparison, or the object not meant to be described, is affirmed in its place. Thus one finds here the concealment of the real nature of a thing and the ascription of an alien and imaginary character to it.

7. Aprastutapraśaṁsā (Indirect Description)

Indirect Description occurs when the object under reference is described by implication through the description of something irrelevant to the context.[2] Viśvanātha, following Ruyyaka, accepts this figure also when an effect is justified by a cause or vice versa, either under a similarity or a contrast. When the description of something not connected with the context (*aprastuta*) serves to point to the object, which is meant to be, described (*prastuta*) it is Aprastutapraśaṁsā.

An example of Aprastutapraśaṁsā is given here from SVC.

कस्यान्तरं न भविता सवितारमुखेः
पूर्वां दिशं पुनरुपेतमुदीक्ष्य तुष्टम्।
रात्रौ प्रसुप्तमखिलं किल जीवजातं
स्वस्वेषु कर्मसु नियोजयितुं पुरस्तात्।।

SVC. XIV 1

---

1. प्रकृतं यन्निषिध्यान्यत् साध्यते सा त्वपह्नुतिः। KP. 377
2. अप्रस्तुतप्रशंसा या सा सैवं प्रस्तुताश्रया।। KP. 383

In this verse Swāmi Vivekānanda's arising is the principal theme (*prastuta*), whereas the description of the sun is only the secondary theme which is not connected with the context (*aprastuta*). The former is suggested by the latter and hence Aprastutapraśaṁsā-alaṁkāra.

8. Arthāntaranyāsa (Corroboration)

Corroboration is that in which a general or particular proposition is corroborated by another proposition, either through similarity or through difference.[1]

An example of Arthāntaranyāsa :

श्रद्धालुरासीज्जननी तदीया धर्मप्रियादर्शवधूर्विशुद्धा।
अजीजनत्सूनुमतो नरेन्द्रं बीजानुरूपो ध्रुवमङ्कुरोऽपि।।

SVC. I 16

Other examples are : I. 4, 9 III. 25 IV. 13, 20, 23 VI. 49 IX. 11 X. 14, 21 XI. 24 XII. 10, 38 XIV. 24, 42, 53

9. Utprekṣā (Poetic Fancy)

Poetic Fancy consists in presuming that the object under references is identical with a similar object.[2]

An example of Utprekṣā :

ताराः सुराणां कुसुमोपहारा नक्तं वियत्प्राङ्गणमाभरन्ति।
उस्त्रैः सुधांशुस्त्रिदिवीविधातुं भुवं सुधासान्द्रतलां करोति।।

SVC. I 37

Some other examples are : II. 43 VII. 75 IX. 4 XII. 29 XIV. 8, 9, 20 XVII. 4

10. Udāttam (The Exalted)

The description of prosperity exceeding all ordinary experience is Udātta or when the actions of the great are represented as subordinate or collateral to the subject in

---

1. सामान्यं वा विशेषो वा तदन्येन समर्थ्यते।
   यत्र सोऽर्थान्तरन्यासः साधर्म्येणेतरेण वा।। KP. 406
2. सम्भावनमथोत्प्रेक्षा प्रकृतस्य समेन यत्।

hand, it is Udātta.[1] By the description of the prosperity or abundance of a thing we exalt its greatness and by subordinating the great we exalt the greatness of the object under description.

An example of Udātta is given here.

लङ्कारथ्याः सुरभिसलिलैर्नागराः सिक्तवन्तः
सालंकारैः पुनरुभयतस्तोरणैः सज्जिताश्च।
राजास्माकं नयनरुचिरः केवलं योगिपूर्वः
प्राप्तो जिष्णुर्मुदितहृदया भाषमाणाः समानाः।।

SVC. XIV 3

11. Upamā (Simile)

Simile occurs when different things having a common similarity are compared.[2]

An example of Upamā :

इत्थं विचाराहितमानसेन हितः स्वधर्माम्बुनिधिर्जगाहे।
ईशोऽस्य विश्वस्य परो नियन्ता यन्ता रथस्येव धृताश्वरश्मिः।।

SVC. I 2

Some other examples are : I. 7, 11, 26 X. 3, 19, 26 XIV. 21

12. Ullekha (Allusion)

When the same object is looked upon by different people as different things, it is Ullekha.[3]

An example of Ullekha :

धर्मस्यावासभूमिः प्रभवपदमिदं नित्यशो दर्शनानां
नानावीरैः सुधारैरविरतभवनात्स्वस्ति कालादनादैः।
विश्वप्रेमप्रकर्षः प्रकृतिमधुरिमा मार्दवं भावनानां
एभिर्लोकस्य कर्तुं प्रभवति सततं नेतृतां भारतं क।।

SVC. XIV 3

---

1. लोकातिशयसम्पत्तिवर्णनोदात्तमुच्यते।
यद्वापि प्रस्तुतस्याङ्गं महता चरितं भवेत्।। *Sāhityadarpaṇa,*
2. साधर्म्यमुपमाभेदे। KP.
3. बहुभिर्बहुधोल्लेखादेकस्योल्लेखः।

13. Kāvyaliṅga (Poetic Reason)

When a reason is implied in a sentence or in a word it is termed Kāvyaliṅga.[1]

प्रतिगृहं पूजनमाञ्जनेय वीरस्य तस्याभिमतं तदासीत्।
स्वतन्त्रतावीर्यपराक्रमाणां प्रतीकरूपः स हि दिव्यतेजाः।।

SVC. I 1

Another example is : SVC. XIV. 10

14. Lokokti (Popular Saying)

According to Keśava Miśra, *Ukti* is of four types[2] Viz. loka, cheka, arbhaka and unmatta. *Lokokti* is the imitation of a popular saying.[3]

An example of *Lokokti :*

बलं जीवनं दुर्बलत्वं च मृत्युः बलं शाश्वतं सादलं सिद्धिबीजम्।
बलं सौख्यकृद् दुर्बलं च दुःखं बलान्यर्जयध्वं ।।

SVC. XIV. 33

15. Vikaswara (Expansion)

A general statement supports a special statement and a special statement again supports that general statement.[4]

An example of Vikaswara :

इह हि मनुजस्यान्त्यं लक्ष्यं जगत्पतिरुच्चते
विषयपदवीमध्यारूढेऽमृतं न समश्नुते।
अनुमृगतृषं धावन्ती काऽऽप्नुते हरिणी जलं
प्रभवति महान् धर्मो नेतुं नरं परम परम्।।

SVC. X 33

---

1. समर्थनीयास्यार्थस्य काव्यलिङ्गं समर्थनम्। *Kuvalayānada*, 121
2. लोकच्छेकार्भकोन्मत्तभेदादुक्तिश्चतुर्विधा। *Alaṁkāraśekhara*, P. 7
3. लोकप्रवादानुकृतिर्लोकोक्तिरिति गण्यते। *Ibid.* P. 257
4. यस्मिन्विशेषसामान्यविशेषः स विकस्वरः।
एकविशेषसमर्थनार्थमुपात्तस्य सामान्यस्य
समर्थनार्थ विशेषान्तरस्याप्युपादानं विकस्वरालङ्कारः। *Alaṁkāra-muktāvalī*, P. 35

In this verse one special statement is made that only God is the ultimate goal of man and that cannot be achieved by a man who is attached to the sphere of the objects like the deer who runs after a mirage cannot get water at all. To substantiate this general statement, a special statement is made *i.e.* only *Dharma* can help in attaining the highest goal of life.

16. Vinokti (Privative Description)

It is *Vinokti* when it is stated that without a certain thing the object described is defective.[1]

An example of *Alaṁkāra* :

वाणीयमस्य प्रसृताऽचिरेण देशेऽखिले येन जना विना तम्।
स्वं मेनिरे वञ्चितमेव चित्तमभूच्च तेषामधिकाधिकोत्कम्।।

SVC. XIV 41

17. Virodha (Contradiction)

When something is said to be contradictory, even when there is no contradiction—it is the figure Contradiction.[2]

नुतिरियमतिभक्तिः कास्ति दीनस्य भिक्षो-
रपरहरितमित्वा चेन्मया किञ्चिदुक्तम्।
जनिभुवमधिकृत्य प्रायशः सा प्रशंसा
श्रुतिविहितसृतेर्वा भारताध्यात्मशक्तेः।।

SVC. XIV 2

18. Viṣama (Uneven)

It is the figure Viṣama when two unequal things are said to be related.[3]

तद्वैभवं! सोऽप्यसमो जनौघो विज्ञानक्लुप्तिर्मनसाऽप्यचिन्त्या।
तज्जीवितं कर्ममयं नवं क्व क्व भारतं दीनतयाऽऽवृतं नः।।

SVC. IX 31

---

1. विनोक्तिश्चेद् विना किञ्चित् प्रस्तुतं हीनमुच्यते। *Kuvalayānanda*, P. 59
2. विरोधः सोऽविरोधाऽपि विरुद्धत्वेन यद्वचः। KP.
3. विषमं वर्ण्यते यत्र घटनाननुरूपयोः।

19. Vyatireka (Reciprocal)

When the upameya excels or falls short of the upamāna, it is Vyatireka.[1]

उन्नतं शिखरमस्ति हिमाद्रेः स्वामिनोऽपि च समुन्नतं मनं।
आदिमं जडमशान्तकठोरं शान्तिपूर्णमपरं मृदुबोधवत्।।

SVC. VII 76

20. Śleṣa (Paronomasia)

Paronomasia occurs when, in a sentence the same words have different meanings which are capable of giving different meanings to the sentence.[2]

ज्ञानासिरात्तस्वचरित्रकञ्चुकः
सोपासनो विश्रुतमार्गणो गुणी।
उष्णीषशीर्षण्ययुतः पदातिगः
स्वयं नियन्ता जगतीं जिगाय सः।।

SVC. XII 51

21. Samāsokti (Brief Speech)

It is the Samāsokti if the irrelevant is also exemplified when the relevant is stated.[3]

न भारतं युद्धसमुन्नति स्या न्न चैति निद्रावशतामिदानीम्।
शक्तिः पुनः कालमियं विजेतुं संत्यक्तनिद्रः खलु कुम्भकर्णः।।

SVC. XIV 30

22. Sahokti (Connected Description)

When a single expression by the force of term denoting conjuction (*saha,* or its equivelent) singifies two facts, it is Sahokti, provided Hyperble is at the basis of it.[4]

---

1. आधिक्यमुपमेयस्योपमानान्यूनताथवा व्यतिरेकः। *Sāhityadavpan Kārikaā* 700
2. श्लेषः स वाक्य एकस्मिन् यत्रानेकार्थता भवेत्। KP. 379
3. समासोक्तिः परिस्फूर्तिः प्रस्तुतेऽप्रस्तुतस्य चेत्। *Kuvalayānanda*, 61
4. सा सहोक्तिः सहार्थस्य बलादेकं द्विवाचकम्। *KP.* 412

एकान्तमेकान्तरसस्य तस्य स्वतन्त्रबुद्धेः स्थिरचित्तवृत्तेः।
ज्ञानस्य लिप्सा वयसैव सार्धं वृद्धिं गता शुद्धविचारशक्तेः।।

SVC. 1 20

23. Svabhāvokti (Natural Description)

When the form and action of children etc. are described as they are, it is Natural Description.[1]

अपीपिडच्चित्रकरीभिरात्सप्रसुं मुहुः प्रश्नपरम्पराभिः।
श्रुत्वा न तर्कानुयोगयोग्यान्वस्तून्यसौ वेश्यगतान्यभांशीत्।।

24. Saṁkara[2]

ज्ञानज्योतिर्नाशितध्वान्तजालं
सानन्दाकं श्रीविवेकाख्यदीपम्।
संस्कुर्वन्त लोकमालोकपूर्णं
सीमातीतस्नेहसारं नतोऽस्मि।।

SVC. I 3

25. Saṁbhāvanā (Supposition)

Saṁbhāvanā is a conjecture for tha attainment of something else with the thought, "if it were so".[3]

कालोऽयं कठनिश्रमस्य भवतो भ्रातर्वचः श्रूयता-
मुत्थाय क्रतुमारभस्व समये मन्येऽतिनिद्रं तव।
माता प्राप्तनिजासना बलवती तन्द्राभिभूता मनाक्
तस्या आयतिरुज्ज्वला परमसौ युष्मत्प्रयत्नोश्रया।।

SVC. XIV 34

26. Saṁsṛṣṭi (Conjuction)

When poetic figures (more than one) exist independently of and distrnctly from one another in one substratum, either

---

1. स्वभावोक्तिस्तु डिम्भादेः स्वक्रियारूपवर्णनम्। KP. 411
2. अङ्गाङ्गित्वेऽलङ्कृतीनां तद्वदेकाश्रयस्थितौ।
   सन्दिग्धत्वे च भवति सङ्करस्त्रिविधः पुनः।। SD. 63
3. संभावना यदीत्थं स्यादित्यूहोऽन्यस्य सिद्धये। *Kuvalayānanda*, Verse 126

in a sentence or in a stanza, it is Saṁsṛṣṭi.[1] This collocation of poetic figures is like the mixture of seasame and rice.

An example of Saṁsṛṣṭi of Rūpaka and Utprekṣa :

आहोस्विदद्य मिलिता नवकर्मगंगा
ज्ञानार्णवेन महतासह तादृशेन।
यस्मिञ्छतान्यवतरन्ति तरंगिणीनां
यत्रावगाहनवशादमृतत्वलाभः।।

SVC. II 47

27. Dṛṣṭānta (Exemplification)

Dṛṣṭānta is the reflective repersentative of the common attribute, the object of comparison and the standard of comparison.[2] The two sentences which constitute Dṛṣṭānta possess reflective correspondence not only between the properties of the two sentences but also between the entities, which consequently stand to each other in relation of upameya and upamāna, and between other circumstances connected with them, if any. This figure has been used by our poet in the following verse:

संसारमंगलमसंभवमेव भाति
शिक्षोन्नतो न भविता महिलागणश्चेत्।
वैहासाध्वनि खगाः परिपुष्टदेहा-
श्छिन्नैकपक्षतिरयाः कथमुड्डयन्ते।।

SVC. XVI 24

Other examples are : I. 50, III. 43, IV. 12, 17 X. 17, 20, 33 XII. 57 XVI. 24.

28. Nidarśana (Illustration)

When an impossible relation of things is taken to constitute similtude, it is Nidarśana.[3]

1. सेष्टा संसृष्टिरेतेषां भेदेन यदिह स्थितिः।
2. चेद् विम्बप्रतिबिम्बत्वम् दृष्टान्तस्तदलङ्कृतिः। *Kuvalayānanda*, Verse 52
3. अभवन्वस्तुसम्बन्ध उपमापारकल्पकः। *KP*, 381

स देशभक्तिं हृदयेषु यूनां
सञ्चारयनु दिव्यगिरा जगाद।
अहो प्रभाता रजनी सुदीर्घा
प्राच्यां नवोऽभूदरुणोदयोऽयम्।।

SVC. XIV 28

Another example is : SVC XIV. 1

29. Nirukti (Derivation)

Nirukti is an artificial explanation of the derivation of a word.[1]

परस्त्वमसि चन्द्रमा नभसि भारतस्योदित-
स्ततोऽजनिषताखिलाः सरुचितारका निष्प्रभाः।
नरेन्द्र इति विश्रुतो भवसि राजभिः पूजिता
जिताहितबलस्य ते सततराजता राजते।।

SVC. XIV 24

30. Pariṇāma (Alternation)

Pariṇāma is a figure in which what is superimposed (upamāna or āropya) serves the purpose of the object of superimposition (*upameya* or *āropita*).

समाजस्य यतीन्द्राणां मूलं विश्वप्रसारिणः।
महामहीरुहस्यासीद् रामकृष्णाश्रमात्मनः।।

SVC. VII 10

31. Praśnottara (Question and Answer)

का पुण्यभुः समुचिता जगतीतलेऽस्मिन्
किं स्थानमत्र परमेश्वरलाभसिद्ध्यै।
नृणां च कर्मफलभोगपदं किमास्ते
तत्रोत्तरं शृणुत भारतभूरियं नः।।

SVC. XIV 15

Another example is : SVC. XIV 16

---

1. निरुक्तिर्योगतो नाम्नामत्यार्थत्वप्रकल्पनम् *Kuvalayānanda*, Verse 164

32. Rūpaka (Metaphor)

Metaphor is the figure when there is identification between the object compared and the object to which it is compared. Here there is identification between Svāmi Vivekānanda and the light of knowlege.

ज्ञानप्रभानिधिरयं जलधिं विलङ्घ्य
यन्नीतवानमितहिन्दयशोतिदूरम्
तस्मादसावनभिषिक्तनृपोत्तमोऽभू-
दस्माकमुन्नतमिह ध्रुवमुत्तमाङ्गम्।।

SVC. XIV 9

Other example are:

I. 1 III. 67 (Parampartitarūpaka). 71 IV. 6 VI. 35

33. Preyas (Lovely)

The Preyas is a felictous expression. Later rhetoricians accept this figure where a feeling (*bhāva*) or sentiment (*rasa*) is subordinated to something else. Hemcandra treats *Preyas* as a kind of *Guṇībhūtavyaṅgya.*

An example:

लोकैः समर्चि हरिचन्दपुष्पमाल्यैः
धूलिर्धृतास्य पदयोः शिरसि स्वकीये।
सच्छत्रचामरपताकमथास्य पुर्यां
यात्रा समारभत विश्रुतराजचिह्नैः।।

SVC. XIV 6

34. Mudrā (Impress)

When some other object is indicated by the words which denote the object under description, it is the Mudrā.[39]

An example :

रिक्थानुरूपसमलङ्कृतभव्यवेश्म
न्यायोजिते निखिलधर्मसभाविभागे।
उद्धर्षिणी रिजमतप्रथिमाभिमाना
नानापथप्रथितपण्डितमण्डलीयम्।।

SVC. X 1

In this verse the word *Uddharṣiṇī* denotes the metre Vasantatilakā along with the person who is delighted.

Conclusion

From the above analysis of the *Alaṁkāras* occuring in SVC it is understood that the author of this epic poem is a brilliant poet of modern time. I do not have any hesitation in saying that his epic-poem is one of the best poems of our time. One can easily find a spontaneous overflow of the powerful feelings taking it origin from the emotion recollected in tranquility. The poet is as master of Sanskrit literary criticism. He has made an in-depth study of the priciples of poetry escpecially the principles of the Alaṁkāras. He uses Alaṁkāras only when they help in *rasaniṣpatti.*

Paṇḍit Tryambak Bhandrakar likes to combine several figures in one verse and to mingle them in such a way as to make it difficult to discern what is the predominant image in the mind of the author. There are also stanzas some of which contain and admixture of a few figures of speech and some contain a congregation of a few of them independently. All these illustrate his proficiency in the use of Alaṁkāras and it is clear that he paid a great importance to them in his *Mahākāvya.* They add chram to his speech and enhance the gravity of its sense.

Bandinaḥ Svadeśacintā of Prabodha Kumar Mishra*

I. Introduction

Bandinaḥ Svadeśacintā is an important translated work in modern Sanskrit literature. The original work is *Bandira Svadeśacintā*, a famous patriotic poem in Oriya composed by Paṇḍita Gopabandhu Dash. It is an immortal creation of a *daradikavi* 'an emotional poet'. The work bears heart-rending cries of a freedom-fighter who had sacrificed his life for the freedom of the motherland. The poem written by Dash, the Oriya patriot saint of pre-Independence days, during the jail-term of two years from 1922 to 1924 in Hazaribag Jail, tell us his reactions of men, things, places and affairs as the railway train swiftly carried him from Orissa towards Bihar. He repeatedly tells his readers not to worry about his being in jail and asks them to view the struggle for Indian independence as a moral war between the right and wrong, and his patriotic soul often cries out in agony for the suffering of millions he has left behind in Orissa, thus transforming his utterances into noble poetry. His spontaneous flow of heart is reflected in his poems *Kārākavitā* written in prison. A chapter of this book of poems is translated into Sanskrit verses. It is available now in the form of a book entitled *Bandinaḥ Svadeśacintā*. In this paper, I have made an attempt to study this translated work.

II. Paṇḍita Gopabandhu Dash, the Original Author

Paṇḍita Gopabandhu Dash (1876-1928), popularly

known as *Utkalamaṇi* 'the gem of Orissa' was a prominent person in the literary history of Orissa. He was an eminent national leader, freedom fighter and a poet of great popularity, an inspiring orator, a noble social worker and a far-sighted eductionalist. In Orissa Paṇḍita Gopabandhu was essentially a devoted servant of humanity. The patriot had started his literatry career as a poet. The little that he produced in his student days was so marked with individuality as to attract special recognition from no less a personality than Radhanatha Ray, the demigod of Oriya literature in those days. But after passing out of the university, Gopabandhu became so immersed in various nationalistic activities that he completely forgot poetry, his adolecent love. Gopabandhu came back to poetry, the old love of his student days. He wrote two small books inside the Hazaribag jail. One is *Bandira Ātmakathā* or the soliloquy of a prisoner. In this book, he tells us his reactions to men, things, places and affairs. Without any attempt to heighten the effect through embellishments of any sort, the simple verse used in this book turns into a noble poetry, charged with the galvanizing outpourings of a great heart. The other book that Gopabandhu wrote in Hazaribag jail is *Dharmapada,* describing the heroic sacrifice of his own life by the boy-architect of that name, in the interest of his class, while engaged in the construction of the temple Konarka. These two poems have become as popular in Orissa as folk-poetry. Artistically they are not of a very high order, but what moves the ordinary reader so deeply about them is the nobility of the ideals and the purity of emotions they expressed. Gopabandhu and his associate took up literature as the means of propagating their ideas and ideals. They wrote histories, poems, plays and innumerable essays in their zeal to awaken in the hearts of their people a patriotic conciousness, the desire to live again as free men and revive the glories of their forebears. The result has been quite an appreciable body of literary works with a distinction of its own.

III. Content of the Poem

The poem begins with a touching description of the sweet wind blowing slowly and slowly outside. The jasmine flowers are smiling in happiness and the mad bees are playing with them happily. The wind is sometimes entering into the room of the jail like a messenger through the small holes of window and hides himself immediately after giving the secret information. The poet becomes happy by its soft touch. Some memories of past days come to his mind. The poet especially remembers the evening when he was moving in the bank of the river Bhārgavi at his young age. By the touch of the wind the waves in that river are also dancing. The women folk from the nearby village come and collect water. The poet remembers the cowherd boys who come back to the village with cows at evening and at the time play flute in a very sweet voice. The marketers come back to their villages after marketing. Young maidens come to the temple of goddess Yogeśvarī and offer their *pūja*. Some of them make quarrels with each other, some play games and some collect flowers of Bakula tree. Somewhere a brother with a heavy load of things goes with his sister to leave her at the house of her father-in-law on a bridge. When evening comes he orders her sister to put her steps quickly. But the young lady with a child in her hands is not able to walk quickly because of the heaviness of the thigh. Looking at such an interesting scene, the naughty boys of the village laugh at her. Birds (*vāduri*) come flying from different places and get together on the branches of *punāṅga* tree loaded with ripe fruits.

All those incidents which were happening at home like the treatment of guests, offering *pūja* to deities etc. come to the mind of our poet. But the consoles himself by saying that there is no point in remembering all those sweet incidents in a jail.

The poet addresses to the wind of spring and requests to give him the news of the southern part of Orissa and to make him happy. The poet being extremely happy considers the wind to be a messenger and thinks that he might have met some of his relatives and might have collected important information on his way of coming. Then the poet imagines that the wind has come on a particular route and visited the places like Śrīkṣetranilācala (the place of the Lord Jagannātha), Satyabādikuñja, Śākhigopal (Gopīnātha), the Āśrama of the poet, river Ṛṣikulyā, Clikā (a beautiful lake of Orissa), the temple of Liṅgarāja, Khaṇḍagiri, Mahānadī at Cuttack, Bārabāṭi (a fort on the bank of the river Mahānadī). By addressing to the wind the poet expresses his love for his native places, his sympathy for the poor and downtrodden. He also expresses his agony and feelings of sorrow about the downfall of Orissan culture and heritage. He wants to know from the mouth of the wind about the problems of the farmers and the people of forests. At the end, the poet requests the wind by saying that he has visited many places of religious merits, so it should touch his head and make his heart cold which is burning by the fire of sorrow in the jail.

IV. The Translated Work

Bandinaḥ Svadeśacintā is a small work of seventyone pages. There are only seventyone verses. The special characteristic feature of this work is that it includes Sanskrit translation in verse in Devanāgarī, original Oriya version in Hindi, and in Oriya and also the Sanskrit version in Oriya script, perhaps, to give it a big shape, and to some extent, facilities the readers. At the end on page 69 a list of *Subhāṣitas* (Gopalbandhu's good, noble and inspiring sayings) is appended. The verses are composed in the metres, viz. *Mandākrāntā, Vasantatilakā, Upajāti, Indravajrā* and *Upendravajrā.* The translator has tried his best to express the thoughts and feelings of the original author as exactly as possible. He has exhibited his talent in his translation in maintaining Gopabandhu's original thoughts and lucid style. It is interesting to say that Paṇḍita Mishra has maintained the same rhythm in his translation what we find in the original poem. The work begins with:

मन्दश्चायं मधुरमलयः शीतलो वाति सारः
मल्लीवाला स्मितमुकुलिता दोलिता भृङ्गरङ्गैः।
लभ्यो वातायनपरिसरे माधवो वक्रभङ्ग्या
किंवा गुप्तचर इव वहिर्वार्त्तिकां याति दत्वा ।। (p. I.)

V. The Translator

The translator Paṇḍita Probodha Kumar Mishra is an Oriya. His place of birth is Sarapada, a village at Bodhanga in the district of Cuttack in Orissa. He had passed *Śāstrī*, *Sāhityācārya*, Sanskrit *Biśārada* and *Raṣṭrabhāṣākovida*. He is an eminent Sanskrit poet and scholar. He is serving in some Sanskrit Vidyālaya and offering his valuable services towards the pious cause of Sanskrit language and literature.

VI. Significant Features of the Work

The poem had some significant features which have made it very popular. In the following verses we will see how poet's delicate heart feels heavy pain and becomes very eager to know the conditions of the poor and neglected farmers who toil hard on their land but are unable to feed their children in peace.

चक्रावर्त्तैर्गुरुपरिगतैः धूलिपत्राणि नीत्वा
व्योम्नि प्रेम्णा चरसि वहते! ह्युत्तराशामवाप्य।
दृष्टं किंवा जनगणसुखं दुःखकं तत्प्रदेशे
तेषां चित्ते पतिनवनवं चेतनं लक्ष्यसे किम्।। (p. 59.)

Whirling the dead leaves, twigs and the dust
of the red earth up into that sky,
Ready to move northward
you must have looked in playful glee.
Tell me, O wind, what you saw there
in the dark land, the story of the poor.

Do those people suffer still?
Or have they been awakened to their lot?

स्वक्षत्रे यः जनयति कृषिद्रव्यकं दुःखदीर्णः
दारासुतैः सह बत! कदा तुष्ट-चित्तः भुनक्ति?
को राजा नो गणयति सखे! पुत्रवल्लोकजातं
राज्यप्राणां निखिलसुखदां लोकते न प्रजां तु।। (p. 60.)

The farmer toiling hard on his land,
bearing the pain of the sun and the rain,
is he able to feed his children
without any fear of the ruler?
Does the ruler there think for a moment;
'They are my children, my kith and kin,
their well-being is my life's aim,
in their happiness lies my own?'

विना प्रजाशक्तिमिहास्ति नो गतिः
नृपस्य वा श्वेनपोतभावकः।
पजाजलोद्बिन्दुभिरेव शोभते
सुराज्यसिन्धुर्नृप एवं धारकः।। (p. 69.)

'Where does the ruler's strength lie
if not in the people he rules?'
The ruler is not to the ruled, never,
what the hawk is to the dove.
People are drops of water, but together
they form the ocean of the State.
The ruler is but a current, nothing more.

प्रजा तु यत्रातिभयेन 'भोज्यकं'
प्रदाय कालं नयति स्फुट सखे!।
न जीवने चास्ति धनेऽधिकारकः
कथाऽधिकारोऽपि तथा विडम्बितः।।(p. 52.)

The people of that land offer
worship and sacrifices to their deities
and pass their days in fear.

No voice they have to protest against oppression
and their lives and property are not their own.

यस्मिन् वंशे कथमपि न वा दृश्यते क्षीणपुण्यात्
सौभाग्यं तत् प्रमदविधुराः राजलोकस्तथाऽपि।
ग्रीष्मे शैले ज्वलति हुतभुक् वर्षकीं लोकपूर्य्यां
स्थानं चान्यत् सरति तु पशुः क्वैव शक्तिः प्रजानाम्।।

(p. 53.)

Having done no good to anyone ever,
the family of the rulers of the land has had
no luck, no love, no happiness.
Still its members do indulge in drinking
the dark wine of cunning and craft,
and close their eyes to life's realities.
Forest fires blaze in summer alone,
but the people suffer all the year through.

Now, the following verses give us a clear picture of a poet who remembers birds, animals, flowers, fruits, ponds and lakes and expresses his love and sympathy for all of them. He declares that all that is sweet and simple in man derives from Nature and is cast in her mould. For him, the world of nature is the abode of Lakṣmī, or beauty. It is sacred, beautiful and wondroud. There is none to rule or to be ruled. So Nature is heavenly, divine and pure.

स्वच्छन्दं वा प्रसरति गिरेः पादयोः स्वच्छधारा
हीराहारभ्रममनुरणन् 'शुभ्रतोया' प्रवाहः।
नित्यं गान्तः पिकशुकखगाः चक्रवाकाः मरालाः
नानापुष्पैः मधुरविपिनं यत्र रागं तनोति।। (p. 54.)

There at the feet of the mountains flow
freely and ever-transparent streams.
The bright bodied river flows there,
a string of diamonds around the forest's neck.

Every day the birds sing–
cuckoos, cakravākas, cranes

and geese, parrots and mynahs.
Decked with many a flower and fruit
the forest arouses in the human heart
sacred feelings of sympathy and love.

सरसि दोलितशुभ्रसरोरुहे
भ्रमर एव सुगुञ्जति मञ्जुलम्।
विहरतीह च कृष्णमृगव्रजः
सुतटिनीतटकानन उत्सुकात्।। (p. 55.)

In ponds and lakes sway white lotuses;
bhramaras hum their soft, sweet tunes.
The kṛṣṇasāra deer roam playful and free
in the verdant lawns on the river bank.

नित्या साध्वी सुरतरुगता मालती माधवी च
सद्भार्य्यावत् पथिकहृदयं स्निग्धछायाप्रदानैः।
शस्योदभारैः विहसति मही श्यामला तोषयन्ती
माधुर्य्यं वा सरलतरलं दिव्यरागप्रसन्नम्।। (p. 56.)

The kind-hearted mālatī and mādhavī creepers
in the arms of the deodars and teaks,
like loyal and ideal housewives, comfort
the wayfarer with cool shades.
There are green earth always smiles,
her body adorned with tender plants.
All that is sweet and simple in man
derives from Nature and is cast in her mould.

विचित्रचित्रः कमलालयः सदा
निसर्गकासद्युतिरेव मोहिनी।
पवित्रितं यत् सकलं कलान्वितं
प्रभावमुक्तं ननु शासकस्य वा।। (p. 57.)

Sacred and beautiful, the abode of Lakṣmī,
wondrous is the world of Nature.
None is therein to rule or to be ruled.
So is she heavenly, divine and pure.

वनादवनान्ते खलु कन्दरे सखे!
सलीलगत्या वहसि स्वभावतः।
कदा च तप्तस्तु सुशीतलः कदा
कदा तु रौद्रातपजर्जरो भवन्।। (p. 58.)

You must have moved from forest to forest
from vale to vale, understood, free,
blowing warm here and cold
there and not elsewhere.

The poet remembers Khandagiri, a broken hill, the city of Cuttack, the river Mahānadī and the fort Barabati. He feels pain in saying that the Barabati, which was the abode of the heroes of Utakal, got changed into a grave of valor and courage. He addresses the wind who was a witness of the glorious victory of the king, Gajapati when he had returned from his battle and it is that wind who had carried all those sounds of his victory in all ten directions. All these make us aware of our past glory. A poet who is a helpless creature in a jail does not find any other way except remembering all those noble incidents and expressing it through his poems to create social consciousness.

उन्मुक्तायां वियति रचयन् खण्डशैलस्य रीतिं
मार्गे रुद्धः कथमपि महानिम्नगाभिः स्वभावात्।
वेगव्याजप्रगुणितगतिः ह्यादृतिं नो त्यजेस्त्वं
प्रेम्णा पाशैः क्षणमपि जनः कर्मठश्चेद् विलम्बी।। (p. 42.)

You must have flown in joy, in style
in the vast open sky above the Khandagiri hills
Did Cuttack stop you on the way?
Did the river Mahanadi,
attired in the blue waters?

You must have pretended haste and hurry
her friendly welcome you could not reject,
However busy, one lingers about,
before finally parting with one's love.

वक्षः स्फीतं ननु विचलितो वीचिहारस्तु तस्याः
तीरे शष्फाः स्मितसुविनताः वीक्ष्य चाङ्गे विकारम्।
लोके या त्वं ह्युपगतशुचा सर्वथा 'वारवाटीं'
शूरव्रातप्रवारवसुधा शैर्य्यहीनाद्य भाति।। (p. 43.)

Mahanadi's heart must have swollen with joy,
the waves must have risen high;
the islands must have lowered their heads
and shyly smiled at her reactions.
There you must have seen the Barabati fort
and felt very sad to see it in ruins
Once the abode of the heroes of Utkal
now it's the grave of valour and courage.

कालो यातो नवतलगृहे भूपयात्रावकाशे
राज्ञः तावत् स्पृशति पवनं स्वेदसिक्तं च भालम्।
विन्दुव्रातं लपनभरितं नेत्रमार्गावलीढं
सिंचच्छीतप्रसरसरणैः मौक्तिकं तत् जहार।। (p. 44)

There in the nine-storeyed palace once,
when for battle the king was leaving,
a breeze carried forth the river water.
and sprinkled it on the queen's sweating brow.
All those drops of love's nectar,
the moons that glistened in her eyes,
the breeze carefully gathered those pearls,
without spilling a single one on the floor,
and took all of them away with him.

जित्वा युद्धं गजपतिरहो ह्यागतः जैत्रघोषैः
अर्ध्यस्थाल्या नृपतिमहिषी वन्दते स्मालिसंघैः।
भेर्य्यस्तूर्य्य मलय! नर्दिताः कम्पितं केतनं च
जैत्रोद्घोषं नयसि विदिशं त्वं नु वासन्तरम्य।। (p. 45.)

When the Gajapati returned from battle
and victory was so loudly proclaimed,
the queen and her maids greeted him

with flowers and lamps in golden plates.
Conches, pipes and flutes blew,
the banner of victory flew high in the sky.
O wind, you carried those sounds of victory
in all ten directions, echoing loud.

वन्दापनादीप्तप्रदीपनर्त्तनैः वामाङ्गवासः प्रविकम्पनैस्तथा।
सम्मोदिता भव्यवराङ्गनाततिः त्वद्धृष्टतायै व्यपदेशरोषिणी।।

(p. 46.)

सौभाग्यरङ्गे खलु तत्र वात! वा
दिष्ट्या सुरम्यं ह्यभिनीतमादरम्।
हा! वारवाटीमधुना विलोकसे
स्वप्नं नु सत्यं किमहो निबोध मे।। (p. 47.)

You made all those lamps dance,
and women's sarees fall from their heads;
naughty as you were, O wind,
those fair ladies chided you
albeit in pretended anger.

You had played a role in that glorious drama
at the Barabati fort in the past,
and now you see the palace in ruins.
Who can say it is real or just a bad dream!

Subhāṣitas

स्वदेशभूमौ ननु लीयतां तनुः
स्वदेशलोका मम यान्तु पृष्ठतः।
स्वराज्यमार्गे यदि गर्तमस्ति वा
मदस्थिमांसे परिपूर्णमस्तु तत्।। 1।।

कुपौरुषं कातरतामलामसं
रणेन वीरो म्रियते च मारयेत्।
न वीरभालेऽस्ति नु पृष्ठभङ्गतो
न वा म्रियेत स्फुटभीतिशङ्कितैः।। 2।।

प्रजार्थसृष्टि विहिता स्वयम्भुवा
प्रजार्थवृष्टिर्निहिता शुचिस्वरैः।
प्रजार्थमेवं रविचन्द्रतारका
प्रजाशिवार्थं तटिनीप्रवाहकः ॥ 3 ॥

VII. Appraisal of the Work

We all know that translation is a difficult task and that too of a piece of poem into Sanskrit from regional language. But Paṇḍita Mishra has achieved tremendous success in his endeavour and has given us an interesting piece of translation which gives special aesthetic pleasure. The striking feature of this work is that the translator has been able to express exactly author's feelings and thinkings with same amount of sensitivity. His language is as flowing as it is in Oriya. The style is simple and lucid. Another noteworthy feature of this work is that while the original author has used only one metre throughout the work for expressing his feelings, the translator has used five Sanskrit metres, viz. *Mandākrāntā, Vasantatilakā, Upajāti, Indravajrā,* and *Upendravajrā.* He has also maintained all those figures of speech in his translation. A good translation must be faithful to the original and avoid the pitfalls of over-expressions. The excellence of thought and beauty of expression of the original should not be lost in the rendering. The translator should not also be tempted to indulge in elaboration of extra ornamentation in his attempt to improve upon the original. But translator has kept all these points in view and the result is a fine piece of literary creation. The old but in a new form and in a new dress. But the beauty is as young as it is in the original creation.

Conclusion

Paṇḍita Prabodha Kumar's translation of Utkalamani Gopabandhu's Oriya poem, *Vandira Svadeśacintā* for the first time is undoubtedly an important contribution to the field of modern Sanskrit literature. As far as I know, nobody has made such an attempt to translate this Oriya *kāvya* into Sanskrit. It is, therefore, true that Paṇḍita Prabodha Kumar's such an attempt is of special importance in this direction. His effort is highly successful and deserves appreciation. By doing this he has not only brought this valuable piece of Gopalbanahu's immortal poem to the scholarly world of Sanskritists but also enriched the existing stock of modern Sanskrit literature. From this point of view, Prabodha Kumar has given commendable service to the literature of our divine language.

Mīrālaharī of Kṣamā Rao*

I. Introduction

Mīrālaharī is an excellent piece of poem composed by Paṇḍitā Kṣamā Rao who has carved a niche in the history of modern Sanskrit literature for her substantial contribution to the field of Sanskrit poetry. After Ganga Devi, Paṇḍitā Kṣamā enriched it to a great extent by her valuable works. She stands out for her substantial contribution among the poetesses of modern period. It is understood very clearly that she has modelled her *Mīrālaharī* on the well-known *laharīkāvyas* like *Saundaryalaharī* of Śaṅkarācārya, *Gaṅgalāharī* Paṇḍitarāja Jagannātha. It also falls in the line of biographical poems, as the poetess intends mainly to portray the character of Mīrā, her noble activity and the special features of her life. It is the only poem, to my knowledge, composed on the life of Mīrā which has come down to us in the form of *khandakāvya.*

In 1944 Paṇḍitā Kṣamā had brought out this short poem, consisting of 135 verses composed in the *śārdulavikrīḍita* metre. The work is divided into two parts which depict the sublime life of Mīrā, a cult figure, who had married to a prince, but being consumed by the intense contemplation of Kṛṣṇa forgot everything else of the world and created a history of her own.

At present, two editions of this work are available. One is accompanied with a Sanskrit commentary written by the

*. The paper published in Śabdākhyajyoti, Prof. Vijay Pandya Felicitation Volume.

poetess herself explaining the verses in easy Sanskrit and with a lucid English rendering of the verses. The other one is without the English translation. Though it is a small work, still it is one of her best works. The poem is distinguished by certain pleasing characteristics, such as, elegant diction, charming vacobulary, appropriate selection of metre, interesting figures of speech, vivid descriptions, precise presentation of the theme and the poetic quality which is of a high order.

II. Life Sketch of Mīrābai (1504-1546)

As we know, the name Mīrābai evokes a very complex and paradoxical image, a multifaceted personality in whom polarities meet. To the egocentric, vanquisher Rajput community which prided itself on its deep-rooted royal tradition, social customs and hierarchial caste system, Mīrā is a self-assertive, non-conformist reble who had tarnished the image of the royal family of Sosodia. To the faminists she is the most liberated woman and to the whole world she is the greatest of the devotees of Lord Kṛṣṇa for whom she sacrificed everything in her life. She is a gentle figure, clad in white saree with ektara in hand, dancing in deep ecstasy, singing the glories of God, drinking deeply the divine nectar and unmindful of her physical surroundings.

Mīrā was born into a Rajput royal family at Pandu village on Medta, some time in July 1504. Her great grandfather; Rao Jodha Singh, who is credited with founding the imperial town of Jodhpur had granted a Jagir of twelve villages to her grandfather, Rao Doodha Singh. In 1462 Rao Doodha Singh founded Medta and subsequently made it, his capital. Mīrā was the daughter of Rao Doodha Singh's second son, prince Ratan Singh. She lost her mother in childhood and was reared by her maternal aunt who lived in the nearby village of Kudki. She was married at the age of twelve to prince Bhojaraj, the eldest son of the famous Sesodia king of Mewar, Rana Sanga. A spell of gloom fell on Mīrā when around 1523, her husband died. A few years later, her father-in-law, Rana Sanga was severly wounded fighting with the Mughal invader, Babur and succumbed to his injuries. Earlier her father, Rana Ratan Singh had died fighting bravely in the battle of Panipat. Rana Ratan Singh, Mīrā's elder brother-in-law succeeded the throne after the death of Rana Ratan Singh, however, ruled for only three years. Rana Ratan Singh's cousin Vikramaditya who succeeded him was worse. Noticing her traumating experience in Mewar, her elder uncle Rana Biram Dev who was then the ruler of Medta, took her to his palace in 1931. Rana Biram Dev and his son Jayamal were quite impressed by Mīrā's poetic gifts and let her live the religio-poetic life the way she wished. For about seven years Mīrā continued with her poetic work undisturbed. But she was again in trouble in 1538 when her uncle lost his kingdom. Mīrā then resolved to go on a pilgrimage and visited Dakar Pusparaja, Vṛndāvan and finally took shelter in Dwarka, once the seat of lord Kṛṣṇa. She died in 1546 in the temple of lord Kṛṣṇa.

Numerous legends have clustered around Mīrā's life-long quest for lord Kṛṣṇa as a lover (not of a devotee for God). It is said that once watching a marriage procession she demanded of her mother to tell her who was her (Mīrā's) bridegroom. As she could not be satisfied with the answer, the mother showed her the idol of Lord Kṛṣṇa and said, "your groom is Lord Kṛṣṇa". Mīrā, it is said, believed therefore none but Lord Kṛṣṇa to be her husband and even after marriage clung to that faith relentilessly. Mīrā is a Rajput queen who experienced innumerable hardships, persecution, calumny in her path of devotion. She is the greatest of mystic poets who trod the path of *bhakti* and took *madhurabhāva* to its highest peaks. She is the ideal lover who surrendered herself to lord Kṛṣṇa in deep devotion and immeasurable love.

At a time in the 16th century when the lord feminine evoked only the image of someone physically beautiful, delicate and graceful and mentally meek, gentle and docile, Mīrā was the first feminist in the broadest sense of the term, who broke away from the narrow bonds of tradition, rigid social and religious customs, class and caste distinctions and discriminations and sought absolute freedom. She surounded all the physical, territorial sexual, mental and spiritual barries and limitations. Her protest is not a halfhearted slogan-raising interspersed with a few symbolic gestures. Her very life is a translation of the protest into action and the fulfilment of her ambition, a reaching-out to the highest goal of her life.

III. Theme as Presented in the Poem

The poem begins with the description of the beautiful city called Kurkhi in the country of Malawa, its golden dome of the palace, roads and its lake. Then about Mīrā who decended from the noblest warrior family with all the auspicious marks on her body and who from her very childhood showed a most wonderful fascination for the ambrosia of Lord Kṛṣṇa name. In that town, Ratan Singh, father of Mīrā had reigned who had adhered strictly to the ethics of the warrior race, and always cherished his subjects as his own children by giving them education, means of livelihood and patronage.

In one night, Mīrā of five years had stood at a palace window with her young companions when she saw a procession moving slowly on the highroad surrounded with a golden palanguin amidst a blaze of hand-torches and accompanied by a band playing superb instrumental music. In that palanquin a newly wedded bride and a bridegroom were sited smothered with garlands. It was for the first time Mīrā saw such large crowd and immediately asked her mother about that thing with surprise. Her mother told her that it is a marriage procession. Then Mīrā asked about her own marriage and her husband. Mother jokingly said that Kṛṣṇa is her husband pointing to Lord Kṛṣṇa's image placed in a corner. Hearing mother's speech in detail, meant merely to humour the child, Mīrā took it seriously as though it were a preceptor's advice and she placed her faith in it with deep devotion. She lost all her interest in what was going on outside and when, everyone was engrossed, she, unnoticed by anyone, went quietly near the Lord Kṛṣṇa's image. From that day onwards, a great change took place in the life of Mīrā. She did not play with her doll and did not take interest in any other activities except worshipping her Lord of love. Getting up alertly even before someone rises she stirs out and going to a quiet pond, plunges into the cold water. After the ablution, she returns home, carrying herself a bowl of water for her worship. She was arranging carefully his toilet with great care by sprinkling numerous perfumes and offering him in worship golden ornaments, jewels, flower wreaths and other necessary things. Finally she was getting completely lost in the stream of nectar like hymns of Lord Kṛṣṇa. As time elapsed, the image of the Lord became an object, of an unsatiated delight to her eyes. One day the king who hearing about his daughters great doings, went to the harem to see Mīrā and got surprised to see her activity. The king who was strictly martial and had no faith in the worship of god, was greatly distressed and made immediate plans for her marriage. After an investigation the king decided to give Mīrā to Bhojaraj, son of Sanga of Chitor in marriage. On an auspicious day of spring, Mīrā's daily ritual was disturbed by the noise of her bridal procession. Following the kṣatriya custom, Ratan Singh celebrated the wedding, characterised by the presentation of swords with a great pomp. After the marriage was over, Mīrā went to her husband's house with several festivities, but she thought of nothing except her Kṛṣṇa. There at husband's home, Mīrā though scolded with very bitter and harsh words, did not swerve from her path of faith. Her husband's low-minded sister tried hard to convert Mīrā's mind but failed in her efforts.

When Mīrā was of thirteen, completely innocent and unsophisticated, she attained her puberty on one beautiful day in spring. The occasion of Mīrā's attaining womanhood was celebrated in the palace. A particular day for her first love meeting was fixed and the bridal chamber in the girl's inner apartment was decorated with proper care. After the function is over, during the midnight, when the young prince eagerly went to the nuptial chamber, he saw it empty and became dejected. Then, thinking that his beloved was hiding somewhere playfully, he became all the more passionate and searched for her everywhere, but his effort was in vain. Finally, he entered softly her chamber of worship. There, he saw the princess sleeping on the bare floor in front of Lord Kṛṣṇa's image. Thinking that she was pretending to be asleep, he tried to kiss her face. But Mīrā awakened by her soft touch, did not give any chance and told him that her husband is Kṛṣṇa only and so she should be forgiven. This news of Mīrā's attitude to the prince spread in the king's palace. The prince's sister intending to sully Mīrā's character misguided his brother and informed that Mīrā is having some love affair with some-body else. The prince became very angry and at midnight he went to Mīrā's apartment with a sword in hand accompanied by his sister and with a heavy heart, he stood at the door for a moment and overheard the conversation with a man. This confirmed his belief in his sister's wicked words and bursting with rage he kicked the door open and rushed to kill Mīrā, who was communing with the Lord. His sword slipped off his hand and dropped on the floor of itself. When he had recovered himself, he dragged his wife and a discussion arose between them. Then crying with disappointment for getting no response from her beloved Lord, Mīrā drpped down on the floor. As the husband's sister tried to raise Mīrā, she was stopped, by some one invisible and so she confessed her wicked trick. In the temple, the king's daughter-in-law soon setteld herself and performed the Lord's worship without restraint from her husband. Many people came to see her dance. The great Moghul emperor Akbar had come in a medicant's guise. The prince was very much angry with Mīrā for this incidence. There was a quarrel between Mīrā and her husband which led Mīrā to go for a suicide in a river where she heard an unseen voice. She leapt but was at once held back by some one invisible. The Mīrā started towards Vṛndāvan. She accepted honour from everyone on the way. She got back her memory of her previous life there at Vṛndāvan and was continuously engaged in search of Kṛṣṇa here, there and everywhere. One day her husband came there to take her back and Mīrā came back with him. The beautiful city of Chitor which since Mīrā's departure had been broken hearted looked bright and happy. Having regained her great independence from her noble minded husband she duly performed her austerities without interruption. Then, by adverse blow of destiny her noble husband died and her brother-in-law arranged all sorts of wicked plots after attaining the position of a ruler. But, whatever he plotted with a sinister motive turned out for her good. He presented her with a pretty bowl containing poison but that turned out to be nectar. He sent a casket of snakes and that turned into a golden image of Lord. A bed full of nails turned into a bed of flowers. Though maltreated in this manner, Mīrā bore everything with patience and remained happy. After getting the advice from Tulsidas, she went again to Vṛndāvan where she became more and more absorbed in silent meditation singing continuously the glory of Lord. She grew old. On a holy day at the end of her Puja she breathed her last. In the midst of dance she left her surface of the earth and vanished into the sky and became one with her Lord.

IV. Figures of speech

The verses of the *Mīrālaharī* are adorned with numerous figures of speech which, in fact, enhance the beauty of the poem. Everyone of them is characterised by learning and acquaintance with the niceties of rhetoric.

Upamā (I.2, 45, 54, 56, 85)
Rūpaka (I.1, II, 37, 38)
Sandeha (I.3)
Utprekṣā (I. 12, 73, II.12, 18, 19)
Paryāyoktam (I. 13)
Arthāntaranyāsa (I.14)
Atiśayokti (I.15, 74, II.37)
Saṁkara (I.17, 51, 75, II.22, 32, 36)
Suddhasandeha (I.21)
Saṁsṛṣṭi (I.22, 23, 39, 67, 90, II. 17, 21, 23, 28)
Yathāsaṁkhya (I. 15, 59, II. 3, 20, 29)
Aprastutaprasamsā (I. 38)
Kāvyaliṅgam (I. 42, 47, 66, 73, II, 8, 24, 26, 31)
Prativastūpamā (I. 46)
Śleṣa (I. 53)
Samuccaya (I. 55)
Bhāvasabalatā (I. 62, 89, II. 12)
Vibhāvanā (I. 64)
Tulyayogitā (I.73)
Samāsokti (I.73)
Sahokti (I.82)
Preyas (II.9, 10, 13, 15, 16)
Ākṣepa (II. 30)
Bhāvodaya (II. 13)
Bhāvika (II. 25)
Parisaṁkhyā (II. 40)

Figures of speech which have added a listing colour to the composition of Kṛamā Roa, are noteworthy features of her creative genius. They not only reflect the subtle naunces of her creativity but also her depth of knowledge in the science of poetry. We will see some of them here in the following page.

1. Example of Prativastūpamā

धावल्यं सितनीरजं त्यजति किं पङ्केऽपि नित्यस्थितं
सौभाग्यं विजहाति किं हिमगिरिश्च्छन्नस्तुषारैरपि।
कान्तिं मुञ्चति किन्न हीरकमणिर्लोष्ट्रैश्च सन्दूषितः
किं चित्रं यदि धर्मतो न चलिता मीरापि तत्तर्जनेः।। I-46।।

2. Example of Dṛṣṭānta

कः शङ्केत सुशुभ्रता हिमगिरेः श्यामायितस्याम्बुदै-
स्तेजः पुञ्जकरालतां दिनपतेर्ग्रस्तस्य वा राहुणा।
किं चित्रं यदि राजसूनुरनघां बुध्वा वधूं दूषितां
देवागारमकारयत्सुरुचिरं तस्यै बहिः स्वालयात्।। I-75।।

3. Example of Tulyayogitā

दृषृश्चेन्महिमा विभोरणुरिदं विश्वं विभात्यात्मन-
स्तन्नेत्रस्य सुचारुता यदि मेदा हा पुण्डरीक क्व ते।
तत्तेजो यदि का सहस्रकर ते तेजस्वितायाः कथा
नित्यानन्दमयाननं यदि विधो किं शब्दसाम्येन ते।। I-41।।

Style and Language

Paṇḍitā Kṣamādevi's style of composition is simple and sweet. It is compact and clear. It is mainly natural and devoid of artificiality. Her language is also simple but endowed with charm and sweetness. Obscure words are not found at all in her composition. Lucidity is tha main feature of Kṣamā's style and language. For an example :

वात्सल्येन किमागता निजशिशोः साश्नाद्यशोदा स्वयं
सम्प्राप्ता किमु रुक्मिणी यदुपतेः सांनिध्यमुत्कण्ठिता।
राधा रासविनोदिनी विलसितुं किं प्राप भूयो भुवं
गोपी गोपसुतस्य कापि पुरतो लास्याय किन्नु स्थिता।। I-21।।

The following verse of Kṣamāroa deserves attention :

जन्मारभ्य सुखोषिता क्व नृपजा शय्याय क्व वा भूतलं
क्वाङ्गनां सुकुमारता क्व च तपःक्लेशोऽपि तत्रादृशः।
संस्कारों बलवत्तरः सुकृतिनां जन्मान्तरोपार्जितो
येनैकान्तिकभक्तियोगमहिमा शिखां विना लभ्यते ।। I-20 ।।

It reminds the following verse of Kālidāsa in the *Kumārasaṁbhava*

मनीषिताः सन्ति गृहेषु देवतास्तपः क्व वत्से: क्व च तावकं वपुः
पदं सहेत भ्रमरस्य पेलवं शिरीषुपुष्पं न पुनः पत्रिणः ।। V-4 ।।

Description of Nature

Kṣamādevi is fond of Nature. Description of Nature constitutes an important part of her creativity. In this poem, *Mīrālaharī*, our poetess has described the beauty of spring in the following verse :

आराद्भूरिमनोरमा वसुमती रेजे सपुष्पोदमा
वल्गन्ति स्म विकासिपद्मवदनाः श्रीपद्मिनीनां गणाः।
सौभाग्याङ्कपरागयुक् सुमनसस्तेनुः प्रियान्दोलनां
सञ्चेरुः प्रमदावनेषु मधुवाः पूर्वर्तुदिव्योत्सवे ।। I-53 ।।

Metre

As Kṣemendra instructs in his *Suvṛttatilaka* that the *Śārdūlvikrīḍita* is preferred in the praise of a king's valour, Paṇḍitā Kṣama has very rightly selected the *Śārdūlavikrīḍita* metre for this poem *Mīrālaharī*. It helps in depicting the strong character of Mīrā, a fascinating figure in Indian legend and history.

बालेन्दुः किमयं विभाति न दिवा तत्कान्तिरेतादृशी
किं वा कैरविणी परं निशि हि जागर्ति संहासिनी।
मूर्तिः किं कनकद्रवोपखचिता तस्याः कुतो विभ्रया
इत्येनामवलोक्य कौतुकवशश्चक्रे विकल्पाञ्जनः ।। I-3 ।।

The mental change of Mīrā is very nicely depicted in the following two verses :

या खेलाभवने स्म खेलति पुरा पुत्रीकृता पुत्रिका
सेदानीं रुदतीव दूषितमुखी कोणे क्वचिल्लीयते।
शीघ्रं भोजय मामिति प्रलपति क्षुत्पीडिता सारिका
शश्वल्लालितगोगणश्च तनुते हम्बाखं विह्वलः ।। I-23 ।।

म्लानं तन्मुखतुल्यनीरजमसौ पश्चन्नलिः खिद्यते
तत्संशिक्षितभूरिखेलनशुनीं नृषां पिकी शोचति।
तत्कण्ठानुरवां मृगी नवशुकीमप्रेक्ष्य हा दूयते
दूरस्थे निजसंश्रये जनिमतां स्नेहानुबन्धोऽद्भुतः ।। I-14 ।।

III. Epigramatic Sayings

Mīrālaharī contains a number of pithy and epigramatic sayings. Some of them are presented below :

I. संस्कारो बलवत्तरः सुकृतिनां जन्मान्तरोपर्जितो
यैनेकान्तिकभक्तियोगमहिमा शिक्षां विना लभ्यते ।। I-20 ।।

II. सूचीं लोहमणिर्यथा सुजनतां सौजन्यमाकर्षति ।। I-73 ।।

III. धर्मात्मा ज्ञयमाः प्रशंससि शठं किं देवभक्तः शठः ।। I-00 ।।

IV. मा शोकं वह दैवतरत्र्यमखिलं जातस्य मृत्युर्ध्रुवः ।। I-1 ।।

V. नूनं निश्चितवेतसा तृणसमः कृषाचलानां गणः ।। I-32 ।।

VI. पुण्यज्योतिरुदीर्य लोकतमसो विच्छेदमातन्वती ।। I-33 ।।

VII. दुर्लंहध्यान्यपि निरस्तरन्ति तपसेत्यादर्शयत्कर्मभिः ।। I-34 ।।

VIII. भूरिक्लेशकराः पराश्च नियमा व्यर्थाः कलावत्यपि ।। I-42 ।।

Conclusion

There is no doubt about the fact that Paṇḍitā Kṣamā Roa's *Mīrālaharī* is a marvellous poem, a khaṇḍakāvya of higher type. What impresses one most is the poetic beauty hidden in the presentation of the emotions and charming excellences of the verses characterised by the depth of imagination and vivid power of description. Poetic grace prevails throughout the poem. The verses show the grace of her style, the elegance of her expression and her command over the meter used for versification. In this small poem our poetess depiects nicely the important features of Mīrā's strong personality, her dedication, her super natural devotion, unimaginable sufferings and the difficulties she had to undergo for achieving her highest goal of life. The ocean of powerful fellings of Paṇḍita's heart have riched us in the form of some waves about Mīrā in this poem and therefore the title, *Mīrālaharī* is appropriate one. The fruit of Paṇḍita's powerful creative genius is wonderful and is always appreciable.

Vyastarāgam of Digambara Mahāpātra

The stream of Modern Sanskrit literature is flowing like that of the river Ganges but unfortunately, it meets with a number of impediments on the way of its extension. Day by day the old problems are becoming stronger and stronger and the new ones are also coming up. For a creative writer it is very challenging to write in Sanskrit. He has to face a number of problems. The problems, which a creative writer encounters, are typical in case of Sanskrit, because Sanskrit is no more a language of communication. With these problems which stand on the way of its growth and development, the writers are endeavoring somehow to expand the frontiers of Sanskrit and the walk with their contemporaries so that Sanskrit would not die in India. The literatures of regional languages have been also influencing them. As a result, Sanskrit literature of today has accepted many changes and is taking new forms. Consequently, it has been able to get a status of its own, which is significantly different from that of the classical literature in Sanskrit. One of the significant changes which has made a noteworthy mark in the field of modern Sanskrit literature is the growth of minor poems. Though such growth creates in our minds some sense of satisfaction with the feeling that the neglected Sanskrit literature is getting enriched day by day, nevertheless, it is alarming for all of us. This type of growth will not help us in achieving our expected goals. What a literary critic observes is that because of such growth of literature seriousness and aesthetic sensiblity of the writers are perishing day by day and in its place a craze for quantitative growth is raising its head.

No doubt, time plays a major role in briging the changes in literature and Sanskrit cannot remain isolated without being influenced by it. The age of science and technology has made us busmore. The impact of the materialistic culture has made us restless for collecting and preserving the materials in order to make our life comfortable and enjoyable. The aims of life which are enshrined in the cultural dome of our literature have almost lost their significance in today's life. The poet of today therefore prefers to go away from the traditon and to take a fresh breath in the firmament of modernity. He likes to compose small poems rather than a big poem, *Mahākāvya* or a *khaṇḍakāvya*. Similarly, the readers of Sanskrit Literature, who are less in number in comparison with the readers of other languages, also prefer to read small poems which do not consume their precious time and result in instant pleasure (*sadyaḥ paranivṛtti*). Unfortunately nowadays we have more writers than readers. There are other reasons also, for which preference is given by the poets to the small poems. Not only the influence of Western poetic culture has paved the way of small Sanskrit poems but our old tradition of *muktaka-kāvyas, kośa-kāvyas* also have exercised tremendous influence upon the modern poets. The poets of today take inspiration from the great poets like Bhartṛhari. Jagannātha and others who have significantly contributed to enrich the field of Sanskrit literature. So, in the twentieth century Sanskrit poetry-literature (*padya-kāvya*), minor poems have been occupying a major portion. Their significance has been gradually realized by many well-established poets who have already carved a niche in the field of modern Sanskrit literature by writing *Mahākāvyas* and *Khaṇḍakāvyas*, etc. but, it seem that slowly and slowly they are also getting attracted towards minor poems. As a result, thousands of collections of short Sanskrit poems have captured the market of literature.

A critical study and a proper evaluation of such works from the literary point of view is a desideratum. But, it is very necessary to examine the status of the current Sanskrit Literature. I have made a small attempt in this paper. The *Vyastarāgam* of Digambar Mahāpātra, a collection of modern Sanskrit poems, is attempted here for a study. The collection embodies variety of poems, which focus on different trends of compositions in Sanskrit. It is a collection of minor poems carefully composed by Paṇḍitarāja Ācarya Digambara Mahāpātra. The poems are short, sweet and understandable. Keeping in view the standard of present day Sanskrit students and the light moods of the present day readers, the poet has written the poem which I hope, will be appreciated by the intellectuals as well as common readers. The poems of this collection are free from artificiality and sophisticated verbatim. They are plain and natural.

The collection contains 62 poems in all. Of them some are composed in the traditional metres and some are *gītas*, lyrics. The poet has presented them into four headings, viz. *Satya-ullāsa, Śiva-ullāsa, Sundara-ullāsa* and some *Prakīrṇa-ślokas* (miscellaneous verses). There are 14 poems under *Satya-ullāsa,* 13 poems under *Śiva-ullāsa,* 15 poems under *Sundara-ullāsa* and 20 stray verses under the heading of *Prakīrṇa-ślokas.* There are in all 234 verses composed in different metres along with 20 *gītas* (lyrical poems) which are composed in the style of medieval Oriya poetry with Oriya metres. However, the classification of poems made by the poet does not bring home any logical sense and it seems superficial. The poet begins this work as per the age-old literary tradition with devotional enumeration of truth, good and beauty in the form of *Vastunirdēśātmaka-maṅgalācaraṇa.*

यद् वागर्थविचारणैः प्रतिपदं काव्येषु संसेव्यते
ब्रह्मानन्द-सहोदरोक्तिभिरलं यद् व्याहृतं पण्डितैः।
ब्राह्मीस्मेरमुखोदितं च यदहो सारस्वतं शाश्वतं
तत् सत्यं शिवसुन्दराञ्चितमिहोल्लासे समुज्जृम्भते।। (P.1)

In this verse the poet has explained the nature of truth in a poetic way. It has brought out his philosophy of truth. Truth is the essence of utimate reality known as *Brahman* which prevades[1] the entire universe.

The noteworthy feature of this poem-collection is that it embodies traditional as well as modern poems; metrical as well as non-metrical compositions, *Ślokas* as well as *Gītas*, group-poems as well as single verses and dialogue-poems, *saṁvāda-kāvyas* as well as non-dialogue-poems. So it is a kind of *Kośakāvya*. It will not be out of place to say that our poet has established himself by composing a *Mahākāvya* on the life history of Surendra Sai, a great hero of Orissa. But, perhaps not being fully satisfied with the big poem or keeping in view the interest of readers he shifted his interest and experimented with the minor poems.

The title *Vyastarāgam* is significant as it clearly suggests the diversity of themes and a variety of fluctuated emotions those come and go being transitory in nature. It may be translated as a tuneless melody. What gives us more pleasure is that we find a good mixture of devotional, cultural, social and personal poems in this collection. The verses and the lyrics are plain and they directly express their meanings. There is a little scope for implication or suggestion. The plain verses open up their beauty very easily and are not able to capture the minds of the enthusiastic readers.

In this work the poet has covered a very wide range of topics for the composition of his poems. As a true representative of his time and as a keen observer of our complex society, the poet has tried to draw the word-paintings to the things, incidents and situations those have thrilled his sympathetic heart. He does not limit himself to any particular story, person, place or incidence. The poems

1. Published by Umesh Chandar Mahapatra, Puruṇāpaṇi, Cuttack, Orissa, 1990.

are composed in different phases of time (in case of some poems, the dates are given at the end of the poems but they are not arranged chronologically). We find a variety among them. Starting from the eulogy of the Lord Jagannātha, the poet stops at the end with an extension of his good wishes for the peace, pleasure and prosperity of the entire mankind on the occassion of India's republic day. There are some poems on deities; some on divine personalities, some on Orissan cultural heritage, and some on miscellaneous topics. The poet is an ardent devotee of the Lord Jagannātha to whom he praises next to his introductory prayer. I cite here one stanza to show the form of his poems :

महासिन्धोस्तीरे गजपतिपुरे नीलशिखरे
धराधाम्नि प्रोद्यद्-रुचि-रुचिर-रूपं कृतपदम्।
सुभद्रावामस्थं वरद-बलभद्रेण सहितं
जगन्नाथं नाथं सकलजगतां नौमि सततम्।। (P.1)

This reminds a popular verse of *Jagannāthāṣṭakam.*

न मे हव्यं द्रव्यं न हि किमपि चार्घ्यं तव कृते
न मे जज्ञे ज्ञानं न च जपविधौ नैव नियमे।
न जाने ते पूजां विविधविधिना मन्त्रमहितां
प्रभो! जाने मात्रं त्वदनुसरणं दुःखहरणम्।।

verse, 5 (P.2)

The collection includes secular, religious, gnomic and also didactic poems, which prevent our monotone. Some poems seem to be the product of spontaneous overflow of his powerful feelings, while some of them appear to be methodical leading to the artificial fancy. Nevertheless, the poet has invested his poems with some motives, imageries, exquisite verbal melodies and pictorial fancies which have substantially contributed towards their charms.

He has composed some *prahelikās (riddles)* which will be interesting to children. As we know, *Prahelikā* is one of the seven varieties of *citra-alaṁkāra*,[1] which is defined in the *Agnipurāṇa* as composition exciting curiosity in the assemblage of the learned. It is two-fold : *Sābdī* and *Ārthī*. According to some,[2] it has sixteen varieties.

1. भ्रमरः कुसुममतिः
   आमेरिकापुरे पतिदेवता
   को वेत्ति ह किं भवति (p.46)

2. स एव कुत्सितो वरः
   याचते यो धनं कन्यापितरम्
   ततः कोऽस्ति नीचतरः? (p. 53)

Though the peoms are not rich in sentimental flavour still some are worth remembering. An example of *Sambhoga-śṛṅgāra;*

विलोक्य हास्यं मृदु षट्पदो मुदा
पिबत्यमन्दं कमलाधरामृतम्।
क एव लोके स्मितशोभितं मुखं
विनोपभोगं विजहाति मन्दधीः। (p. 82)

---

1. गोष्ठयां कुतूहलाध्यायी वाग्बन्धश्चित्रमुच्यते।
   प्रश्नः प्रहेलिका गुप्तं च्युतदत्ते तथोभयम्।
   समस्या सप्त तद्भेदा नानार्थस्यानुयोगतः।।
   द्वयोरप्यर्थयोर्गुह्यमानशब्दा प्रहेलिका।
   सा द्विधार्थी च शाब्दी च तत्रार्थो चार्थबोधतः।
   शब्दावबोधतः शाब्दी प्राहु षोढा प्रहेलिकाम्।।
   Bhattacharyya, Suresh Mohan, *The Alaṁkāra section of the Agnipurāṇa*, (critically edited), Firma klm Private Ltd. Calcutta, 1976, p. 165.
2. क्रीडागोष्ठीविनोदेषु तज्ज्ञैराकीर्णमन्त्रणे।
   परव्यामहने चापि सोपयोगाः प्रहेलिकाः।।
   एताः षोडश निर्दिष्टाः पूर्वाचार्यैः प्रहेलिकाः।
   Daṇḍin's *Kāvyādarśa* with the com. of Jīvānanda Vidyāsāgara Bhaṭṭācārya, and Introduction and English translation by Narayana Aiyr, pubd. by R.V. Rama Swamy Sastrul & Sons, Madras, 1952, PP 262-266.

प्रभात-मन्दानिल-चञ्चलाकृतिः
सहस्रधाम्ने प्रमदेव पद्मिनी।
समर्पयत्यात्मनिवेदनं भृशं
विवस्वते प्रस्फुरिताननना सती।। (p. 82)

न भूतपूर्वा भविता न नास्ति वा
त्वया विना मेऽन्यतरा हि बल्लभा।
इतीव भृङ्गः कलगुञ्जनच्छलान्
निवेदयन् भाति च चाटुचञ्चुरः।। (p. 83)

Like all beautiful poetry, the poetry of Paṇḍita Mahāpātra is an expression of his powerful feelings. The poet is neither a serious thinker of ivory tower nor a propagator of armchair philosophy, which has a little relevance in today's life. He is not an artist of artificiality like many Sanskrit poets who live in the world of mere fancy and go far away from reality. The art does not exist for the sake of art and descriptions based on superfined imaginations do not exist for the sake of descritpion. Paṇḍitta Mahāpātra chooses poetry as a medium for communicating his varied and rich experiences of life, for describing the beauty of the nature, for narrating the present day problems of our society, and for duly pointing out what is good and what is not good in our society. The dictum—"Poetry for the sake of life" seems to be his motto and therefore he does not circumscibe the field of his poetry to a limited sphere. He simplifies his poetry to make it accessible to many of his *samānadharmās*. He has never wanted to remain in the world of dreams but concerned himself to remain in close touch with the realities of life and socity. Being a critic of life, his poetry covers a wide field and also being idealistic, it is replete with the thought of welfare of the universe. His verses do not have just ordinary descriptions but at the center, rich and intense emotions coupled with an honest and edifying vision are observed. For mere description he would have chosen prose and not poetry as his medium.

Paṇḍita Mahāpātra has introduced himself as a social thinker who has a deep concern for the society and its welfare. A wide range of topics that Paṇḍitarāja selects for his composition provides him a good opportunity to give his opinion on many social problems. His keen observant eyes visualize the maladies of the society. He has been hold enough also to criticize those maladies openly so that it may bring some good result to the society. He is not a mere silent observer making a note of the events in a diary but also suggests a remedy for them. Śrī Mahāpātra's searching eyes discover the prevalling evil in the society and we find him talking about the downfall of moral laws and of growing discipline among people. He has noticed many other evil elements, which are responsible for the degeneration of our society. The moral values are to be made strong so that an evil wind cannot shake the beautiful fabric of our society. Our poet has given much thought to these social problems and wants the conscientious people about their poisonous fruits in future. On the one hand, he ridicules these elements in general, while on the other, he rouses public consciousness by preaching the moral values like *satya, śiva,* and *sundara* so that this kind of evil trend cannot get any public support. There may be development of moral behavior. Society may be free from menacing evils. The poetry has been made an instrument of that criticism. He says with heavy pain :

दन्दह्यते खलु विलोक्य मदीयचित्तं
विश्वं विषाक्तमधुना विधिना वियुक्तम्।
स्वार्थाय जीवनधनस्य लुठन्ति मूल्यं
मर्त्या यदीह किमहो कथयाम कुत्र।। (p. 37)

Our poet is abundantly affected by the lose of morality in the society. The world is now poisonous and is separated from its creator. Selfish people are increasing and they are involved in the corruption. What the poet says is not new and everybody knows that thing but as in a particular manner a poet pictures that phenomenon it becomes appealing. Here is an example :

रुन्धन्ति सत्पथमसत्परिपोषयन्तो
निन्दन्ति नीतिनिपुणान् विषमुद्गिरन्तः।
गेहे वहिश्च कलहं खलु योजयन्ति
प्रायः खलाः कलियुगे बहुलीभवन्ति।।

गेयं स्वराष्ट्रमहिमानमपाचरन्ति
ध्येयं त्यजन्त इह दुष्कृतमाश्रयन्ति।
पेयं विचार्य च मुदा मदिरां पिबन्ति
प्रायः खलाः कलियुगे बहुलीभवन्ति।। (P. 72)

सुन्दरता नास्ति रमणीवदने
विभीषिका विडम्बना च यत्र।
दूरदर्शनस्य जायते लालसा
न पूर्णता कामभोगस्य तत्र।

अहो सर्जनम्,
आलेख्यचित्रणे प्रकृतिकृपणा
भवन्ति सकला नास्ति नयनम्।। (p. 109)

The poet Mahāpātra has great love for his motheland, Orissa. His ingenious fellings find fine expressions in many of his sweet verses. For example :

जननी मे जन्मभूमिर्महीयसी चिरम्, (p. 9)
भजामहे चाजीवनं स्वदेशमातरम् (p. 9)
अयि देशमातर्मम तवाङ्केऽनुपदं सुखं कदुष्मे वसामि। (p. 11)

It is not merely the tradition established by the Sanskrit poets, which leads Paṇḍita Mahāpātra to describe the varied aspects of nature that has always attracted the hearts of Sanskrit poets, but it is Śrī Mahāpātra's sensitive heart which makes him see wonderful elements in every aspect of nature. A sensitive poet cannot remain blind to the lovely phenomenon of nature, which is the wonderful creation of the creator. He has tried to bring to the notice of the nature-lovers, the sublime and subtle features of poetry through his descriptions. He has given fanstastic description of early morning and also has unfolded its hidden beauty along with the beauty of the rising sun. He has appreciated the inexpressible and unthinkable design of the supreme creator. In so far as the natural descriptions are concerned, we find them to be infused with beauty and novelty endowed with keen power of observation. He has described the beautiful and sweet aspects of nature. He has given enlivening and touching scenes. He also brings unity between humanity and nature.

The following stanzas give a picture of the feelings that he has for the nature :

प्रदोषकाले परिलक्ष्य सङ्गमं
तमःप्रभामण्डलयोः परस्परम्।
निभालये सृष्टिमिमां यदोऽतुलां
प्रभो! त्वदीया स्मृतिरेति मां तदा।।

निसर्गता नीलकलेबरेऽम्बरे
परेसहस्त्राः परिदृश्य तारकाः।
विभावयेऽवाङ् निभृतं यदा हृदि
प्रभो! त्वदीया स्मृतिरेति मां तदा।। (P. 12)

The poet has profound love for trees, forest, birds, animals and environment. His sensitive heart does not tolerate to see the destruction of these elements, which are perishing day by day. He warns the public and advises not to destroy our natural treasure. The poet gives an attractive description of the forest in the form of a definition. There are plenty of references to the flowers like *padma, kamala, mālatī, tamāla, mādhavī, aśoka, karṇikāra, bandhujivaka, saroja, rucaka,* and birds and animals like *titiri, ghūka,* etc. (P. 14)

The poetry of Paṇḍitji is also adorned with the mythological and historical allusions, which are useful for explaining and justifying the poet's intention.

Poetry is the mirror of poet's mind. It gives a clear reflection of his thoughts, ideas, viewpoints, his attitude and approach towards life. The poet strongly believes that the *Brahman* is the supreme reality and all other objects are false appearances being the fabrications of *māyā*.

The poet believes in *Karma* as a potent force, which shapes one's fate, and as the highest religious duty it leads to happiness. That *karma* is nothing but *Dharma*. A man has to enjoy the fruits of his action in this phenomenal world.

The poet has used some words, which are not used in the common Sanskrit language. But he has also given their meanings *i.e.* the synonyms in the footnotes so that a reader will not take the pain to open the pages of dictionary. I think, he has used the words for the purpose of metrical perfection and to maintain short and long order in the structure of some verse.

The style of the poet is simple, sweet and devoid of long and complex compounds. Therefore it can be said *vaidarbhī*. Some *guṇas* like *śleṣa, prasāda, mādhurya* etc. are present in his style.

Similarly the language is simple and sweet. He has used the selective words, which are generally used nowadays by the Sanskritists. Even a post-graduate student can understand his verses. The language is free from grammatical errors and perfectly expresses his feelings. The verses are marked with perspicuity and clarity.

The poet makes use of a good number of poetic figures, which adorn his speech and create special charm. A fine example of *Utprekṣā-alaṅkāra* is given.

याऽऽशीर्वादसुधाप्रदाननिपुणा प्रज्ञानुकम्पानिधिः
सिद्धेः संप्रतिपत्तये च सुकृतां साक्षादिवालम्वनम्।
मर्त्त्यानां श्रुति-नीति-भूति-पदवी-दिग्दर्शिनी या स्थिता
मन्ये सा न तु मानवी कलियुगे श्रीमा परा देवता॥ (p. 143)

It will not be an exaggeration if I say that the poet Mahāpātra's diction is one of the instruments, which garnish his poetry. No one can miss the melodious flow along with scholatic perfection that has been there in the presentation of his thoughts in the form of verses. He has tried to adopt whatever was good in tradition and to incorporate whatever is acceptable in the name of modernity. He is one of the rare poets who have accepted both tradition and modernity equally without being extremely partial to any one.

The poet seems to be influenced by the great poets like Kālidāsa, Bhaṭṭi and others as in some sentences we get the shadow of their linguistic expression.

The collection clearly shows that the poet is well-versed in metrics. To make his poetry charming, he has made use of different metres. He has mainly used the well-known metres like *Śikhariṇī, Śragdharā, Vasantatilakā, Upajāti* and *Śārdūlavkrīḍita* etc.

There are varieties of materials like a variety-store, which could attract the people of all types and of all tastes. Among the many varieties of poems, mention must be made of modern topics like *Monāliśahāsyam, Alampickrīḍā* etc.

The poet tried to dub some Oriya versions into Sanskrit. I know that there was a hot lyric. i.e. *ame e kulare galu ki se kulare galu.* (we are neither in this bank nor in that bank); we are neither men nor women. For many years this lyric was current in Orissa and it was creating a flood of laughter. It was a poem on eunuch. Our poet has tried to present the content of that poem in Sanskrit. I give here some verses.

The poet has given a number of pithy and epigrammatic sayings, which emphasize moral and social values. A few of them are produced here as specimen examples :

प्रवृत्तिरापद्यत एव भूतये
निवृत्तिरास्ते सततं विभूतये। (P. 14)
कर्मैह हि धर्म एव। (P. 62)
वृणोति वीरो मरणं सकृन् महा–
नुदारधीर्जीवन एव सिंहवत्।। (P. 137)

The *Vyastarāgam* of Paṇḍitarāja Mahāpātra is, therefore, a notable contribution to the field of modern Sanskrit literature. It embodies, the social sensibilities with excellent stylistic elegance and conceptual subtleties. The topics like Indian culture, ancient civilization, scientific adventures, importance of Sanskrit, beauty of natural objects, patriotism, worldly pleasures, and various dimensions of human life have been aptly portrayed with its natural niceties with a view to make the readers conscious about themselves and their surroundings. The efforts of the poet are successful in depicting the interesting features of human life, which appeals to modern tests, because of its rich varieties, brilliance of its fancy and great warmth of its feelings. The poetic genius of Mahāpātra has bloomed at its peak in the delineation of human emotions. We find in him both traditionalism and modernism in equal measure. He is a man of traditional spirit having a heart of modern sensibility. The poet has given a new direction to follow to bring manifoldness of modernity in the field of Sanskrit literature. Since Mahāpātra's poetry has its roots in the soil of Orissa, his poetry reflects the various aspects of cultural heritage of Orissa.

This *Kāvyasaṁgraha* of Mahāpātra is a valuable addition to modern Sanskrit literature. The collection looks like a garland made of numerous flowers of different colours. The merit of the collection lies in the fact that it presents us short and sweet poems like chocolates and they are free from the load of scholastic jargon. This type of poems, I hope, will receive the appreciation in this age when we are trying to make Sanskrit a *Lokabhaṣā*, language of people instead of *Devabhāṣā*, language of gods.

Use of some *deśi* words not intelligible to the Sanskrit readers who are not acquainted with this kind of usage. Moreover, the staunch Sanskritists may also not sanction this type of usage.

Some of the stanzas of Mahāpātra remind us the verses of some great poets. The poet has borrowed even some lines.

In this collection some stanzas are bellow the mark. They may be interesting to the children but not to the connoisseurs, for whom poetry is a source of some extraordinary pleasure *(brahmāsvādasahodara)*.

Such type of poems exhibits the poet's craze for the physical growth of the collection. *Kimataḥ paraṁ syāt, Hemahāriṇī, Madhure'vasare* etc., to mention a few.

No doubt, the poet has made meticulous efforts of give a life to his fluctuated emotions whenever he had found something special in the sphere of *satya, śiva* and *sundara*. In depicting the pictures of trinity he has followed the natural style of his own not being bound by the literary principles those are propounded in the texts like the *Aucityvicāracarcā*, the *Kavikaṇṭhābharaṇa* etc. Nowadays Sanskrit poets in general are not following them strictly. Keeping in mind the need of the society and the time, the Sanskrit poet feels impractical to follow the principles of the rhetoric texts. At the same time it is also a fact that all the poets of the present generation do not have the potency to compose their poetry in a traditional structure. This is perhaps one of the reasons why modern Sanskrit literature has got a new shape. As a result the dignity that Sanskrit had in past is decreasing day by day. Though we cannot avoid the changes, which are prevailing in the domain of literature, we should not also compromise with the status and dignity of Sanskrit languagge. Paṇḍitarāja Digambara Mahāpātra is one of the few poets of modern India, who rightly deserves our hearty appreciation for his traditional and modern approach that we observe in the collection of his poems.

Sudāmacaritam of Puṇḍarīkākṣa Miśra

I. Introduction

Sudāmā, a poor Brahmin of Dwāpara age, who has occupied an important place in the literary history of India, is a well-known figure. His unique character, simplicity, innocence, dedication, devotion and religious attitude have attracted the attention of many Sanskrit poets who have written small as well as big poems on his life. The *Bhāgavata-Mahāpurāṇa* is the first poem which has nicely depicted the character and personality of Sudāmā.

The *Sudāmacaritam*[1] of Puṇḍarīkākṣa Miśra is an interesting *khaṇḍakāvya* in Sanskrit. As the title denotes, the poem deals with the well-known Sudāmā who had the fortune of having an intimate friendship with the Lord Kṛṣṇa. Though the small episode of Sudāmā does not give much scope to compose an epic poem still the Sanskrit poets have attempted to compose *mahākāvyas* and *khaṇḍakāvyas* on this popular theme. I have been able to collect four poems on this theme.[2] Miśra's work distinguishes itself from its

---

Journal of The Oriental Institute, Vol. 55, Nos. 1-4, September 2005-June 2006 Issue, pp. 89-98

1. *Sudāmacaritam* of Paṇḍita Puṇḍarīkākṣa Miśra, Lokabhāṣā-Pracāra-Samiti, Puri, Orissa, Date of Publication is not given.
2. I. *Sudāmacaritam* of Paṇḍita Bahora Pathak (*Mahākāvya*), Ed. Gopabandhu Mishra, Sanskṛita Prasāra-Pariṣad, Ara, Bihar, 1997
   II. *Sudāmacaritam* of Śrīsālirāmacandra Ray, Sanskriti Prakashan, Dharwad, 1957
   III. *Sudāmacaritam* of Indradeva Dwivedi, (*Mahākāvya*).
   IV. Refer to Footnote I.

counterparts for the reason that the poet has treated the theme in a beautiful and interesting manner for the glorification of the relationship between Lord Kṛṣṇa and his devotee Sudāmā.

The poem contains only five cantos, bearing significant titles which indicate the subject-matter of the cantos in an aphoristic manner and are given at the end of the cantos. There are 500 verses (80 in first, 94 in second, 84 in third, 112 in fourth and 130 in the fifth). The theme of the poem is taken from the *Bhāgavata-Mahāpurāṇa*. The poet has given the form of a poem to a simple story by making some innovations for the purpose of making it interesting and enjoyable. He has tried in this poem to bring to the notice of the readers the ultimate aim of an ardent devotee and the fruit of his sincere devotion. The objective of the poet is to make people aware of the noble character of Sudāmā, a simple house-holder who inspite of his extreme poverty and noble conduct could achieve the love and compassion of the lord of universe while great yogis, sādhakas, wise and enlightened ones fail. The poem commences and completes with the prayer to the Lord Jagannātha.[1]

II. Author

The author of this poem is Paṇḍita Puṇḍarīkākṣa Miśra (1918-1987), who was born on 18-3-1918 in the village of Jayarampur in the district of Bhogarai in the Balasore of Orissa. After completing his primary education in his own

---

1. (a) स्मरन् जगन्नाथपदाम्बुजद्वयं
लिखामि किञ्चिच्चरितं मनोरमम्।
इदं सुदाम्नो भगवद्गुणावली-
विमोहितस्यात्र विशुद्धचेतसः।। I.1, p. 1
(b) श्रीमज्जगन्नाथपदारविन्दे
स्मृत्वा सतां ब्राह्मणपण्डितानाम्।
शुभाशिषञ्चास्य मया सुदाम्नः
भक्तस्य वृत्तं निखिलं समाप्तम्।। V. 30, p. 101

village, he went to Udayanath Sanskrit Mahavidyalaya for his study and then to Bhogarai Shyamasundar Sanskrit College at Kanitara, West Bengal and passed *Sāhityācārya* in 1939 from Utkal Sanskrit Samiti with the first class. He served as a teacher in Jagadeshwara Sanskrit school at Khuluda only for eleven months and then became the head of the department in Bhogarai Syamasundar Sanskrit college in 1940. He became the Principal of that college and retired from his service in 1982. He served as Honorary Professor in the department of *Sāhitya* in Śrī Jagannātha Sanskrit University, Puri, Orissa from 1982 to 1987. He had been awarded with a number of prizes for his valuable service to Sanskrit literature but among them the President's certificate of honour is the most important one. This eminent scholar passed away on 9-7-1987 but he has left behind some immortal works which speak of his dedication and devotion for Sanskrit language and literature.

III. Summary

The first canto of the poem is entitled *Dāridryavarṇanam* (description of the poverty). In this canto, the poet describes the extreme poverty of Sudāmā, his single-minded devotion for the Lord, his begging, Sumati's dedicated service and their peace and satisfaction in the family.

The second canto is entitled *Dwārikāgamanam*. In this canto, there is a description of Sudāmā who remembers the name of Hari at early morning, goes for the collection of flowers for the worship of the lord, eats food prepared by her loving wife Sumati out of the old stock of savings of alms, goes for begging. Sudāmā comes back with frustration without getting anything, informs about the non-availability of alms in the village and listens the pathetic words of Sumati who inspires him to go to Kṛṣṇa, the lord of Vaikuṇṭha as he was his childhood friend and studying with him in Sāndipani's residence. But Sudāmā does not get ready to meet Kṛṣṇa with the view that Kṛṣṇa is a king and he may not care for a poor fellow. Finally, Sudāmā gets ready to go to Dwarika, the place of the Lord Kṛṣṇa.

The third canto is entitled *Haripurapraveśa*. It gives a picture of Sudāmā's difficulty on the way of his going to Dwarika. First he comes across a river on the way, where he does not get a boat to cross the river. After some time, an old man comes with a broken boat and is not ready to take him up but after a humble request he finally agrees. The wind becomes silent. The boat does not meet any kind of misfortune and he reaches the bank of the river safely. By saying politely to boatman that he had no money to pay and promising that he will pay all his dues at the time of his return, Sudāmā proceeds towards Dwarika. On the way, he enters into a dense forest, where three thieves come and snatch away that bundle of rice and throw it on earth. Sudāmā does not lose heart and proceeds further uttering the name of Hari and finally reaches the place of his destination. There he asks the guards about the right way to go to the capital city of Kṛṣṇa. He is guided in the right direction by the guards, who just laugh at him without giving any sense of respect and importance.

The fourth canto entitled *Śrīkṛṣṇadarśanam* describes that Kṛṣṇa, the omniscient one came to know about the coming of his best friend Sudāmā. He immediately calls on his servants and Satyabhāmā, his wife and informs them that he had a very good time because his best friend Sudāmā has come to meet him. He also orders them to be ready for his proper hospitality. By saying this, Kṛṣṇa himself proceeds to receive and welcome Sudāmā. He embraces him closely with profound love and affection.

The fifth canto is not given any title. It describes how seriously Kṛṣṇa, the lord of the universe thought about his problem of poverty after the departure of Sudāmā who did not ask him for anything. Then Kṛṣṇa called on Lakṣmī and requested her to make Sudāmā free from his miserable condition. Lakṣmī carried on her duty accordingly. Sudāmā reached his village and became surprised to see a big bungalow in place of his small cottage made of leaves. Sumati was made known about the arrival of Sudāmā. She washed and prayed on the feet of Sudāmā with great reverence. But Sudāmā did not recognize her and asked about her introduction. Sumati convinced him that she is his wife. She narrated the incident that in the absence of him she did not find the way of survival. So she went to the river for suicide. But at the time of attempting suicide, a man informed her about his coming. So, she left the idea and came to see him but was surprised to see this change. After knowing all these from Sumati, Sudāmā still didn't take any interest in all those precious things. At that time, Kṛṣṇa himself came there with his consort Lakṣmī and told him to enjoy the things given to him and to come to Vaikuṇṭha, when the time of his life will be over in the mortal world.

IV. Story in the Source

The theme of the poem is taken from the *Bhāgavatapurāṇa*, where the story is given as follows:

Śrīkṛṣṇa had a Brahmin friend, who was conversant with the knowledge of Vedas. That Brahmin was not attached to the objects of the sense and was of peaceful soul. Betaking to a householder's mode of existence, this Brahmin's wife was emaciated with hunger.[1] One day that pious lady devoted to her poor husband approaching him with a haggard

---

1. कृष्णस्यासीत्सखा कश्चिद्ब्राह्मणो ब्रह्मवित्तमः।
विरक्त इन्द्रियार्थेषु प्रशान्तात्मा जितेन्द्रियः।।
यदृच्छयोपपन्नेन वर्तमानो गृहाश्रमी।
तस्य भार्या कुचैलस्य क्षुत्क्षामा च तथाविधा।।
पतिव्रता पतिं प्राह म्लायता वदनेन सा।
दरिद्रा सीदमाना सा वेपमानाऽभिगम्य च।।
ननु ब्रह्मन्भगवतः सखा साक्षाच्छ्रियः पतिः।
ब्रह्मण्यश्च शरण्यश्च भगवान्सात्वतर्षभः।। *Bhāgavatapurāṇa*. X.79; 6, 7, 8, 9

countenance, said, "I am sinking and my limbs are trembling. I heard that the Almighty Lord is your intimate friend. Go to that Lord who is the best refuge of the pious people. He shall give an abundance of wealth to you". Śrīdāmā then made up his mind to go to Dwarika. He spoke to his wife as follows—"O blessed lady! Have you got in the house anything worthy of presentation to Kṛṣṇa? If so, let me have it. Thereupon, soliciting from the Brahmins four handfuls of flattened rice, she bound them in a piece of cloth and gave the bundle to her husband as a present for Kṛṣṇa. Having taken the bundle of flattened rice for presentation to Kṛṣṇa, Sudāmā started for Dwarika, and anxiously meditated in his mind on the way as to how he should have a sight of Kṛṣṇa.[1]

However, Śrīdāmā arrived at the city of Dwarika and having passed by three barracks of soldiers and having crossed three high-ways crowded with Brahmins, Śrīdāmā went near the places of the Andhakas and Vṛṣṇis whose lord was Acyuta. Then Śrīdāmā, entered a residence out of the sixteen thousand residences of the queens of Śrīhari. Entering the precincts of the residence, the Brahmin seemed to enjoy the ecstasy of realizing Brahma. Acyuta, who was lying on the bed of his dear beloved wife, having seen Śrīdāmā from a distance hurriedly rose up from the bed, and coming near to him, delightfully embraced him with his two arms. Having touched the body of his dear friend, Acyuta was highly enraptured, and tears of joy began to flow from his lotus-like eyes.[2] Thereafter Śrīdāmā took his seat on his bed, Kṛṣṇa

1. अप्यस्त्युपायनं किंचिद्गृहे कल्याणि दीयताम्।
याचित्वा चतुरो मुष्टीन्विप्रान्पृथुकतण्डुलान्।
चैलखण्डेन तान्बद्ध्वा भर्त्रे प्रादादुपायनम्।।
स तानादाय विप्राग्य: प्रययौ द्वारिकां किल।
कृष्णसंदर्शनं मह्यं कथं स्यादिति चिन्तयन्।। *Ibid.*, 13, 14, 15

2. तं विलोक्याच्युतो दूरात्प्रियापर्यङ्कमास्थित:।
सहसोत्थाय चाभ्येत्य दोर्भ्यां पर्यग्रहीन्मुदा।।
सख्यु: प्रियस्य विप्रर्षेरङ्गसङ्गातिनिर्वृत:।
प्रीतो व्यमुञ्चयन्बिन्दून्नेत्राभ्यां पुष्करेक्षण:।। *Ibid.*, 18, 19

himself collected the things for the adoration of Śrīdāmā and washed his feet with water, took the water with which the feet of his friend has been washed on his head. He then smeared the Brahmin with heavenly perfumes, sandal paste and saffron. Thus delightfully worshipping his friend with incense and rows of lamps, Kṛṣṇa offered him betel, and then asked him the question regarding his welfare. Then the queen herself with her maids began to serve Sudāmā by way of fanning him, who was clad in tattered rags emaciated and lean. Thereupon the members of the seraglio seeing this unclean Brahmin, appearing like an *Avadhūta*, so delightfully welcomed and adored by Kṛṣṇa of unsullied renown, were struck with wonder. Thereafter having held one another by the palm of their hands, Kṛṣṇa and Sudāmā began to talk about those sweet adventures of their childhood, when they lived together in the family of their spiritual preceptor. The Lord Kṛṣṇa said that he was versed in all righteousness. Having come back from the family of the preceptor, to whom he did pay a handsome fee, he has married to a wife worthy of himself. Though he is constantly leading a householder's mode of life, yet his heart is not enslaved by selfish desires, and he is not attached to riches, materials and money.

Śrīkṛṣṇa reminded him of an interesting incident that had happened in past when both of them were staying in preceptor's residence. They had gone to fetch some fuel sticks. Suddenly storm came and heavy shower of rain fell. The sun got set in the sky, and immediately the cardinal quarters were pervaded with deep gloom; the ground get deluged with water and they could not discern anything. During that heavy pouring of rain, they were sorely struck with drops of rain and were driven by strong gusts of wind, then failing to discern the direction to be followed, and being sorely oppressed; they wandered there holding each other by the hands. Coming to know their miserable condition, the preceptor Sāndīpani went out in quest of them before the rising of the sun. Then the preceptor found them in that miserable plight. He told "For my sake you both have undergone great misery. Life is very dear unto created beings, and you have disregarded that life for me. In this manner good disciples should pay their debt of gratitude to their preceptors with a pious intention. May your desires be fulfilled? Your knowledge of the Vedas will not waste away in this or in the next world". Then Kṛṣṇa asked: "What present have you brought for me from your house? Even very small particle of food collected by my devotee out of affection, becomes sufficient for him. On the contrary abundance of eatable gathered by men having no reverence for me is useless." So spoken to by Śrīkṛṣṇa, out of bashfulness Śrīdāmā did not offer those four handfuls of flattened rice to the lord of the universe. Then Śrīkṛṣṇa himself took out the said bundle of flattened rice from the ends of the tattered cloth of Śrīdāmā. Seeing the contents of the bundle Śrīkṛṣṇa became very much pleased and ate one handful of rice. When he was on the point of taking another handful to his mouth, the goddess of prosperity swiftly caught the hand of the Supreme Lord. That night Śrīdāmā lived in that residence of Kṛṣṇa and there eating and drinking palatable dishes and potions, he was overjoyed and thought himself transported to heaven. At the break of the following day, Śrīdāmā started for his own home, having been greeted by his friend. When proceeding on his way back to his home, Sudāmā was enraptured on remembering his meeting with Kṛṣṇa. He did not get any wealth from his friend. But, he was very happy with the treatment of Kṛṣṇa. He came to proximity of his own house, which to his surprise found to be surrounded on all sides by chariots resplendent like the sun, the fire and the moon. He found it furnished with beautiful pleasure gardens and groves, swarming with melodious singing birds, and with expanses of water with decorated blooming lotuses and lilies. Beholding his own house crowded with persons decked with ornaments and, women having eyes resembling those of a gazelle, Sudāmā was astonished beyond measure to see the thatched cottage becoming so metamorphosed into this extensive and beautiful place all around. When Śrīdāmā has been thus revolving in his mind, persons of both sexes as beautiful as celestials, came out of the palace and welcomed him with songs accompanied by musical sound of various instruments. Having heard that her husband has come back, his wife Sumati became transported with joy, and hurriedly came out of the house like the goddess of prosperity incarnate is coming out of her own abode. Beholding her husband, she began to shed tears of joy and her voice was choked with profound emotion. Then considering her husband to be one, worthy of her adoration, she bowed down unto him and embraced him with her eyes closed. Having seen his loving wife like heavenly goddess, shine in the midst of maidservants and decorated with necklaces of gold, Śrīdāmā was struck with great amazement. He was overwhelmed with joy and entered his own house, which was furnished with hundreds of pillars made of jewels like an abode of the celestial king. His heart was full of joy. He began to enjoy those luxuries with his wife but his heart was not very much attached to those enjoyments. He gradually liberated himself from the material influence and at the end of his life attained to the status of the lord.

V. Critical Appreciation

The poem is composed in five cantos which bear significant titles. They are of moderate length; the shortest is of 80 verses and the longest of 130 verses. There are 500 verses in all. The significant features of this work are given below:

(a) Characterization

In this poem, there are only three main characters namely Sudāmā, Sumati and Kṛṣṇa. There are other minor characters like a boatman, thieves; Satyabhāmā and Lakṣmī. We find them very natural in their worldly life and accept the truth of life. Sudāmā is a man of extreme simplicity, patience, strong determination, single-minded devotion, truth and righteousness. Though very poor, he is very happy. He is represented in the poem as a man who completely surrenders everything to god aid satisfies himself with the thing he gets without deliberate effort.[1] Though his friend is the Lord of the universe, he does not take any interest in approaching him for wealth and prosperity. His best quality is his strong faith in God. He is a fatalist. But he does his action without desiring anything as directed in the *Bhgavadgītā, karmaṇyevādhikāraste ma phaleṣu kadācana.*

Sumati, his wife, is equally simple, devoted and dutiful. The service of husband according to her is the best duty of a wife. She is a woman of strong determination and noble character.[2] She is very good by heart and intelligent. Kṛṣṇa, the God of the universe, is represented as *Bhaktavatsala.* He has great love for his devotees.

(b) Rasa

The sentiment of this *kāvya* is *Śānta.* As the poem deals with the story of Kṛṣṇa other sentiments do not find any place in this poem. Even the *śāntarasa* does not find fullest exposition. But different emotions are nicely depicted.

---

1. अकिञ्चनः सन् न मुखेन याचते
धनं प्रदेहीति वचो न भाषते।
न वाधिकं कामयते महाजने
प्रफुल्लचित्तो विचरत्यसौ सदा।। *Sudāmaacarita* I. 40, p. 8

2. (a) मनोरमेयं बत तैलवर्जिता
नितान्तहीनाभरणा सती सती।
निजोपभोगै रहिता दिवानिशं
कदोपवासेन दिनान्ययापयत्।।
(b) प्रियस्य सौख्यात् सुखिनी भवत्यसौ
तदीयदुःखान्नितराञ्च दूयते।
स्वकीयकष्टं प्रतिवेशिनः कदा
न वक्ति सा भावरता भ्रमादपि।। *Ibid.*, 1. 16 & 19, p. 4

(c) Metres

The poet employs one metre in one canto with a variation at the end. A metrewise break-up of the poem is presented below:

Canto Nos.	Metre
1	*Upendravajrā*
2	*Upajāti*
3	*Vasantatilakā*
4	*Upajāti*
5	*Upendravajrā*

Besides, in the closing verses of cantos, *Sragdharā*, *Vasantatilakā*, *Vaṁśastha* and *Upajāti* metres are used.

(d) Figures of speech

Paṇḍita Miśra follows the *Vaidarbhī* style. He avoids the use of long compounds. His style is easy and elegant. Sweet composition and clear expression of thought are the special characteristics of his presentation which give a reflection of his personality. The clarity of thought is clearly seen in the verses of his composition resulting in the clear picture of simplicity and devotion. His diction is refined and beautiful. He is very natural in his description without any kind of verbal jugglery.[1] His language is simple and sweet. Even an average scholar of Sanskrit will not find any difficulty in understanding and enjoying the poetic beauty of his poem.

(e) Pithy and Epigrammatic Sayings

The poet gives us a good number of pithy and epigram-

---

1. पद्मिन्या विरहावसाननिपुणः सूर्यो महान् नायकः
पूर्वोर्वीधरमागतो विधिवशादेतौ पुनर्हृष्टवान्।
दूरीकर्तुमयं जनस्य विपदं शक्तो न वा वर्तते
मित्रत्वं परिरक्षितुं प्रकटितं किं स्वागतो दूरतः।। *Ibid.*, I. 0, p. 16.

matic sayings which stress mainly the moral values. A few of them are reproduced by way of specimens.[1]

(f) Poet's learning

The poet has good command over the grammar also. He is well-acquainted with the Purāṇa literature especially the *Bhāgavatapurāṇa.*

(g) Innovation

Though our poet has mainly taken the story from the *Bhāgavata,* he has made necessary innovations to make his poem interesting. He has given both the names but in the *Bhāgavata* hero's name is given as Śrīdāmā. He has introduced some of the episodes of boatman, presence of the thieves on the way and their threatening etc. which are not given in the original story of *Bhāgavata.* The poet has also introduced the episode of leper who was bitten by his wife. He at many places follows the *Bhāgavata* line of presentation and drops the lengthy dialogue of Kṛṣṇa that he had with Sudāmā.

VI. Conclusion

The present poem belongs to the category of mythological poems. The hero of the poem is Sudāmā and the title of poem is given after the name of its hero. It centres around a minor plot of Sudāmā's sincere devotion and Kṛṣṇa's great love for his devotee. Though in the second page, it is written that

---

1. (a) लभे न लज्जां सुमणेः समाश्रया-
ल्लघुर्हि काचः श्रयते परां द्युतिम्। *Ibid.*, I. 6.
(b) सुखेषु दुःखेषु च तुल्यमानिता।
सतां जनानां भवतीह सर्वदा।। *Ibid.*, 1. 13
(c) सतां हि निष्ठा परमं धनं स्मृतम्। *Ibid.*, I. 41
(d) दरिद्रता सद्गुणमण्डिते जने
स्थितापि सम्मानधनं हि रक्षति। *Ibid.*, I. 42
(e) एको दरिद्रोऽस्त्यपरश्च राजा
विधेर्विधानं न विवेचनीयम्।। *Ibid.*, I. 43

Sudāmacaritam is a *Mahākāvya*, the structure of this poem does not fit perfectly to the structure of a *Mahākāvya*. There are many things the poem lacks. It does not follow the definition of the *Mahākāvya* as given by Viśvanātha Kavirāja in his *Sāhityadarpaṇa*. There is no doubt about the fact that Paṇḍita Miśra has infact made a small but valuable contribution to the field of modern Sanskrit literature.

Poetry of Keshab Chandra Dash

Bhinnapulinam (separate shore) is a collection of poems written by Keshab Chandra Dash. The work is published by Smt. Subhadra Dash, Puri, Orissa in 1995. It is an important contribution of Prof. Dash who has made a place of his own among the contemporary poets of outstanding merit in the history of modern Sanskrit literature. As a poet of profound depth, Dash is well-known for exploring a new dimension of Sanskrit writings. His creative works collections of poems, stories, and the novels, suffuse with deep philosophy of life and aesthetic strength of beauty. The present work is not an exception.

The title of this work is suggestive. It conveys the condition of a shore (may be an individual soul or a loveer) is separated from the sea, and the sea, to my mind, is *Brahman*, or *Priyatamā*. But, the state of that separation is focused by the suggestive title.

After a thorough study of this work, I came to this point that this *kāvyasaṁgraha* is important for two reasons : Firstly, it represents a true picture of modernity which is really expected from modern Sanskritists who have a distinct departure from the traditional approach. Secondaly, it brings forth the aesthtic sensibility of today's man, who is surrounded by a variety of problems under the different types of social pressures, and gives vent to his feelings in a manner which is modern in its true sense.

The present paper attempts to highlight some of the significant aspects of Dr. Dash's poems. The title itself speaks many things. I think, the title suggests *Brahman*, the supreme reality as a sea and an individual soul who is separated from it and undergoes different types of pains and pleasures as shore. The title also suggests a person who is separated from his sea probably his wife after having an intense union with her. Here the word *pulinam* brings home this idea very significantly and represents the condition of his being, his passions, his emotions, feelings, experiences and frustrations. The poems of this collection give us some glimpses of poet's associations with not only his sea but with all other things, which are very closely associated with him. It may be understood as the stroy of a separate shore, which puts forth its experience about what it has achieved and what not, with reference to its relation that is has with the sea. It may be understood also how the shore loses identity after having an union with the sea and comes back with a sense of frustration seeing the sea standing as it is without having any significant change in it.

It is interesting to note here what the poet himself says about this work : "It is a symbolic, not of pragmatic silence with an abiding quests for perfection. This strikes a delicate balance between existential agony and spiritual aspirations. This is interlaced with several conflicting ideas and motifs. Integrity of vision for renewal of human spirit is sharp in this collection. In the realm of Sanskrit poetry this stands rare with remarkable depth." (cover page, back side)

The work is a small collection of 35 poems. The titles of the poems, *Bhinnapulinam 2. Antardhvani 3. Āṣāḍhamāyā 4. Āviṣkāraḥ 5. Saṁjñā, 6. Purohitaḥ 7. Subhecchā 8. Aparacchandaḥ 9. Adhikāraḥ 10. Tattvamasi 11. Navajanma 12. Viraticitram 13. Nepathyacandrikā, 14. Nagnamalayaḥ 15. Puṣpacchāyā, 16. Abhāvaraṅgaḥ 17. Vicchinnagahvaram, 18. Niśīthaniśvāsaḥ, 19. Niṣkūlam, 20. Kītajhaṅkāraḥ, 21. Bhimarāgaḥ, 22. Tanvamtaram, 23. Darpaṇam, 24. Alamkāraḥ, 25. Virutiḥ, 26. Anvārambhaḥ, 27. Mārgaḥ 28. Vicchinnanemiḥ, 29.*

Manmasssmitam 30. *Niḥsaṅgaparibhāṣā*, 31. *Ghūrṇikalā*, 32. *Utsavaḥ*, 33. *Priyāmsuḥ*, 34. *Caitanyacandrikā*, 35. *Madhudīpaḥ*.

From this list of titles, one can slightly grasp the contents of the poems. But, he can have a bare idea which underlies the structure of many of the poem. Though in case of a few poems, the given titles do not convey anything, neither any essence nor any emotional content. Yet, I hope the readers would get some hints befitting their thoughts. Some titles are very simple like *Antardhvani, Āviṣkaraḥ, Purohitaḥ* etc., but some others like *Nepathyacandrikā, Naganamalayaḥ, Ābhāvaragaḥ, Vicchinnagahvaram, Nishtihanivāsaḥ*, etc. are not comprehensible. What they convey is not easy to understand. it seems that the poet has taken some extra care to exhibit modernity through the titles of his poems. But it also frustrates its readers who come for finding out the unique pleasure of poetry and finally move only in a barren land.

The content is an important substance of poetry. Without a theme or content a poem cannot be composed. It is not possible to create a poem out of nothing. The beauty, sweetness and artistic value, which are the essentials of a good poem, depend mainly on the content of the poem. To my mind, the content is the land on which the poet like an expert builder develops a fine structure of building by using his own creative genius. In case of the traditional poems in Sanskrit the content–aspect becomes very clear from their titles whether you talk of a *Mahākāvya* like *Śiśupālavadha, Subhadrāharaṇam*, or a *Khaṇḍakāvya* like *Meghadūta* or a *Dṛśyakāvya* like *Uttarāmacaritam* or *Muktakakāvyas* like *Sāradāharanam*, etc. But in case of modern Sanskrit poems the essence of the content is not easily grasped. It is also a part of modernity.

In many of the poems of Dr. Dash, what I observe is that the poet has picturised his feelings that has grown in him in different contexts and different situations. As these poems have been composed in different points of time and in different moods, so the feelings, which are subjected in these poems, are varied. But all of them essentially belong to a category of personal experience which includes some of the fragments of his childhood, his youth, his village-life, his love-life, his ambitions, his desires, his passions, his frustrations and his understandings of some of salient aspects of life. One can easily notice a great structure of individual experience on the plane of which these poems have grown like the flowers of a garden.

The *Bhinnapulinam* in fact gives us some glimpses of Dr. Dash's wide experience which is not limited to any particular context, time, situation or incident. The *Bhinnapulinam* is the first poem of this collection. A few lines of this poem give us fair idea of his feelings.

Some significant aspects do get reflected in the thought-structure of his poems. The poems are individualistic and they reflect his own sorrows, loneliness, desire etc. We may call them 'Individual Poems'.

Everybody knows that the poet is above all an artist. His art has some distinct features of which the style is one. It makes his identity and also decides his place among the poets. When we talk of Dr. Dash's style, I will prefer to call it 'modern' which has its own characteristic. It is free from metrical chains and traditional bonds and boundaries. Though the *Prāsādikatā* is found in his compositions, still I hesitate to call it *vaidarbhī* style for the reason that one should not mix the modernity with the traditional approach. But it is interesting to note that his style is not devoid of the figures of speech. Occasionally we find some figures of speech in the compositions of Dr. Dash and they naturally beautify his poems. The poet very nicely employs the figures like Upamā, Utprekṣā, Rūpaka, etc. Some of the examples are given below. Some of the similes of Dr. Dash are worth noting– *asthiha carvāmi tṛṣārtakukkura iva* (p. 34) *Candro māṁ paśyati vṛddavaidya iva* (p. 35) *purātanacatupatha iva ahaṁ tu nirvavaḥ* (p. 36), *Jalaśunyakūpakuṇḍalīva apuyā bhavati vāsarasya māyā* (p. 37), *Tvamiha dṛśyase pariṇataśasyakṣetre yathaikā hataśeṣa .... nirjhari Niṣkūla .....* (P. 38), *sammukhe in meghonnati vilupyate vimuktavarsane navoḍhāyāḥ lajjākaṭākṣo yathā madhuyāminīdarpaṇe* (p. 46), *Paramadya vicchinnoham sakaṭasya nemiriva* (P. 55)

Some of the examples of *Rūpaka* are : *Āsā atra tamasātaṭiṇī jīvanam sākṣāt laghuyaṣṭiḥ (Caitanyacandrikā,* P. 67)

In some poems the poet's feelings of pain have been expressed in a very touching and natural form. For exmples : *mṛtamuhūrtasya nārikelam dhṛtvā ahaṁ tu prārthaye ātmananiṁ mama yantraṇācinheṣu anvisya pīyūṣam (Subhecchā* P. 13)

The poet satires at the existing social maladies in some of his poems. For examples :

Mārjanī tu asamarthā ātmānaṁ saṁkarium gomayam tathāpi ghoṣayati mānavatāsaṁvidhāne śāntirapi sāiyasvādhikāraḥ (adhikārah. P. 18)

Dr. Dash is a lover of nature. In the poem, *Nepathya-candrikā* he has described the evening in modern manner which is siginficantly different from the traditional type of presentation. It definitely arrests the attention of a delicate reader, who is truly a lover of poetry.

Vānaprasthai ratimāṅ saṁjātah bālavibhākaraḥ / sāṁdhyaklinnagaganataḥ askhalat tārakāyaḥ caraṇavalayaḥ / purātanavihim pratyāgataḥ kukkurāṇām kāmārtakalahai (nepathyacandrikā, p. 25)

What makes Dr. Dash distinct from other poets and gives a special place to him among the poets of today is his wide range of experience. His expressions have a special feature that marks his poetic individuality and his thought-structures. Mainly he does not express his ideas in an ordinary manner but a manner that is sufficiently striking and charming. For example :

Paraṁ kva madhu kva vā madhumatī? surabhiprasāraṇanimmitaṁ muktamiha sarvatra gaganaṁ/ vistiṇavitānatale smin uḍḍinasya svatantratā kutaḥ? sammukhe me parvatasindhiṣu nirjharaḥ krandati avagahya svakiyasya bandhyapratirūpe madhudipakalpanayā. (Madhudipaḥ, pp. 69-70)

A significant feature of his poems is that the poet has very competently created sophisticated imageries, which bring a special status to the structure of his compositions as well as expressions of feelings. We give here some of the examples :

sīmāvalaye sīdatīha mahāvṛkṣaḥ ātmanaḥ pracarāśailīṣa vilāsaprapañcaṁ sthūlayitaṁ tvarate sanyasī / (Darpaṇam, p. 45) *Aṅgaro ham śeṣabhasmibhavanam pratikṣe (Vicchinnanemiḥ,* p. 56)—*ullanghanamuhurtaamanvisaya jalanidiḥ rarangasarvasva (ghurnikale,* p. 61)—*tvamatra prekṣālayaḥ aham ca pratikṣālayaḥ vyavadhāne ghurṇiratra samparkavalayaḥ (ibid,* p. 62)

Gītīmayatā is a distinct feature of Dr. Dash's poems as they wear an extra ornament because of his lyrical way of expressions characterized by simple and sweet language, on which he has a perfect command. For example :

Eyam mālā eyamapi mālakāraśailī sāmañjasyasaṁpādane tapasaḥ praṇāti (Caitanyacardrikā, p. 68)—*jirṇayānaviratiriyam tvamiha viharasi yathā yaṣṭibhāravāhiṇi dinadarmakari / dūrāt pratiyase sākṣāt bhūkamadalitā parityaktadarī (Viraticitram,* p. 23)—*adhya tu aśrubinduṣu me dṛsyate pratibiṁbaṁ tava edamiha anubhavaḥ avaśiṣṭasamayasyaṛkte haritapraṇavaḥ (Nepathyacandrikā,* p. 26)—*nidritaspandaneṣu layacumbiṁ tādātṁayasya kunjavanī nisithaniśvasitirapi praṇavapraṇayini (sithaniśvāsaḥ,* p. 36)

The extreme difficulty in the mode of expressions sometimes spoils the beauty of some poems. One important feature is that in some poems the sentences do not form a unity. In some poems even if unity is there, it does not strike spontaneously as it should be. When the process becomes laborious, the labour of the reader stands on the way of his realization of aesthetic pleasure for which the entire activity of art aims at. For example :

Mastakasindūretava sandhyā vatrarati abhābvaḥ krīḍati punaśca maṅgalasūtre te (Anvārambhaḥ, p. 51)

I cannot but say that Prof. Dash's presentation has a new dimension and a new mode. Some of the sentences though appear very sweet and charming, lack the substance of meaning. What does the poet want to convey by all those sentences is not understood at all. Since the meaning is the most important element on which the entire edifice of poetic structure is based, it should be revealed easily. If it remains hidden in the body of words and does not reach to the connoisseures, then the entire process fails miserably. Excessive craze for hiding the meaning in the sophisticated structure of words does not help in creating aesthetic value. I cite here some of the sentences just for example :

ātmalinadigvalayasya madhuparka śpastāyate tārakāviyoge, (p. 4) purṇamāsīlajiāvaguṇṭhane avathanti āṣāḍhasya chāyā āviṣkṛtya nijatve nagnatam, (p. 5)

Dr. Dash has significantly contributed to a new trend of Sanskrit poetry and has been successful to a great extent in influencing many of his successors who have tried to imitate him. Dr. Dash's poems have their own designed and many inferior in comparison with their counterparts composed by the poets of regional languages. Though the writings of Dr. Dash, Sanskrit language seems to have been refreshed and revitalized. It will not be an exaggeration if I say that the Sanskrit language has been given a new life and a new force by Prof. Dash who has completely dedicated his valuable energy for enrichment of Sanskrit language and its literature. Which collects some precious aspects of his experience and preserves them in the form of his poems. I hope, it will be highly appreciated by the poets and poeticians equally and will secure a dignified place in the history of modern Sanskrit literature. At the end, I like to conclude this article by the follwing words of Dr. Dash who has expressed about the aims of his life.

The blind current swallows the road.
Neither dead nor non-dead is seen.
Only shouting embellishes
a dying personality,
A divisive geography
as if a taste
of a pregnant belle
develops deformations (Andhasnota, p. 67)

*

Translated Literature in Sanskrit

Translation is an art because it is a *kauśala karma*. Though not mentioned in the list of sixty four arts translation may be included in the *kāvyakalā*. Nobody can deny the importance of translations in today's world. Although deviation is inevitable, there is no doubt that translation leads to literary innovations on its own right. Translation is a rewriting of an original text. All rewritings, whatever their intention maybe, reflect a certain ideology and as such manipulate literature to function in a given society in a given way. Rewriting helps in the evolution of literature. It can introduce new concepts, new genres and new devices. So the history of translation studies is the history also of literary innovation.

The art of translation has played a significant role in the spread and preservation of knowledge throughout the ages. With the dedicated labors of talented translators at crucial points of history, much of the treasures of the Eastern and Western thought and literature have survived. The phenomenal advance of science and technology in our times has added new dimensions and a sense of urgency to the art of translation. Translation has become an indispensable tool and a means of wider communication in the first shrinking world of today. It provides the means for breaking the existing language barriers. So the translator is no longer to be treated as a 'traitor or a 'traducer'. He is a benefactor in bringing the world closer, culturally as well as politically.

The translators have useful function to fulfill. They have a very useful part to play as a means of 'wider communication'. The substances of important works in the several languages of the world are made available across the borders of each language through translations faithfully but intelligibly rendered. It is also a fact that the rhythm and the other beauties of form and other essential parts of poetry can never be brought out in translations and consequently very beautiful things when translated become flat and stale. Rice is not the same as starch in powder form. Orange or pomegranate or mango juice, or essence of roses or jasmine is not the same as an orange or a pomegranate or a mango or a rose or a jasmine flower. The essence may be there, but the beauty of the fruit and the flower is not reproduced in the translated substance.

The Sanskrit word for translation is *Anuvāda*. It means repetition of what is said in a text with a different wording. Translation can be viewed as basically a change of form. When we speak of the form of a language, in this context we are referring to the actual words, phrases, sentences, and other higher units that are spoken or written. It is the structural part of language which is actually seen in print or heard during a speech or a conversation. What happens in translation is that the form of the source language is replaced by the form of the target language. In past, Sanskrit language with an elitist approach to literature was not used for translation from other languages but Sanskrit texts were being translated extensively in different Indian languages. Inter lingual translation from one Indian language into another started quite late in the 19th century.

A question arises : What is it that induced the men, engaged in creative work of the biggest order, to spend part of their energy in translation? This question cannot be adequately answered by saying that translation is a psychic urge that is deeply rooted in certain people. No one will dispute that it is an inner urge. There is a particular cast of mind that makes one a translator. But what is the nature of this urge? It is not a mimetic impulse. The translator is not an imitator, and certainly not a parodist. The pleasure he derives is not histrionic; it is not the pleasure of make-believe or of assuming a role. Nor is the longing to exercise one's powers the decisive factor in the situation. It can only be described as an urge to perform and interpret, as a great conductor interprets the score before him. This interpretation is, in its own way, a creative process. No poet can turn into a translator unless he feels a subtle continuity between the work of original composition and the labour expended on interpreting the work of a kindred soul. In becoming a translator he does not cease to create, nor does his pleasure cease to be personal. Through a remarkable paradox, the self-obliteration that translation involves itself becomes a means of self-expression. The translator has therefore been rightly described as a character in search of an author'; he finds the author first in another and then within himself.

Renato Poggioli puts the matter admirably. Describing the translator as a narcissus contemplating his own likeness in the pool of another's art, Paggioli says: 'through the shock of a recognition primarily psychic in quality, the translator suddenly finds that a poem newly discovered, or discovered anew, offers him an exemplary solution for his own formal problems, as well as an expressive outlet for his subjective experience content. Once we look upon translation as a personal adventure, as a voyage of self-discovery, the age-old controversy about 'faithfulness to the original' falls into a proper perspective. Nothing could be more misleading than the idea that every translator has to choose between two rival schools, between the literalists on the one hand and the apostles of the free rendering on the other. Nor does it help to attempt a mechanical compromise or 'truce' because it is not a question of perpetually balancing between under-translation and over-translation. One error cannot be cancelled by another error; the either-or approach cannot be corrected by the 'little of each' approach.

One has to boldly accept that the formal law of Non-contradiction does not operate in the field of aesthetic experience. Kant grasped this clearly and asserted that every aesthetic judgment is characterized by 'subjective universality'. In the same spirit one must assert that if translation is regarded as an aesthetic process, formal consistency cannot be expected of it. The real trouble with the 'literalists' is that they do not distinguish with sufficient clarity between formal and inner consistency, with the result that in their hands 'faithfulness' becomes a static concept.

The literalists' main contention is unquestionably sound. A translator must translate but not improvise. There are certain things which the translator has simply no right to attempt. For instance, he has no right to skip. Having selected a work, he has no right to pretend that a word or a phrase that he finds inelegant does not exist. He has to stick to his author through thick and thin. The translator has to pray so closely into the author's workshop that he is in danger of discovering much unsavory detail. He may find examples of repetitiveness or of unpardonable weakness for particular words and phrases. But he has no right to leave out anything in the fond belief that it 'makes no difference'. Nor has he any business to 'improve' the original. He cannot do so, anyway; the only thing that he can improve is his version of the original in a different language. He must heed Dr. Johnson's advice; "never sir, try to excel the author you translate". Sometimes radical deviations are sought to be justified on the plea that they 'sound better'. If the musical quality of the original can be retained it is well and good. If it cannot, it has to be sacrificed at the altar of accurate rendering.

We should not forget the fact that Europe first learnt of Kālidāsa's '*Śakuntalā*' from Sir William Jones's translation published in 1789. After this translation something in the nature of a commotion was created among European intellectuals by the discovery of this drama and as a result several editions of this play came out. Its translations also appeared in different languages like German, French, Danish, and Italian from Jone's translation. Goethe was powerfully impressed and paid a magnificent tribute to '*Śakuntalā*'. The idea of giving a prologue to Faust is said to have originated from Kālidāsa's prologue, which was in accordance with the usual tradition of the Sanskrit drama.

Pandit Jawaharlal Nehru informs us that "An English translation of Sudraka's '*Mṛcchakaṭika*' was staged in New York in 1924. Mr. Joseph Wood Krutch, the dramatic critic of the nation, wrote of it as follows: Ȟere, if anywhere, the spectator will be able to see a genuine example of that pure art theatre of which theorists talk, and here, too, he will be led to meditate upon that real wisdom of the East which lies not in esoteric doctrine but in a tenderness far deeper and truer than that of the traditional Christianity which has been so thoroughly corrupted by the hard righteousness of Hebraism . . . . .

A play wholly artificial yet profoundly moving because it is not realistic but real ....Whoever the author may have been, and whether he lived in the fourth century or the eighth, he was a man good and wise with the goodness and wisdom which come not from the lips or the smoothly flowing pen of the moralist but from the heart. An exquisite sympathy with the fresh beauty of youth and love tempered his serenity, and he was old enough to understand that a light-hearted story of ingenious complication could be made the vehicle of tender humanity and confident goodness... Such a play can be produced only by a civilization which has reached stability; when a civilization has thought its way through all the problems it faces, it must come to rest upon something calm and naive like this, Macbeth and Othello, however great and stirring they might be, are barbarous heroes because the passionate tumult of Shakespeare is the tumult produced by the conflict between a newly awakened sensibility and a series of ethical concepts inherited from the savage age. The realistic drama of our own time is a product of a like confusion; but when problems are settled, and when passions are reconciled with the decisions of an intellect, then form alone remains .... Nowhere in our European past do we find this side the classics, a work more completely civilized.' Pandit Nehru further remarks: "There is hardly any translation in English or any other foreign language from the Sanskrit which can be called worthy of or just to the original. Both Indians and foreigners have failed in this work for different reasons. That is a great pity and the world misses something that is full of beauty and imagination and deep thinking, something that is not merely the heritage of India but should be the heritage of the human race."

"The hard discipline, reverent approach, and insight of the English translation of the Authorized Version of the bible, not only produced a noble book, but gave to the English language strength and dignity. Generations of European scholars and poets have laboured lovingly over Greek and Latin classics and produced fine translations in various European languages. And so even common folk can share to some extent in those cultures and in their drab lives, have glimpses of truth and loveliness. Unfortunately, this work has yet to be done with the Sanskrit classics. When it will be done, or whether it will be done at all, I do not know. Our scholars grow in numbers and grow in scholarship, and we have our poets too, but between the two there is a wide and ever-growing gap. Our creative tendencies are turned in a different direction, and the many demands that the world of to-day makes upon us hardly give us time for the leisured study of the classics. Especially in India we have to look another way and make for long lost time; we have been too much immersed in the classics in the past, and because we lost our own creative instincts we ceased to be inspired even by those classics which we claimed to cherish so much.

Translations, I suppose, from the Indian classics will continue to appear, and scholars will see to it that the Sanskrit words and names are properly spelt and have all the necessary diacritical marks, and that there are plenty of notes and explanations and comparisons. There will be everything, in fact, literally and conscientiously rendered, only the living spirit will be missing. What was a thing of life and joy, so lovely and musical and full of imaginative daring, will become old and flat and stale, with neither youth nor beauty, but with only the dust of the scholar's study and the smell of midnight oil.

In spite of theoretical controversy, the process of translation is going on everywhere, since the time immemorial, as a process of communication and dissemination of information. The question of untranslability has too often been discussed in terms of absolute rather than relative equivalence. If one is to insist that translation must involve no loss of information whatsoever, then, obviously not only translation but all communication is impossible. No communication whether intra lingual or inter lingual or inter semiotic can be without some loss of information.

Dryden says very clearly about what should be an ideal aim of a literary translator in the following words:

"A translator that would write with any force or spirit of the original must never dwell on the words of his author. He ought to possess himself entirely, and perfectly comprehend the genius and sense of his author; the nature of the subject, and the terms of the art or subject treated of; and then he will express himself as justly, and with as much life, as if he wrote an original; whereas he who copies word for word loses all the spirit in the tedious translation".

"Translation has two aspects, meaning and flavor. We are almost saying that the translator's work is a continual war between science and art, between precision and intuition, method and feeling."

"It would be almost true to say that there are no universally accepted principles of translation, because the only people qualified to formulate them have never agreed among themselves, but have so often and for so long contradicted each other that they have bequeathed to us a welter of confused thought which must be hard to parallel in other fields of it."

In the Indian multilingual society the anomaly is that while Indian literature is one, writers and readers in one language know very little of what is being written in a neighbouring language of the country. It is therefore, necessary to translate the works whereby Indian writers may come to know one another, across the barriers of language and script, and whereby readers may appreciate the immense variety and complexity of their country's literary heritage. It is great paradoxes that though some consider the activity of translation to be 'an impossible task', humans are known to have been translating since ages. Moreover, translators- rare breed of men of letters—have often been undervalued and have seldom been given the acclaim and commendation due to them. However, if the translator is not noticed, that might suggest that the translated piece has an excellence of its own. Think of the Gujarati, Marathi, Telugu, and Hindi Translators of Sharat Chandra Chatterjee's novels. These translators by their excellent work could so easily cross the linguistic barriers and almost convince us that Sharat Chandra was a Gujarati or a Marathi writer or that he actually wrote in Hindi. Translators are the invisible men of literature. They are a rare breed. They cannot be in it for the glory; it must be love of literature and a sense of loyalty to the languages.

A translator is a true bilingual or trilingual and has more linguistic competence in totality than a creative writer who may know only one language. The translator gains a rich and new experience and attempts literary translation with a pioneering spirit and missionary zeal.. Moreover, if we want to establish Indian literature as one it is possible only through translation. Translations from one Indian language to another reveal the features of commonality in our thought expressed in different Indian languages. It is both for the understanding of the basic unity and wonderful diversities on Indian literature in the Indian situation, the necessity of translation are ineluctable.

Sahitya Academi, the national body of Letters, realizes that if India has to retain its cultural specificity and integrity then all languages must develop as the cultural expression of people speaking such languages. There could be need and motivation for multi lateral communication. Translation is one of the major facilitators of such communication.

In an organization like Sahitya Academi aims at translating the best of Indian literature from one language to another for developing the concept of Indian literature as one literature.

One of the fascinating fields of modern Sanskrit literature is the translations. Study of translated literary works forms an interesting, emerging and challenging area of research in Sanskrit. In past, Sanskrit literary works were translated into several foreign and Indian languages. Today without translations, the study of Sanskrit originals seems impossible. That activity is still going on. But at present we have a reverse trend. A sizable amount of literature in the form of translations of literary texts is available. All those works are neglected and are not subjected for study and research. We are not able to evaluate and appreciate them as we know a little about them except some information. There are more than hundred literary works written in ancient languages like Pāli and Prākṛit, foreign languages like Russian, English, French and German, Indian languages like Hindi, Gujarati, Marathi, Oriya, Kannada, Malayalam, Bengali, Assamise, Rajasthani, Urdu, and Persian etc., which are translated into Sanskrit. It is observed that some of the best minds have endeavored to translate or trans create the seminal works from several other languages into Sanskrit, and have made valuable contribution to the field of modern Sanskrit literature. The Sanskrit writers of twentieth century have prepared significant and commendable works in this direction. They have not only enriched the Modern Sanskrit literature but have given a new life to this dying language. They have also created scope for research in this new field.

Sanskrit has always kept an intimate relation with the popular tongues and the literatures in them. In the modern period, the critical and historical study of Indian literature has induced many a Sanskritist to render into the Sanskrit medium some of the best examples from his own regional literature. These renderings are from ancient as well as modern productions in these languages. Some of the oldest works are translated into Sanskrit from Tamil literature. Following in the footsteps of the famous Vaṣṇava philosopher, Vedānta Deśika, some south Indian scholars have translated the Srivaisnava canonical hymns of the Alwars; Medaepalli Venkataramanacarya of the Girvanasathagopasahasra, T. Narasimha Iyenger alias Kalki of Mysore (*Sahasra-gatharatnavali*) and P. B. Annangarachariar of Kanci have rendered portions of this hymnal collection. The celebrated Tirukkurul has been translated by two writers, whose Sanskrit version is called *Suniti Kusumamālā* and is accompanied by the author's Sanskrit gloss and a more recent and better version in compact Anuṣṭubhas, entitle *Sūktiratnākara,* by Sankara Subrahmanya Sastri. Subrahmanya Sastri translated Tamil didactic classic Naladiyar in his Catuspadi. C. Narayanan Nair translated the Tamil epic Silappadikaram , a Sanskrit poem of six cantos entitled Kanakikovalam. The stories in the *Kathāśataka* of S. Venkatarama Sastri are drawn from vernacular originals. Sesha Sastri presented four hundred proverbs in Sanskrit. The boat-songs, the swing-song, tiruppuhazh, kummi, kolattam, etc., ST G. Varadachariar has put into Sanskrit famous *śataka* poems in Telugu —the *Vemana-śataka,* the

Sumatiśataka, the *Dasarathiśataka,* the *Kṛṣṇa-śataka,* the *Bhāskaraśataka,* and the *Kalahastiśvaraśataka.* G. Sitapati has rendered stay Telugu verses, some of the Telugu *padas* of Ksetrajna which are used for acting in Bharata nāṭya, and also one of the poems in Telugu, Purnamma of Guruzada Appa Rao. Philosophical Essays of Lalit Kumar Shastri from Gujarati in the name of Amṛtadhārā, 1979 are translated by Visnudev Paṇḍita.

One of the bases of Indian national unity is the growth and development of literature. Although the country was divided into various regional units so far as languages are concerned, literature itself had derived inspiration from common and identical sources . In the modern period too, it has evenly absorbed the influence of western thought and scientific progress and has closely followed the national aspirations of the people in various regions. Thus it was that in 1947 we were faced with a more or less anomalous situation while Indian literature was essentially one, it was being expressed in different Indian languages. Due to the insurmountable barrier of languages and script, the people of one region were almost ignorant of the writings in the other regions.

Translation also enriches the literary personality of the creative writer. A writer is naturally eager to read and acquaint himself with the best works in various languages and draw inspiration for his writings. Translation is, thus, the best possible means of knowing a work and imbibing its healthy influence. This is why the best among the creative geniuses have taken to translating works of their choice. No writer is writing all the time. There are frequent intervals during his creative period, when he is engaged in assimilating new experience and drawing fresh inspiration by reading and observing. During such periods of useful fruitlessness translating a master has been helped him to see a new vision or tread a new path.

Here a list of the Translated works is given:

Translation of Christian Literature into Sanskrit

Bible

The New Testament of our Lord and Saviour Jesus Christ from the Original Greek by the Missionaries at Serampore (under the Superintendence of William Carey) 3 Vols. Serampore during 1808-1811

The Holy Bible containing the Old and New Testaments from the original by the Missionaries at Serampore in 1821

The Proverbs of Soloman, School Book Society's Press, Calcutta, 1842

The Book of Genesis and part of Exodus from Hebrew by the Calcutta Baptist Missionaries in 1843

The Book of the Prophet Isaiah, The Baptist Mission Press, Calcutta, 1845

The Proverbs of Soloman from Hebrew , Baptist Mission Press, Calcutta, 1946

The Psalms-Isvariya Stavarthaka Gitasaṁhitā, Baptist Mission Press, Calcutta, 1877

Translations from Hindi Literature

Rasasiddhānta of Nagendra by Amir Chandra Shastri

Vyāmohi of Shyama Vimal by the author himself

Satasai of Bihari by Paramananda Sastri and Prem Narayana Dwivedi by the title of *Saundarya- saptasati*

Vairāgya Sandipani Dohāvali of Kavir, Dadu and Rahim by Prema Narayana Dwivedi

Kāmāyanī of Jaysankar Prasad by Bhagavan Data Sastri 'Rakesha'

Nirmalā of Premcand by Srirama Dave

Dhruvasvāminī of Jaysankar Prasad by Srirama Dave

Pañcavaṭī of Jaysankar Prasad by Radha Vallabha Tripathy

Ramacaritamānasa of Tulasidasa by Prema Narayana Dwivedi

Aṅglaromāñcam by 1.O.Doshi and Harihara Trivedi

Vidyapatiśatakam of Vidyapati by Kasinatha Mishra

Dūr-Vs-Pār of Hariraj Singha deva by Trivikrama Pati

Translations from Persian

Rubayat of Omar Khayyam by Virendra Kumar Bhattacharya

Rubayat of Omar Khayyam by Trivikrama Pati in 75 stanza

Kalapurvodayam—Andhrakāvyānuvāda by Suryanarayana Sastri, 1967

Besop's fables have been translated more than one Sanskrit writer.

Kavitāñjali of Aurobindo by Kapalisastri, Pondichery, 1946

cerāge Dair of Mirza Galib by Nahid Abid;

Translations from Telugu

Gayatri niti gītāvali by T. G. Varadacharya

Gandhisūkti-muktāvali by Cintamani Dwarakesa Deshmukh

Kalapunodaya by Y. Mallikarjuna Rao, (a prose version of a Telugu Romance) .

Manucaritra of Allasani Peddanna by K. Yajnanarayana Diksita

Ekavirā of Viswanatha Satyanarayana by Vasa Subramanya Shastri, 1993

Nāticarāmi Anyasca Kathā of Kaluri Hanumanta Rao by the author himself

Nanhe Muktaka of N. Gopi by Vijaya

Translations from Bengali

Gītañjali by Pullel Ramachandredu . We are informed that five translations of this work have been prepared but they are not available to us.

Meghanādavadha

Caitanyacaritāmṛta- by Bhaskarananda Swami

Translations from English

Hemlet of Shakespeare by S. D. Joshi

Athelo of Shakespear by Rajaraja Varma, 1912

Plays of Shakespear by Laksmana Sastri Tailanga

Plays of Sheakspear by Ananta Tripathy Sarma

Five short stories of Ksama Rao in Anustup metre by the author herself

Thoughts and Glimpses of Aurobindo, Cintanasca Cidunmesa

Naum Argenum, bekaniyasutravyakhanam by unknown author

Principles of Human Knowledge of Barkeley Jñānasiddhānta-candrika

Essays concerning Human Understanding of Lock, Mana-viyajñānaviṣayakaśāstra

Sindhuvadavṛtam, Stories of Sindhbad by Ramasastri

Astācalīyam by Govinda Chandra Pande

Works of Aurobindo by Sribhasyam Vijayasarathi in the name of Avahanam, 1991

Translations from Gujarati

Setubandha Gujarati poems of several poets by Yasvanti Dave

Philosophical Essays of Lalita kumar by the tirtle Amrtadhara

Translations from Oriya

Cilikā of Radhanatha Roy by Khirod Chandra Dash, 1991

Ānandasandhānam of Herekrishna Mahatab by Probodha Kumar Mishra

Ramakānta-kavitā-sañcayanam by Kshiroda Chandra Dash

Dharmapadam of Gopandhu Das by Harekrisna Satapathy

Svacchāsati by Purna Chandra Sahu

Bāji-Rauta of Saci Rauta Ray by Narayana Dash

Vanaharanam of

Bandinaḥ Swadesacintā of Gopabandhu Dash by Probodha Kumar Mishra

Śrīrādha of Ramakanta Rath by Govinda Chandra Udgata

Yajnaseni of Pratibha Roy by Bhagirathi Nanda

Araṇyaśasyam of Manoranjan Dash, by Khiroda Chandra Dash

Stories of by Narayana Dash published in the Kathā magazine

Aruna Ranjan Mishra informs that Ananta Tripathy Sarma has translated Upendra Bhanja's Oriya *mahākāvya, Lavanyavati* of 48 cantos. Bhagavata Prasad Dāsh translated the *Vaidehivilasa,* another great epic of Upendra Bhanja. *Tapasvini,* a *mahākāvya* of Gangadhar Meher (1862-1924) has been rendered into Sanskrit by Umasankar Panda in 1993. *Mahāyātrā,* another Oriya *mahākāvya* by Radhanatha Roy (1848-1980) has been rendered into Sanskrit by Umasankar Panda. His work is entitled *Mahāyātrā Mahākāvyam.*

Translations from Tamil

Kamba Ramāyaṇa (Sri Ramacaritam) by S. Nilakantha Sastri

Tamila Laghukathaḥ of Subrahmanya Bhārati and Kalkikrishnamurti by Rajalakshmi Srinivasan

Translations from Malayalam

Kannakikovalam Sllapattikaram by C. Narayana Nair

Keralabhasavivarta

Mahakavikrtayah

Sitavicaralahari of Kumaran Asan by N. Gopal Pillai

Mayurasandesam of Kerala Varma Valiya Koli Tamuran published under the title Mayuradutam by P.K.Narayana Pillai

Kathasatakam

Translations from Marathi

Jñāneśwarī of Jnaneswara by Sakharama Sastri Bhagavata and M.P. Oka;

Jñāneśwarī by some other person

Kekavali of Moropanta by T. D. Sakurikar in the title Girvanakekavali

Balidanam of N. C. Kelkar by Latkar Sastri

Manobodha

Dasabodha of Srisamartha-ramadasa

Abhangarasavahini

Agnija

Some plays by Palsule

Translations From Kannad

Sārtha of S.L,Bhairappa by Nagraj Rao

Dharmaśrī of S.L, Bhairappa by Janardana Prasada Hegde

Jñānadīpti by Nagaratna

Yugāvatāra of H.V. Shesadri by Suceta Vasuvaja

The above list is not complete. We are confident that many such works are under darkness. I have tried my best to collect and collate the pertinent information about the Indian literary works translated into Sanskrit. There is no doubt in my mind about the fact that the translators who are themselves poets and writers of high caliber have made sublime contribution and enriched the field of modern Sanskrit literature. Because of the untiring efforts of some renowned translators, the Sanskrit literature has extended its horizon and has embodied a substantial amount of literature available in Sanskrit translations. The works like the stories of Tolstoy from Russian, the plays of William Shakespeare from English, *Nirmalā* of Premcand from Hindi, *Rubayat* of Omar Khayam from Persian, Poems of Mirza Galib from Persian, *Gītañjali* of Rabindra Nath Tagore from Bengali, *Yajñaseni* of Pratibha Roy from Oriya, *Sartha* and *Dharmaśrī* of S. L. Bhairappa from Kannad, *Setubandha*, a collection of modern poems from Gujarati, to mention a few titles, are in fact valuable creations. These works would have unknown to the Sanskrit readers if they would not have been translated into Sanskrit. But the problem is that the works of this type are in need of evaluation and appreciation. As far as my knowledge goes, there are no critical and comprehensive studies on this aspect of Sanskrit literature. In the conclusion I have to say that an important chapter in the history of modern Sanskrit literature is in darkness. It is not properly read and appreciated. The translators are to be appreciated for taking the trouble for enriching the field of modern Sanskrit literature. Mahalinga Shastri in the preface of his *Dravidarya-subhasitasaptati* writes: "My experiments in translating English and Tamil poems have shown me that the poetic efforts in the other languages come off beautifully in Sanskrit and even look enriched, more tidy and majestic in the new garb. Every attempt in that line seems to reveal to me the immense potentialities of this most ancient language-its flexibility, roominess surprising aptitude for supplying into felicious moulds of excelling brilliance and brevity. Due to the kinship of the two cultures translation from Tamil into Sanskrit is not literary fit, but an easy walk over into an equally commodious well-furnished adjacent parlor."

REFERENCES

Swain, B. K., *Contribution of Orissa to Post-Independence Sanskrit literature 1947-1985,* Centre of Advance Research in Sanskrit , Sri Jagannatha Sanskrit University, Puri, 2002, p.14

Mukhopadhyaya, Satakadi, *Sanskrite Anudita-sahityam (bharatiya bhasabyo Vaidesikabhasabhyaśca),* Adhunikasanskritasahityasriḥ, pp.39-62

Raghavan , V. *Sanskrit literature in Contemporary Indian Literature,*

Panda, Rabindra Kumar, *Vandinah Swadesacinta,*

Sastri, Kalanatha, *Arvacina Gadya Sahitya* , Rashtriya Sanskrit Sansthan, New Delhi,

Mishra, Aruna, Ranjan, *Sanskrtit Mahakavyas in Orissa after Independence* in Sanskrit Writings in Independent India, pp.241-263

_____ Contemporary Sanskrit Writings in Orissa

Shukla, Ramakanta, *Arvacinasamskritasahityasar-vekṣaṇam* (1997-1998), Presidential Address, Proceedings of the All India Oriental Conference, Thirty ninth Session, Bhandarkar Oriental Research Institute, Pune,

'*The Discovery of India*, p. 164.

समसामयिकसंस्कृतपद्यकाव्येषु राजनीतिरूपचित्रणम्

समसामयिकं संस्कृतपद्यसाहित्यं प्राचीनवन्न केवलं रसभावसौन्दर्यविमण्डितं सत् सहृदयहृदयान्तकरणे लोकोत्तराह्लाददायिनीं चमत्कृतिं संसृजति, अपितु तद् विश्वसाहित्यक्षेत्रेऽपि स्वतन्त्रस्थानमलङ्करोति। अस्यनैकानि कारणानि सन्ति। सत्सु विद्यमानेषु कारणेषु नूतनविषयचयनमपि विशिष्टमेकमुल्लेखनीयं कारणमस्ति। अर्वाचीने संस्कृतसाहित्येऽथवा समसामयिके साहित्यक्षेत्रे कविभिः प्रायो नूतनविषयाः, ये साम्प्रतिके समाजेऽथवा साम्प्रतिके समये सर्वेषां साधारणानुभवविषयास्ते काव्य-वस्तुरूपेण स्वीकृता दृश्यन्ते। इदं सर्वदा स्वागतयोग्यमस्ति। अनेन साहित्यं नूतनमिव प्रतिभाति। तथाचास्याकर्षणशक्तिः संवर्धते। सहृदयाः पाठकाः स्वतो नूतनं, परिदृश्यमानं, सामाजिकं वस्तु प्रति समाकृष्य भवन्ति। तस्मात् साहित्यं न विरक्तिमुत्पादयति। परन्तु विशिष्टसुभोगसाधनरूपेण तदादरणीयस्थानं भजते। यद्यपि प्राचीना विषया नवोनवोन्मेषविशेषशालिनी-कविप्रतिभाबलेन नूतनत्वं धारयन्ते, ते प्रकरणवक्रताऽथवा प्रबन्धवक्रताप्रयोगकौशलकलया मुह्यन्ति मनांसि तथापि नूतनं नूतनमिव, पुरातनं पुरातनमिव। यद्यपि जनस्य व्यवहृतं प्राचीनं वस्त्रं प्रति प्रेम स्वाभाविकं भवति तथापि नूतनं प्रति न कस्याकर्षणमिह जगति। मधुमासे यथा द्रुमास्त एव नवा इव, प्रतिभान्ति तथैवातिपरिचिता विषया विविधरसोपेताः सन्तः शोभामावहन्ति। आनन्दमनुभवति मे चेतः कथयितुं यत् संस्कृतकविर्यः प्राचीनां परम्परां विशेषरूपेण संधारयते स एव नूतनताया अन्वेषणाय अग्रेसरो भवति। समाजस्य वास्तविकतां स्वकरकमलकोमल-लेखनीसहायेन चित्रयितुं यतमानोऽस्ति, प्रकृत्या अनन्तवैभवस्य चित्रणापेक्षया साम्प्रतिकसमाजस्यानिष्टकारकाणां विषबीजसदृशानां विनाशकारीतत्त्वानां चित्रणमधिकं प्राधान्यमर्पयति, नारीणां घनस्तनजघनानां वर्णनापेक्षया समाजस्य विकृतमङ्गमथवा प्रदूषितं परिवेशं, तेन तस्य मूलकारणमाविष्कृत्य कमनीयकाव्यकान्तिमाध्यमेन लोकलोचनमानेतुं प्रतिज्ञाबद्धो भवति, एवं तद्द्वारा कविः समाजस्य सारस्वतसेवां

करोति। तेनैव साहित्यस्य परिसरो प्रतिदिनं प्रवर्धते। अधुनाऽवास्तवकल्पनाराज्यस्य सम्राट् न संस्कृतकविः। स साधारणः, दायित्वसम्पन्नः, सचेतनो नागरिकः। तस्य लक्ष्यमद्य समाजस्य समुद्धारः। सरलया, सुबोध्यया भाषया, सुकुमारशैल्या च सामाजिकं सौन्दर्यचित्रणं तस्य दर्पणविषयः। स प्रकृतस्य द्रष्टा। सत्यस्य स्रष्टा। सारस्वतस्यापि सेवकः। तस्य काव्यं तस्माद् विलक्षणवैभवं धारयते। विषयेऽस्मिन्न सन्देहावकाशः।

तेषु विषयेषु अन्यतमो राजनीतिसन्दर्भः। अस्मिन् लघुनिबन्धे संस्कृतकविभिः कीदृशं राजनीतिरूपवर्णनं कृतं तद् विशदयितुं प्रयासः। यद्यपि स्थालीपुलकन्यायेनात्र सामान्यं किञ्चिदुपस्थापितमस्ति तथापि तदेव संस्कृतकवीनां राजनीतिं प्रति वर्तमानाभिगमं प्रकटयिष्यति। अत्र सूचनामात्रं क्रियते।

दीपको घोषस्तस्य राजनीतिलीलाशताधिकमिति सुन्दरे काव्येऽर्वाचीनसंस्कृत-पत्रिकायां प्रकाशिते अनन्तशक्तिमयीमनन्तकीर्त्तिमयीं च मातरं राजनीतिं नमति।

(14/2, पृ० 1)

भो राजनीते प्रणमामि तुभ्यं पुनः पुनस्ते पदयो प्रणामः,
अनन्तकीर्त्तिरमिताश्च शक्तीः शक्नोमि मातुं न तव क्षमस्व।।1।।
विचित्रवर्णा न विशेषवर्णा विचित्रमार्गा च विशेषमार्गा।
विचित्रचित्ता न हि दुष्टचित्ता भो राजनीते भवती विचित्रा।।
जानीमहे नैव तव स्वरूपं का त्वं नु तन्निर्वचने न शक्तिः।
तस्मादनिर्वाच्यपदाभिधेया वेदान्तमायेव विचित्ररूपा।।

तेन कृता तुलना राजनीत्याः अनिर्वचनीयया मायया साकमधिकां रमणीयतां भजते। कविस्तस्या गहनगम्भीराया महामायास्वरूपाया विचित्ररूपाया रूपं वर्णयितुं स्वसामर्थ्यं प्रकाशयति। तेनैवास्या जटिलस्वभावं द्योतयति। एवञ्च नमस्कारमाध्यमेन तस्या भयङ्करत्वमपि सूचयति। सरलपदावलीयुक्ता कवितेयं सुन्दरं भावतरङ्गं संसृज्य समाजस्य मूलोत्पाटकारिणीं राजनीतिशक्तिं तस्याः प्रभावञ्च स्पष्टीकरोति। अपरमुदाहरणं पश्यामः।

तथैव बटुकनाथशास्त्री खिस्तेमहोदयास्तेषां निर्वाचनावसरे काव्ये (अर्वाचीन-संस्कृतम् 12/2, पृ० 19-20) नेतृणां लीलावलीमतिसुन्दररीत्या वर्णयति। उदाहरणस्वरूपमेकं काव्यम्

आचूडमग्ना अपि कल्मसौधे
हंसच्छदाभं वसनं दधानाः।

निर्वाचनायोत्पतिता धरायां
गृहीतसेवा इव पूर्वदेवाः।। 1।।

स्वपक्षसंरक्षणजागरूका
विपक्षसन्तक्षणचञ्चवश्च।
नियुद्धलग्नान् पथि ताम्रचूडान्
विडम्बयन्तः परितो भ्रमन्ति।। 2।।

उच्चावचैः पक्षबलप्रचारै-
र्निनादिताऽशेषदिगन्तराला।
निर्वाचनाक्षं तिमिरं किरन्ती
कालस्य कन्या विहरत्यवन्याम्।। 6।।

हे देवि! निर्वाचनपेटिके त्वा-
मभ्यर्थयामः शृणु सावधाना।
सुतान् पवित्रान् जनयेः स्वगर्भात्
नैशाचरी माऽस्तु तव प्रसूतिः।।7।।

महाकवेः शास्त्रीमहोदयस्य काव्यमिदं प्रमोदप्रसूनं चित्तोपवने संसृजति। निर्वाचनपेटिका देवीरूपेणात्र समुपस्थापितास्ति।

इच्छारामद्विवेदीमहोदयानां तथैव गीतिकाव्यं राजनीतिविषयकं प्रसादगुणोपेतमपि समुदाहरणरूपेणोपस्थापनं करोति।

भाषणे शूरता कर्मणि क्रूरता।
कीदृशे चत्वरे राजनीतिर्गता।

राजसत्तासमाराधने पण्डितैः
प्रीतिधारैव सामाजिकी खण्डिता।
साधुता मूर्खतेति ध्रुवं दण्डिता
पूजिता लोलुपैर्वञ्चनामण्डिता।।

लुण्ठने वीरता, वञ्चने धीरता, कीदृशे चत्वरे, राजनीतिर्गता।

(समुज्ज्वला-काव्यसंग्रहस्य 'चत्वरे राजनीतिः, अर्वाचीनसंस्कृतम् पृ० 6-27)

श्रीरामकरणशर्मामहोदयाः स्पष्टं वर्णयन्ति यन्नेतारः शब्दजालेन जनान् विमुह्यन्ति। उदाहरणम्-

"शब्दक्रीडामात्रं लीलाः सर्वा सुकृत्रिमा धाराः।
क्रीडन्ति तत्र मञ्चे नेतारश्चाभिनेतारः।। (मानसी, 4)

उमाशंकर शर्मा त्रिपाठी महोदयाः चक्रिचूडामणिकाव्ये गर्दभस्य स्वामिनमित्थं वर्णयन्ति।

''नेता योऽसावधर्मरजको नित्यपानानुभावो
मालिन्यानां धुरि परिवहन् पृष्ठदेशासनोऽपि।
दण्डाघातैर्व्यवसितविधिर्घासमष्टिं व्यकीर्य
प्रजातन्त्र्ये जनमिव खलस्त्वां कदर्थीकरोति।।"

परन्तु काव्यमिदं व्यञ्जनया रजकरासभसम्बन्धोपन्यासद्वारेण प्रजातन्त्रस्य स्थितिः प्रकाशयति। व्यंग्यप्रधानं काव्यमिदं जननायकस्य चारित्रिकस्खलनं विद्योतयति। इयमस्ति नूतना संस्कृतकाव्यपरम्परा। लघुकाव्यानि अत्याधुनिके काले प्रयोजनानि सन्ति। विशेषरूपेण लघुवस्तूनां वर्णनाय लघुलघु काव्यनिर्माणं क्रियतेऽद्याधुनिकैः कविभिः। पठनपाठनाय, भाषाप्रचाराय, समयसामयिकवस्तुचित्रणाय तथा न हास्यव्यंग्यपरम्पराया परिपोषणाय लघुकाव्यानि विनिर्म्यन्ते। ता मनोरञ्जनाय सूक्ष्मवस्तूनां संदर्शनाय च साधनरूपेण व्यवह्रियन्ते कविभिः। अधुना अन्यानि उदाहरणानि पश्यामः, भुवनेश्वरः करस्तस्य दोषशतके काव्ये (पृ०3) राजनीतिप्रभां सम्यक् चित्रयति। एकं पद्यमुपस्थाप्यते।

''दुर्नीतिरुन्नतिपदं परितः प्रयाति
साधु समुन्नतगुणो नतिमैत्ति नित्यम्।
मूकायते गुणिगणः खलराजनीतौ
हे काल पश्य तव चित्रगतेः प्रभावम्।।''

कवेः करमहोदयस्याशयो यत् दुर्नीतिरस्माकं देशे प्रवर्धते तस्यां कारणमस्ति राजनीतिः।

श्रीनिवासरथमहोदयाः 'तदेव गगनं सैव धरा' काव्ये सामाजिकानां दुरावस्थाचित्रमित्थमुपस्थापयते। (पृ० 5)

''जनताकष्टतिः शान्तिसुखहीना
संस्कष्टतिदयाऽतिमलिना दीना।
केवल-निजहित-साधनलीना
राजनीतिरचना स्वाधीना।।

न तुलसीदलं न गङ्गाजलं स्वदते यथा सुरा। तदेव गगनं सैव धरा।।"

पुनश्च द्विवेदीमहोदयेन प्रकारान्तरेण राजनीतेः स्वरूपं प्रदर्शितम्।

"राजनीतिस्वयं कापि मायावती
हिंस्त्रनृत्यान्विता लक्ष्मणाख्ये पुरे।
यच्चकाराप्रियं शूर्पणखाः समं
तत्फलं प्राप सा सत्वरं चत्वरे।।"

(व्यथा, पृ० 5)

पश्य, कथमत्याधुनिकः कविर्जननायकस्य चित्रणं करोति। वेदानन्दमहोदया वर्णयन्ति।

"न जानाति यो नीतिशास्त्रं स नेता।"
न चावैति यो धर्मशास्त्रं स शास्ता।।
मतं राजमार्गे भुजङ्गप्रयातं
कलेरद्य चित्रं प्रपश्यन्तु सन्तः''।।

(त्रिपथगाकाव्यम्, पृ० 25)

राधावल्लभत्रिपाठी महोदयानां नेतास्तवमाला रमणीयास्ति।

"नमस्तुभ्यं नेतृवर्य यत्कण्ठः पुष्करायते।
मदाभोगघनध्वाने राजनीतिकताण्डवे।।
निरुपादानसम्भारमथित्तावेव तन्वते।
चित्रमाश्वासनं चित्रं कलाश्लाघाय ते नमः।।"

(स्तवमाला, सन्धाने पृ० 53)

अस्मिन् प्रसङ्गे निरञ्जनमिश्रस्य लोकतन्त्रशतकम् (भारतोदयः, सितम्बर, 2001) काव्यमपि ग्रहणीयमस्ति। पश्यन्तु कति श्लोकान् तस्मादुदाहृतान्।

''शकारः शासको यत्र राजनीतिस्तु कुट्टिनी।
विट-चेटाः प्रजा यत्र तत्र वेश्या स्वतन्त्रता"।। (पृ० 12)

अपरमुदाहरणम्-

"विघ्नस्य विघ्नभूताय श्वेतवस्त्रधराय च।
लोकतन्त्रस्य देवाय भूयो भूयो नमो नमः।" (तत्रैव)

"वने वने याति यथा मधुप्रियस्तथैव नेता सततं दले दले।
यथा न चम्पे मधुपप्रवासस्तथा न सत्ये वसतीह नेता"।। (तत्रैव)

"काङ्ग्रेसे भारतीये वा राष्ट्रीये जनतादले।
कम्युनिष्टे तथा चान्ये याति नेता स्वलोभतः"।।

(तत्रैव)

कविश्रीमिश्रमहोदयानां मते राजनीतिः कुट्टिनी। तस्मात् वेश्यारूपा स्वतन्त्रता उपमारूपकाद्यलंकाराणां प्रयोगेण कविः हास्यरसमपि संसृजति तथा व्यंग्यमपि करोति।

डॉ० वनमाली विस्वालः स्वकाव्यमाध्यमेन नेतृणां तेषां कपटकौशलं च चित्रयति।

"निर्वाचने खलु विजित्य पदं महान्तं
स्वार्थाय हा प्रतिपदं जनतास्तुदन्ति।
रक्षाछ्लेन वत! देशमिमं मुषन्ति
ह्याखुर्गजाननमहो! कवलीकरोति।।

(सङ्गमेनाभिरामा-काव्यसंग्रहस्थे आखुर्गजाननमहो कवलीकरोति काव्ये, पृ० 11)

आचार्यदिगम्बरमहापात्रमहोदयानां काव्यमुपभोग्यमस्ति।

"न योग्यता नेतृपदाय काचित्
न लोकसेवा न च विज्ञता च।
न जातु शास्त्रनुमता च बुद्धि-
र्यघस्ति किञ्चिद् वद तत् स्वरूपम्।।

(दुर्नीतिपुराणम्, 36)

तथैवः–

"राजनीतिं बुधा आहुर्दुर्नीतेरादिकारणम्।
सम्बन्धश्च तयोर्नित्यम् इत्युक्तौ नास्ति संशयः।। 117।।

दुर्नीती राजनीति साऽनुगच्छति पदे पदे।
सर्वनाशञ्च सर्वेषां कष्टं हा कुरुतेऽनिशम्"।। 115।। (पृ० 20)

कविः डॉ० इच्छाराम द्विवेदीः प्रणवः राजनीतिं तमसया साकं तुलयति। सा तुलना चमत्कारमावहति। अधोलिखिते काव्ये तमः पदं व्यंग्यमस्ति,

"कीदृशमिदन्तमः
वकाः सरःसु समाधौ मग्नाः
हंसानां संकल्पा भग्नाः
राष्ट्रदेवता हृतवस्त्रेयं

भयविकम्पिता रोदिति नग्ना
तुच्छजम्बुकैः
सिंहजनानां व्यर्थीकष्टतः श्रमः
कीदृशमिदन्तमः।। (पृ० 32)

चित्रणमिदं वास्तवमस्ति। तस्मादस्ति रसमयम्। विषमता काव्यबीजमस्ति। प्रतीकात्मिका कविता राष्ट्रदेवताया दुरावस्थां सम्यक् प्रतिपादयति। अस्माकं पूर्वजैः स्वाधीनतासंग्रामिभिः देशस्यास्य समुद्धाराय कृतः श्रमः कथं निष्फलो जातः, कवि तदेव तथ्यमुद्घाटयति। के ते जम्बुकाः? पाठकाः स्वयमेव ज्ञास्यन्ति अनावश्यकी तस्य समालोचना।

बच्चूलाल अवस्थीमहोदयानां राजनीतिचित्रमपि उल्लेखनीयमस्ति। व्यञ्जनया वृत्या कविः नेतृणां कृत्रिमं क्रन्दनं विशेषरूपेणास्माकं नेत्रपथमानेतुं प्रयतते।

"नेता कण्टकशोधनाय यतते स्वस्यैव मार्गस्य यत्
तस्मात् कण्टकजालमेव विकिरल्लोकतन्त्राध्वनः।
लोकोऽयं क्षतजाप्लुताङ्घ्रिरधुना कार्पण्यभष्टददूयते
नेता रोदिति नक्रवाष्पविकलं तत्पीडया पीडितः।।"

(प्रतानिनी, पृ० 171)

अपरे नेतृस्तवाख्ये काव्ये नेतृणां मिथ्याभाषणं तेषां कुप्रवृत्तिं च सुन्दररीत्या कविः वर्णयति। सामान्यमपि वस्तु कविकौशलवशात् मधुरं प्रतीयते। उदाहरणं यथाः–

"आगच्छेत् स समाजवादविभवो यस्य प्रसादात् परं
स्वच्छन्दं विहरन्तु रन्तुमनसः स्वैराधिकाराः स्त्रियः।
इत्थं कूट-कथंकथः प्रवचनैर्मिथ्यावदानक्षमो
नेता मल्लनटोऽक्षवाटमटति द्वन्द्वाय च व्यूहते।।" (नेतृस्तवः)

भागीरथिनन्द शर्मा भारतीयगणतन्त्रे काव्ये किं कवयति पश्यन्तुः

"प्रयति निर्वाचनहुंकष्टतिर्यदा प्रविश्य नेतारः अहोऽत्र संसदः।
वदन्ति नाना मधुरां वृथा गिरम् नटो यथा भाति विभिन्नतां वहन्।।"

डॉ० केशवप्रसादगुप्तोऽपि स्वरचिते 'वेदनाऽनुभूयते' काव्ये समाजस्य विकलाङ्गं विलोक्य वेदनाविदारितः सन् तस्य वर्णनं करोति स्पष्टभाषया। गीतिमयीयं काव्यकलिका प्रभावशालिनी। यथा पठने जायते तथैवास्य भावग्रहणे। उदाहरणरूपेण पद्यद्वयं प्रदीयते।

"कीदृशी निशाचरी वेदनाऽनुभूयते।
आगताऽपि योजना कल्पना प्रतीयते।।

धर्मवादकोटरे माधवो विराजते
क्षेत्रवादकोटरे दानवः प्रमोदते।
जातिवादपोषिता पूतना महीयते
कीदृशी निशाचरी वेदनाऽनुभूयते।।

द्वेषरागकीर्तिता मन्त्रणा सुपूज्यते
कूटनीतिपण्डिता मन्थराऽपि लज्जते।
मन्त्रिणां विमोहिनी वञ्चना प्रगीयते
कीदृशी निशाचरी वेदनाऽनुभूयते।।"

(भारतोदय:, दिसम्बर:, पृ० 20)

डॉ० रवीन्द्रकुमारः पण्डा 'स्वतन्त्रताशतके' राजनीतेरित्थं चित्रं प्रस्तौति। तस्य मते राजनीतिरेका पिशाची। सा जनान् न्यायमार्गं त्यक्त्वान्यायमार्गे चलितुं प्रेरयति।

"देशे स्वतन्त्रेऽद्य कुराजनीतिः
भुङ्क्ते पिशाची संकलाः सुनीतिः।
अन्यायमार्गे चलितुं हि लोकान्
सा राजनीतिश्च ददाति शक्तिम्।।

नवा पिशाची नवराजनीतिः
क्षणे क्षणे सा नवतां विधत्ते।
आयान्ति यान्ति कति शासकाश्च
तथैव सन्तीह सदा समस्याः।।"

(पृ० 25)

नेतारः देशस्य समस्याविषये केवलं प्रलपनं कुर्वन्ति।

सर्वासां समस्यानां समाधानार्थं प्रतिज्ञां कुर्वन्ति। तया प्रतिज्ञया मानवान् मुह्यन्ति। यावत्कालपर्यन्तं निर्वाचनमस्ति तावत्कालपर्यन्तं तिष्ठति सा प्रतिज्ञा, प्राप्ते सिंहासने सत्ताप्रमत्तो नेता सर्वं विस्मरति।

आचार्यदिगम्बरमहापात्रस्य राजनीतिकाव्यं तस्या भयंकरत्वं सूचयति। तस्मान्नमस्करोति ताम्।

"हे राजराजेश्वरि राजनीते!
वन्दामहे दूरत एव नित्यम्।
व्रज व्रज त्वं व्रज राजधानीं
न किन्तु विद्वद्वर-भावधानीम्।।

हे राजराजेश्वरि! राजनीते!
किं ते प्रशस्तिं करवाणि कीर्त्तेः।
अनर्थसृष्टेस्त्वमिहासि बीजं
गृहे गृहे यत्र तव प्रचारः।।"

(जनतन्त्रविमर्शः, पृ० 33)

राजनीतिः देवतायते कविनयने। सा देशेऽस्मिन् सर्वस्यानर्थस्य मूलकारणमस्ति। तया भयभीतः कविरतो वन्दनं करोति। दुर्जनं प्रथमं वन्देति न्यायेनात्याधुनिकः संस्कृतकविः राजनीतिदेवीं वन्दते। तस्य वन्दनमिदं न किञ्चित्प्राप्तये। न तस्य दुःखोपशमाय। परन्तु स व्याजोक्ति-अलंकारेण तस्या राजनीतेः सर्वध्वंसकारणत्वं वेदयते।

यद्यपि लघुलेखेऽस्मिन् केवलं संस्कृतसाहित्ये विद्यमानस्य राजनीतिचित्रणस्य बिन्दु-मात्रमुपस्थापितमस्ति तथाप्यस्मात् सहृदयपाठकाः संस्कृतकवीनां राजनीतिं प्रति सामष्टिकीं प्रतिक्रियां विज्ञातुं शक्नुवन्तीति विश्वासः। आधुनिके काव्यजगति एतादृशी काव्यनिर्माणपरम्परा प्रतिदिनं समृद्धा भवति। अनेन कविः समाजस्य प्रगतये निरन्तरं चिन्तासन्तुलितः संस्कृतकविः दुर्नीतिर्निवाराणाय परमेश्वरपादयुगले भावगद्गदः सन् स्तोत्रकाव्यं न समर्पयति। न वा सः रसाप्लुतो सन् तया भावनया आनन्दकन्दरं प्रविशति सन्तोषाय। स सत्यसुन्दरं वस्तु कलाकौशलकर्मणा सुन्दरीकुर्वन् पाठकानां सम्मुखे तथा परिवेशयते येन ते सूक्ष्मातिसूक्ष्मं वस्तुत्तत्वं ज्ञास्यन्ति तथाच रसानन्दमनुभविष्यन्ति। लघुकाव्यानामियं विशिष्टता यत् तानि यस्मिन् कस्मिन् काले पठनीयानि सन्ति। अस्मिन् युगे समयस्य समस्या सर्वेषामेवास्ति। कारुण्यमपि न कस्मै रोचते।

शृङ्गारचित्रणमपि पिष्टपेषणमिव न सुखविशेषमुत्पादयति। अस्मिन् काले राजनीतिविषयमाधारीकृत्यानि लघुकाव्यानि मनोरञ्जनसाधनानि भवत्यैव। मन्मतेऽत्याधुनिकीयं काव्यनिर्वाणपरम्परा सन्तोषदायिनीति नास्ति शङ्कावकाशः। अर्वाचीनसंस्कृतसाहित्यक्षेत्रे नूतनत्वसंशोधनतत्पराः सुरसिकाः कवयः तेषां नवनवोल्लेखप्रज्ञाप्राबल्येन हास्यरसं प्राधान्यं प्रददति। सरलया, सुकुमारया भाषया शैल्या च संस्कृतभाषायाः प्रचारकार्यमपि ते कुर्वन्ति। राजनीतिसदृशा विषयाः सामान्यानां

जनानामपि प्रिया: सन्ति। ये जना अतिगम्भीरे दर्शनतत्त्वसंवलिते विषये परमानन्दं काव्यरसोत्पन्नं प्राप्तुं न सन्ति समर्थास्ते राजनीत्यादिविषयेषु रुचिं धारयन्ते। अपरञ्च या भ्रान्तधारणा जनानां मन:सु विद्यते यत् संस्कृतं केवलं पौराणिकं भक्तिविषयं साहित्यस्यावयवरूपेण संगृह्यतो सा शनै: शनैरस्माकं कवीनां प्रयत्नैर्विनश्यतीति प्रमोद:।

आधुनिकसंस्कृतसाहित्ये कति व्यक्तिनिष्ठकाव्यानां परिचयः

अपारे कविपरंपरावाहिनि संसारे नवनवोन्मेषप्रतिभाशालिभिः गम्भीरार्थतत्त्व-विद्भिर्महाकविभिर्विनिर्मितानि लोकोत्तरानन्दसन्दोहसमुत्पादकानि मनोहराणि काव्यानि केवलं क्षणिकभावात्मकसुखानुभूतिप्राप्तये न भवन्ति। तेषां रमणीयार्थप्रतिपादकानां काव्यानां मानवस्य चरित्रविकासाय तथा समाजस्य सर्वविधकल्याणसाधनाय संविद्यते महती चावश्यकतेति विषये नास्ति शङ्कालेशः कस्यापि सहृदयस्य मनसि। काव्यं यदि कमनीयकल्पनासन्निविष्टं भूत्वा केवलं मनोरञ्जनसाधनविशेषं भवेत्तर्हि तस्य मूल्यहानिर्भवतीति न संशयः। काव्यस्यासाधारणं प्रयोजनं प्रतिपादयिता मम्मटाचार्येण यथार्थेन काव्यप्रकाशे निगदितं यत् काव्यं जनान् 'रामादिवत् प्रवर्तितव्यं न रावणादिवदिति' व्यवहारज्ञानमुपदिशति। आदिकवेर्वाल्मीकेरारभ्य अद्यावधि कवयो महाकवयश्च तामेव शिष्टपरम्परामनुसृत्य जनान् सन्मार्गे संप्रेरयितुं चरित्रनिर्मातुं च नवरसमयानि सुन्दराणि सुखकराणि काव्यानि रचयन्तीति हेतोः संस्कृतभाषासरस्वती सुतरां समृद्धा भवति। आनन्दवर्धनेन ध्वन्यालोके यद्यपि रामायणरचनायाः कारणं 'क्रौञ्चद्वन्द्ववियोगोत्थः शोकः श्लोकत्वमागतः' इति कथितं तथापि जनानां समक्षं लोकोत्तरं रामसीतालक्ष्मणभरतादीनां चरित्रमेवोपस्थापयितुं महाकविना वाल्मीकिना प्रणीतं रामायणमिति धारणा तु स्पष्टा भवत्येव। अतः कथयितुं शक्यते यत् चरित्र-निर्माणार्थमुत्तमकाव्यानि कवयो विरचयन्ति। चरित्रनिर्माणद्वारा व्यक्तेर्व्यक्तित्वमेव विकसति। विद्यमानेषु पद्यकाव्येषु च व्यक्तिनिष्ठकाव्यानां प्रचलितास्ति संस्कृत-साहित्यजगति सुमहती परंपरा। विशेषतः संस्कृतसाहित्यस्याधुनिके काले परम्परेयं सुसमृद्धा संजाता। स्वाधीनतासंग्रामे प्राणोत्सर्गकृतवतां देशभक्तानां महापुरुषाणां विशालं व्यक्तित्वमाधारीकृत्य नैकानि काव्यानि महाकाव्यानि च विरचितानि दृश्यन्ते। यद्यपि काव्यं गद्यपद्योभयमिति तद्विदो मन्यन्ते तथापि वेदसूक्तान्यारभ्य इतिहासपुराणादिषु प्रस्फुटितः काव्यमार्गः प्रायेण पद्यसरण्यैव प्रसारितः। छन्दोबद्धेषु वाक्येषु गेयपरिस्पन्दः

प्रचुरतरमनुभूयते। गेयगर्भितेषु पद्येषु भावशबलता झटिति चमत्कारमादधाति। सहृदयाः काव्यज्ञा न केवलं पदानि वाक्यानि च काव्यपाठसमये स्वयं व्यक्तमुच्चरन्ति, अपि तु कविस्वभावनिष्ठेन कविना काव्यनिर्माणवेलायां स्वस्मै स्वयं श्रावितं गेयवृत्तम-नुश्रृण्वन्तीवास्वादयन्ति। श्रव्यकाव्यस्य चमत्कारस्तदा वाचकेन स्फुटतरमनुभूयते। अतः कविरत्नब्रह्मानन्दशुक्लमहोदयः कथयतिः-

ते वै जयन्ति नितरां कवयो यदीयां
वाङ्माधुरीमनुसरन्त्यपरेऽधुनापि ।
वाल्मीकि-शोधित-नवीन-कवित्व-मार्गं
व्यासादयोप्यनुययुर्जनजीवनाय ।।

(नेहरुचरितम् १/७)

तथैव त्र्यम्बकशर्मणा कथितम्-

हरन्ति सन्तः कवयो निरन्तरं नितान्तमन्तःकरणस्य दूषणम्।
सरस्वती यद्रसनाङ्गणे गुणैश्चिरं विरन्तुं सरसा रसोमले।।

अस्मिन् लघुनिबन्धे कतिपयानां प्रमुखानां व्यक्तिनिष्ठकाव्यानां परिचयमात्रं प्रदीयते।

महापुरुषाणां चरितानि कीर्तितानि कविभिर्महान्तमामोदं जनयन्ति। आदर्शास्ते जननिवहस्य येन पथा सञ्चरन्ते, यां पद्धतिमङ्गीकुर्वन्ति, यथा वा प्रवृत्तिमन्तो भवन्ति तथैवेतरे प्रवर्तन्ते। ते हि पथिकृतो भवन्ति पथिदर्शाच्च। आभाति च लोकः-'महाजनो येन गतः सः पन्थाः' इति। महाजनानुसृतपथस्तेषां चरितादेव सुज्ञानो भवितुमर्हन्ति, अत एव तेषां चरितकीर्तने विदुषां प्रवृत्तिः। आधुनिकैः सुरगवीकविभिर्गांधि-जवाहरलाल-राजेन्द्रप्रसाद प्रमुखाणां नेतृणां जीवनवृत्तमधिकृत्य भूयस्यः कृतयस्तेषु जीवत्स्वेव प्रणीताः। स्वनामधन्यस्य लोकमान्यबालगङ्गाधरतिलकस्यासामान्येन नेतृपदेन ख्यातस्य सुभाषचन्द्रस्य च चरितानि महाकाव्यद्वारेण लोके चिरस्थायितां नीतानि। इन्दिरागान्धेरप्यनेकाः प्रशस्तयः प्रणीताः प्रकाशिताश्च। दरिद्रभारतस्याशा-तन्तुनिबन्धनबन्धुरस्य कतिपयान् मासानेव देशस्यास्य प्रधानमन्त्रिपदमलंकृत्य स्मरणीयतां गतस्य लालबहादुरशास्त्रिणोऽपि जीवनगाथां कवित्वमार्गेण चर्चितुं च कैश्चन प्रयासः कृतः। मातृ-सेवा-परधर्म-धुरीणस्य कृषकवर्गाधिकारानधिकृत्य कृत-बारडोलीमहासत्याग्रहस्याग्रगण्यस्य शतशः खण्डेषु खण्डितस्य स्त्रक्-सूत्र-न्यायेनैकराष्ट्ररूपे बन्धकस्य लौहपुरुषस्य जीवनविषये महाकाव्यापि विरचितमस्ति। एवमपि भगतसिंह-वीरसावरकर-वीरसुरेन्द्रसायप्रभृतीनां महापुरुषाणां विषये काव्यानि

लिखितानि अद्यापि च लिख्यन्ते। इयं सुमहती परम्परा अर्वाचीनसंस्कृतश्रियं संवर्धयति साहित्यक्षेत्रं च पुष्णाति। काव्यमाध्यमेन सहृदयाः पाठका न केवलमेतेषां महापुरुषाणां जीवनवृत्तं ज्ञातुं पारयन्ति अपितु तेषामवदानविषये सम्यग् ज्ञान लभन्ते। अतस्तेषां प्रति समादरभावः साहित्यमाध्यमेन वर्धत एव।

नेहरूयशः सौरभम्

नेहरूवंशस्य प्रमुखस्तम्भो जवाहरलालनेहरूः विश्वविख्यातो महामानवो विद्यते। भारतीयस्वाधीनतासंघर्षे तस्यासाधारणं कृत्यं विश्वविदितं वर्तते तथैव स्वाधीनतानन्तरं राष्ट्रनिर्माणस्याधारशिलायाः सुदृढीकरणेऽपि तस्य प्रयासः सततस्मरणीयो वर्तते। अतोऽसौ सामान्यजनानां कृतेऽपि श्रद्धास्पदो वर्तते। ईदृशीं श्रद्धामनुभूय महाकविना गोस्वामीबलभद्रप्रसादशास्त्रिणा 'नेहरूयशः सौरभम्' नामधेय महाकाव्यं विरचितम्। वस्तुतः काव्यमेतत् तस्य राष्ट्रहिते कृतकार्याणां कृते कवेः श्रद्धाकुसुमाञ्जलिरेव आसीत्। उक्ते काव्ये नेहरूवंशं वर्णयता कविना राजकौलादारभ्य प्रियदर्शिन्या इन्दिराया पूर्वार्धचरितं यावत् कथानकं वर्णितम्।

न चेति या ना किल राष्ट्रभावना प्रदर्शिनी काव्यकलेवराश्रिता।
कथेयमादर्शचरित्रपद्धतेर्बिभर्ति कालमितयेऽपि गौरवम्।।

कवेश्चिरं मानसमन्थनोद्धृतं रसार्द्रमेतन्नवनीतमोदकम्।
यथा भवेल्लोकमनोहरं तथा तनोतु चित्ते नवराष्ट्रचेतनाम्।।

(नेहरूयशःसौरभम्, काव्यकथामुख, पृ० १५-१६)

इन्दिराजीवनम्

तेन कविना पुनः इन्दिराजीवनमिति चापरं महाकाव्यं विरचितम्। तत्तु तस्य वंशस्योत्तरार्धमिव विद्यते। महाकाव्येऽस्मिन् भारतरत्नभूताया गान्ध्युपाह्वायाः श्रीमत्या इन्दिरायास्तथा च तदात्मजस्य श्रीराजीवगान्धि महाभागस्य प्रशस्तं चरित्रं राष्ट्रहिते तयोर्बलिदानं च काव्यकलालङ्कृतैर्मधुरैः सरसमनोहरैर्भावोन्मेषभव्यैश्च काव्यतत्त्वैर्वर्णितमस्ति। अस्मिन् काव्ये न केवलमिन्दिराराजीवचरितमपितु समाजदर्शनं चापि प्रस्तुतम्। अत्र राजनीतिधर्मप्राजतन्त्रनियतिभवितव्यता अपि व्याख्याताः सन्ति। मानवीयमूल्यानां महत्त्वं, राष्ट्रस्य गरिमा, तत्कृते भारतीयजानानां समर्पणभावना अपि प्रकाशिताः सन्ति। समाजे विकृतराजनीतेर्नर्तनं हिंसायास्ताण्डवं स्वार्थवृत्तिर्यथैव शब्दचित्रैः काव्येऽस्मिन् प्रस्तुतानि सन्ति तथैव मानवजीवनस्य क्षणभङ्गुरता त्यागस्य महत्त्वं राष्ट्रियजीवनं चापि सन्मार्गदर्शनाय चित्रितमस्ति।

कविः स्वयं कथयति यदिदं महाकाव्यं नेहरूयशः सौरभमिव दलगतप्रतिबद्धतया राजनीत्या वा नास्त्यपितु 'चारुचारित्र्यगीतिः', 'सहृदयहृदि वेद्या भव्यभावानुभूतिः' 'मङ्गलानां प्रसूति' श्चास्ति।

न च दलगतनीतिर्नाप्यसौ राजनीतिः
सरसकृतिरियं मे चारुचारित्र्यगीतिः।
सहृदयहृदि वेद्या भव्यभावानुभूति-
र्भवतु कविगिरेयं मङ्गलानां प्रसूतिः।।

(इन्दिराजीवनम्, १९/४३)

कविः धर्मस्य महत्त्वं सुन्दरैः सरलैश्च शब्दकुसुमैर्वणयति यत्तु ग्रहणीयं तथा स्पृहणीयं प्रतिभाति।

को नु धर्मो जनान् शास्ति वै हिंसनं
को नु धर्मो वदेल्लोकविध्वंसनम्।
धर्म आमोदते लोकसंरक्षणम्
धर्म एवाह वै राष्ट्रसंरक्षणम्।।
धर्म आशंसते स्नेहसंरक्षणम्
भ्रातृभावप्रबुद्धैकतारक्षणम्।
राष्ट्रसंरक्षणं, बन्धुतारक्षणं
मानवीयैर्गुणैर्लोकसंस्मरणम्।।

(तत्रैव, १०/२५-२९)

चन्द्रचरितम्

बभूबुर्भवन्ति चैव भवितारो भारतभुवि शतसहस्रशो नेतारः किन्तु 'नेता' पदेऽलङ्कृतोऽस्ति केवलं सुभाषचन्द्र इति तथ्यं सुविख्यातमेव। मनसा वाचा कर्मणा च भारतभूमिसुतः स्वदेशोद्धारहेतोर्यादृशं कण्टकाकीर्णवर्त्मावलम्ब्य यद् यन्महत्कर्म चक्रे तादृशमुदाहरणं न कुत्रापि श्रुतन्न दृष्टं कदाचन। एतदर्थं स एवांशावतार इवाद्यपि लोके गण्यते। अतीवाद्भुता विस्मयकारिणी च तस्य जीवनलीला प्रतीयते यतश्च येन देशान्तरेऽपि सैन्यसंघटनं कृत्वा दिग्दिगन्तस्याप्तमपि ब्रिटिशशासनं विनष्टीकर्तुं भगीरथप्रयत्नोऽकारि तेन तथा च विश्वमहायुद्धेस्तस्य रणव्यूहरचनाऽशियचमत्कारिणीव निश्चीयते सामरिकदृष्ट्या च लोमहर्षिणीव प्रतिभाति। कारणेनानेनैव सुभाषस्य क्षमता प्रतिभासामर्थ्यानि लोके युगे च स्मरणीयानि जातानि। यद्यपि भारतीयानां विश्वासोऽस्ति

यद् गान्धिनोऽहिंसाव्रतेन लभते भारतः स्वतन्त्रतां तथापि राजनीतिज्ञा अद्याप्येवं स्वीकुर्वन्ति यत् सुभाषस्य सशस्त्रक्रान्त्या ब्रिटिशा भयभीताः संजातास्तथा च यदासौ आंग्लीयानां रिपून् स्वपक्षे कृतवान् तदा भाविसंघातसङ्कटं समीक्ष्यैव लन्दनसिंहासनं सहसा विचलितमभूत्। ततस्ते ब्रिटिशा भारताय स्वराज्यं प्रदातुं कटिबद्धा बभूवुश्चेति। एतदर्थं सुभाषस्य जीवनवृत्तं मिथिलेशकुमारीमिश्रेण संस्कृतवाङ्मयेऽवतारयितुं गीतगद्यमयः प्रयासः कृतः। उदाहरणमेकं द्रष्टव्यम्।

दासता वा यापराधीनता व्यस्ता
भारते यत्प्रचलितं हि दुःशासनम्।
ये बहुपीडितं ताडितं तापितं
साम्प्रतं दृश्यते शोषितं जीवनम्।।

विश्वभानुः

भास्वरे भारतनिवास प्रागुदीच्चामुदयमुपलभ्य प्रवृद्धतेजसा भुवनलयमुद्भासयन्तो जगद्देशिकमहिमानमधिगत्य सर्वकालपरोपकारव्रतदीक्षितामितिसविषयीभूतानां ज्योतिर्मण्डले देदीप्यन्तेतरां पूजनीयाः श्रीमद्विवेकानन्दस्वामिपादाः येषां प्रख्यातमितिवृत्तमुपजीव्य निर्मितं महाकाव्यं विश्वभानुः। अस्मिन् सर्गबन्धे प्रबन्धे आजन्मशुद्धस्याफलोदयकर्मणो दयावीरस्यास्य महामनीषिणो गुणशीलचरितवर्णनमिषेण सनातनवैदिकसंस्कृति-स्रवन्त्याः पूर्वमहिमा वस्तुगत्या अनुरञ्जितो भवति। भाविभारत-भविकार्थमभीप्स्यमानस्य महार्थस्य प्राप्तये स्वामिपादैरुद्बोधिता पद्धतिरपि तत्त्वार्थध्वनिभरितैः पदनिचयैः प्रकाशिता दृश्यते। काव्यमिमं पदवाक्यवृत्तगत-माधुर्येणोप्रक्रियमाणां रसभावनिबन्धनामनुभूतिं हृदि समुद्भासयति। पञ्चपञ्चाशदधिक-पञ्चशतैः श्लोकैर्निबद्धे विश्वभानौ षोडशमन्तिमं च विहाय इतरेषु पद्यसङ्ख्य। प्रतिसर्गं पञ्चविंशत्या नियता। सर्गान्तदीर्घवृत्तपरिपाटी तु प्राचीनेषु केषुचिन्महाकाव्येष्विवात्रापि बाह्यशोभामात्रमिति नादृता। अनुष्टुबुपजातिवंशस्थवियोगिनिपुष्पिताग्रावसन्ततिलका-पृथ्वीसमाख्यैः सप्तभिर्वृत्तैर्निबद्धेस्मिन् काव्ये प्रतिसर्ग वृत्तभेदोपादानाय निर्बन्धो न दृश्यते।

एवमेव विश्वभानौ षट्सु सर्गेषूपजातिः, चतुर्षु वसन्ततिलका, त्रिषु वंशस्थं, त्रिष्वनुष्टुप्, द्वयोर्वियोगिनी, द्वयोः, पुष्पिताग्रा, एकस्मिन् पृथ्वी चेति पश्यामः। रीतिरस्य काव्यस्य स्वभाविकीति यत्र कुत्रापि द्रष्टुं शक्यते। यथा–

विजित्य मायां हृदि सारदर्शिनः
समस्तलोकोदयचोदिताशयाः।

सुदुर्लभाः सन्ति विशुद्धनाविकाः
सनातने तत्त्वविचारसागरे।। (विश्वभानुः १/९)

बन्धपारुष्यरहिता शब्दकाठिन्यवर्जिताः नातिदीर्घसमासा च वैदर्भीरीतिरेवात्र प्रायेण दृश्यते। क्वचिद् गौडीयापि संघटना विषयानुगुण्येन समुपात्ता। यथा–

भ्रमरूपमरीचिकाहरी परिखीभूतपरार्ध्यनिर्झरी।
मुनिमानससोदरी परि स्फुरतात् काशिपुरी पुरीश्वरी।।

(तत्रैव २/२३)

आलङ्कारीकैः सार एवं प्रदर्श्यते–

शब्दो विवक्षितार्थैकवाचकोन्येषु सत्स्वपि।
अर्थः सहृदयाह्लादकारिस्वपन्दसुन्दरः।।

एवं विधानि विवक्षितविशेषाभिधानक्षमाणि पदानि वर्णनेषु प्रयुञ्जानः कविधर्मज्ञः काव्यकर्ता चमत्कारमादधाति। परिवृत्तिं यत्र पदानि न सहन्ते शब्दन्यासनिष्णाताः पाकगुणं पश्यन्ति। विश्वभानौ द्राक्षापाकः प्रायेण परीक्षकैरनुभवितुं शक्यते। अग्निः शुष्केन्धनमिव, स्वच्छजलं वस्त्रमिव, चित्तं व्याप्नुवन्ति प्रसादभूयिष्ठानि पदानि रसदीप्त्या बहुत्र सहृदयहृदयान्याह्लादयन्ति।

इन्दिरागान्धीचरितम्

भारतदेशस्य प्रधानमंत्री श्रीमती इन्दिरागांधी कोटिशो जनानां पूजनीयाऽभिवन्दनीया च। विशालस्य जम्बूद्वीपान्तर्गतस्य भारतभूखण्डस्य महापरिमाणस्याधिकदशानि वर्षाणि सफलं शासनमस्याः कमप्यसाधारणं गुणगरिमाणमाविष्करोति। भारतीया जनाः कथं सुखिनो भवन्तु, कथं च दैन्यं दारिद्र्यं वा परिहरन्त्वितोयमनारतं चिन्तयति स्म। तेषां दैन्यादुद्धारः समुन्नतिर्वा प्रधानमन्त्रिणी प्रथमं कृत्यमित्यभ्युपैति। एतदर्थमेव तथा विंशतिसूत्रात्मक आर्थिकः कार्यक्रम उद्भावित प्रवर्तितश्च। अस्मिन् महाकाव्ये पञ्चविंश सर्गाः सन्ति। काव्यस्य प्रारम्भे पूर्वपीठिका प्रदत्तास्ति। तत्र सत्यव्रतशास्त्रीमहोदया काव्यस्य प्रयोजनमित्थं वदन्ति।

विशुद्धबुद्धेर्जनताप्रियाया
दिगन्तविश्रान्तयशः कथायाः।
हृद्यं विदुष्याः शुभमिन्दिरायाः
गीर्वाणवाण्या चरितं ब्रवीमि।। (श्लोकः ७)

प्रतापराणायनम्

ओगेटि परीक्षितच्छर्मभिः राणाप्रतापनृपतिचरितमत्यद्भुतमुररीकृत्य विरचितं प्रतापराणायनं नाम विशालं महाकाव्यम्। रुचिररससमन्वितेऽपि विविधवर्णन-वर्णच्छ्व्यभास्वरेऽपि अस्मिन् काव्ये न कविना काचिदपीतिहासः विकृतिमापादितः। अत एवायं काव्यग्रन्थः सन्नपि रुक्षविवेचनवर्जितः भावानुबन्धी रसस्यन्दी इतिहासोऽपि भवति। प्रायशस्त्रिशतवर्षेभ्यः प्राक् परकीयमोगलसाम्राज्यावलितभीषणपरतन्त्र्यक्रकच-पाशवशात् अनल्पपीडिताया बहुव्यथिताया अतिनिर्विण्णाया भारतभानुः कन्धरां विमोचयितुं कराङ्गुलिपरिमेया एव नृपतयः संस्कृतेर्जीवातुभूता इव, प्रयत्नानां परा-काष्ठां व्यदधुः। तेषु अन्यतमः महाराष्ट्रेषु लब्धजनिः स्वनामधन्यः शाहसूनुः छत्रपतिः शिवः। तत्पूर्वं च राजस्थानराजपुत्र स्वप्रतापपराभावितपारतन्त्र्यध्वान्तः राणाप्रतापः। विरलतरा हि एतादृशानां महाप्रभावाणां पुरुषाणामाविर्भावा भवन्ति, ये हि क्षणमात्रमपि अविश्रम्य, सोढ्वा च शारीरानपि क्लेशान् बहुतरान्, स्वातन्त्र्ययज्ञकुण्डेषु तिलशः स्वात्मविसर्जनं कुर्वन्तः स्वदेशार्थमात्महोमं विदधते। शिवछत्रपतिमुद्दिश्य नैकानि महाकाव्यानि महाकविभिः प्रणितानि। तेषु 'क्षत्रपतिचरितं' महाकाव्यं सुप्रसिद्धमस्ति।

महाकविः ओगेटि परीक्षितशर्मामहोदयः राष्ट्रभक्तस्य राणाप्रतापस्य विक्रमैकरसं प्रत्यवायसङ्कटं चरितमत्युद्भुतमतिपावनं हृदि ध्यायं राणासमीपतां समासादितुमिव तन्निवासपरिपावितपांसूनि चित्तोड-उदयपुरादि-दिगन्तराणि, तत्पूजितएकलिङ्गेश्वरादि-देवतामन्दिराणि, तद्विहितपराक्रमस्थानानि हल्दिघाट्याद्याख्यानि च दर्शं दर्शं, तत्रत्येभ्यः ग्रामवृद्धेभ्यश्च राणाप्रतापस्य वीराद्भुतकथायुताः गाथाश्च श्रावं श्रावं, प्रत्नमपि ऐतिहासिकं घटनाक्रमं नितान्ततृषितेन संवेदनक्षमेण तन्मयेनेव हृदयेन मनश्चक्षुषा च साक्षादिव अन्वभूत। स एवानुभवो वस्तुगत्या वाचामगोचरोऽपि, अर्थसार्थः शब्दराशिरभवदस्मिन् महाकाव्ये। किं तावत् प्रयोजनमस्य काव्यस्येति स्वयं कविनिम्नलिखितैः पद्यैः स्पष्टीकरोति।

यावत् वाणी चिरं तिष्ठेत् तावद्राणायनं भुवि।
लोके निद्राणजन्तूना कर्तव्यं शासयन् ध्रुवम्।।

यावदर्कः चरेत् शून्ये भारतं जगतीतले।
तावद्राणायनं भूयात् लोककल्याणसिद्धये।।

देशभक्तं महावीरं कथं मे पूर्वसूरयः।
विस्मृत्य कृतवन्तो यत् लोके काव्यचयं महत्।।

राणाजीवितमुद्दिश्य काव्यं नास्तीति संस्कृते।
अपवादात्मकं वाक्यं निरस्तु कवयाम्यहम्।।

(प्रतापराणायनम्, पृ० ११)

ब्रह्मानन्दशुक्लमहोदयः स्वकीये काव्यरत्ने महापुरुषाणां गुणकीर्तनमित्थं करोति।

ये मानवा मनुजतां परिपालयन्तो
राष्ट्रोन्नतौ निजधियं विनियोजयन्ति।
ते वन्दनीयचरणा उभयत्र नूनं
लब्ध्वा यशोऽतिविमलं सततं जयन्ति।।

येषां मनो न रमते विपुलेऽपि वित्ते
नैवात्मजे न च कुले न च लोकसौख्ये।
नाना-विभूति-कलनां ललनां विहत्य
ते सर्व-विश्वहृदयाःसुतरां जयन्ति।।

तेषां प्रशस्तयशसां किल वर्णनाय
बद्धादरोऽपि नहि वेद्मि निजात्मयोगम्।
पूता भविष्यति ममापि मतिस्तथापि
मत्वेत्थमेव चलितोऽस्मि गतिं विधातुम्।।

(नेहरूचरितम्, १/११, १२, १३)

श्रीस्वामि-विवेकानन्दचरितम्

युगपुरुषस्य विवेकानन्दस्य प्रभावशाली व्यक्तित्वमपि संस्कृतकवीनां हृदयान् समाकर्षति। एतदर्थं गद्यरूपेण पद्यरूपेण च नैकानि काव्यानि महाकाव्यानि च तस्य जीवनोपरि विलिखितानि दृश्यन्ते। विश्वभानोश्चर्चा अस्माभिः पूर्वं कृतास्ति। अपरमप्येकं महाकाव्यं श्रीस्वामि-विवेकानन्दचरितनामधेयं त्र्यम्बकभण्डारकरेण विरचितमस्ति। तत्तु काव्यनायकस्य विवेकानन्दस्य जीवनदर्शनमतिस्पष्टं करोति। भावपूर्णं सरल-पदावलियुतं वैदर्भीरीतिमण्डितं महाकाव्यमिदं व्यक्तिनिष्ठकाव्येषु स्वतन्त्रस्थानमर्हति। उदाहरणमेकं प्रदीयते।

श्रीरामकृष्ण-युगमुज्ज्वलमेकसंस्थं
जातं जनेष्जननि विश्वजनीनमुच्चैः।
वन्दे तमन्धतमसावृतजीववृन्दे
प्रज्वालितो जगति येन विवेकदीपः।।

(श्रीस्वामिविवेकानन्दचरितम् १/१)

लौहपुरुषावदानम्

भारतस्य स्वातन्त्र्यसंग्रामे महात्मागांधि-जवाहरलालप्रभृतिनेत्रन्तरवत् वल्लभभाई-पटेलस्य 'सरदार' इति यथार्थेनोपाधिना प्रसिद्धस्य योगदानं न कस्माच्चिदपि न्यूनमुपेक्षणीयं च। राष्ट्रीयमहासभाया नायकेषु गांधि-जवाहरौ स च मूर्धन्या अभवन्। स्वातन्त्र्यलभनान्तरं विभाजनादिभिरुपसर्गैः सर्वथा विशृंखलीभूतस्य भारतराष्ट्रस्य प्रशमनादिभिर्दाढ्तापादनेन नैकशतराज्यानां संघठनेन च कोऽपि निरतिशयो विशेषः स्फुरत्येव। वल्लभो राष्ट्रीयमहासभाया निष्ठावान् सदस्यस्तया प्रवर्तितेष्वान्दोलनेषु चान्यतमः सैनिकः सेनानी चावर्ततेति तज्जीवनचरितप्रसंगेन मद्यनिषेधवैदेशिकवस्त्र-प्रत्याख्यानलवणनिर्माणसविनयादेशभंगप्रभृतीनां संघर्षाणां विस्तृतं वर्णनमत्र लभ्यते। वल्लभचरितप्रसंगेन च राष्ट्रीयमहासभाया महात्मानो गांधेश्च सकलोऽपि स्वातन्त्र्यसंघर्षेतिहासोऽत्र समासत उपवर्णित इति। कतिपयाः श्लोकाः प्रदीयन्ते।

स्वातन्त्र्यमेवामथ भारतमाडुढौके
दीनं सुदुर्गतमसङ्ख्यतया विभिन्नम्।
तद् ये यता उद्धरन् निजबुद्धिरज्ज्वा
मुख्योऽस्ति वल्लभ उदारमतिस्तु तेषाम्।।

गौराङ्गदुर्नयजयक्षतसंघभावं
राज्येषु नैकशतकेषु पुनर्विभक्तम्।
यो भारतं स्वनयसूत्रबलेन नद्धं
चक्रे स शुक्रगुरुधी-विभवः प्रशस्यः।।

वित्तादिलाभपरिलुब्धधिया मयेयं
नोदीर्यते चपलचाटुकृतिः प्रभूणाम्।
यातश्चिराद्दिवमुदारमनाः सधुर्यै-
र्विस्मारितश्च खलु यः स तु किं प्रयच्छेत्।।

तस्यावदात-महिमा महनीयकीर्ते-
र्मूर्तेश्च विस्मयकरप्रतिभाभराणाम्।
श्रीवल्लभस्य जनवल्लभजीवनस्य
गन्मानसं कुतुकि सच्चरिते करोति।।

(लौहपुरुषावदानम्, पृ० ७-८)

एतानि महाकाव्यानि आधुनिकसंस्कृतसाहित्यस्य प्रतिनिधिभूतानि सन्ति। एतेषां

साहित्यक्षेत्रे स्वतन्त्रं स्थानमस्त्येव। महाकवयः काव्यनायकानां चरित्रं, जीवनं, गुणावलिं तस्य समाजसमुद्धाराय चोल्लेखनीयं योगदानं च सरलया भाषया, प्रसादगुणोपेत-वैदभरित्या उपमारूपकादिसुमनोहरैरलङ्कारैर्मण्डयित्वा तथ्यपूर्वकं चित्रयित्वा जनानां सम्मुखं समुपस्थापिवन्तः। सहृदयाः पाठकास्तान् सर्वान् पठित्वा न केवलं तेषां महापुरुषाणां विषये सम्यग्ज्ञानं लप्स्यन्ते अपितु ताभिः काव्यकृतिभिरुद्बुद्धाः सन्तो समाजहिताय संप्रेरिता भविष्यन्ति। धन्या इमे कवयो यदीयाभिः कृतिभिः संस्कृतसाहित्यं सम्प्रत्यपि भूमण्डलवर्तिसकलान्यसाहित्यं विजित्य विजृम्भते।

लोकोत्तराः प्रियतराः कृतयो रसार्द्रा
भावोन्नताः कृतिवरैरभिनन्दनीयाः।
विद्यावदातहृदया ललिता यदीयाः
स्तोतुं न तान् भवति कस्य मनः प्रसारः।।

*

Appendix

वन्दिनः स्वदेशचिन्ता

मन्दचायं मधुरमलयः शीतलो वाति सारः।
मल्ली-वाला स्मित-मुकुलिता दोलिता भृङ्गरङ्गैः।
लभ्यो वातायन-परिसरे माधवो वक्रभंग्या
किंवा गुप्तश्चर इव बहिर्वार्तिको याति दत्वा।। १।।

बाहारे बहइ केड़े सुशीतल
मधुर मलय मन्द मरुत।
नवमल्लीकढ़ि मुरुकि हसइ
भ्रमर दोलाए प्रेमे ता वृन्त।।

कवाट फाङ्करे चाहिंले बाङ्करे
थरे थरे आसे चोरा पबन।
से कि गुप्तचर बाहार खबर
देइ लुचि चालियाए बहन।।

स्निग्धस्पर्शैः पुलकितवपुर्भाति मुग्धं मुहूर्तं
जागर्त्येवं स्मृतिरतितरा हृत्पटे चारुचित्रं।
भार्गव्या वै तरुणसमये तीरदेशेऽभ्रमं वा
सायंवातं वकुल-सुरभि-स्फारितं सेवमानः।। २।।

से स्निग्ध परशे निमिष सम्भाषे
तापित प्राण मो पुरे पुलके।
केते सुखस्मृति जागे ए अन्तरे
केते चारुचित्र नाचे पलके।।

मने एवे आसे तरुण वयसे
बुलिथिलि येबे भार्गवीतीरे

पुनाङ्क बकुल, सौरभ सङ्कुल
सुबास शीतल सञ्ज समीरे।।

कृशाङ्ग-तोयासु च खेलति स्फुटं
सुमञ्जुला वीचिततिः मनोरमा।
सुकुञ्चितं कुन्तलमेव दक्षिणं
किमेव पल्ली-वनिता प्रसारयेत्।।३।।

क्षीणतीया नीरे खेले धीरे धीरे
सुमंजुला लघुलहरीमाला।
दक्षिण दिगकु कुञ्चित-कुन्तल
मेलाइ देइछि कि पल्लीबाला?

ग्रामीण-बाला कलसी-भरं जलं
यद्वा नयेद् वारि-विभङ्ग-कारितैः।
स्फीता तु तन्नील-मणि-प्रभान्विता
उर्मिद्युतिः संप्रसरेत् सुदूरकम्।।४।।

ग्राम समिन्तिनी चहलाइ पाणि
कलसरे येबे निअन्ति भरि।
नीलमणि दाम प्राय से लहरी
खण्डदूर क्षणे याए प्रसरि।।

गोपालबालः मृदुवेणुवादनैः
गोष्ठात्तु धेनुं नयति स्वधाम वा।
हृष्टास्तु यान्ति व्यवसायिनो गृहं
भञ्जीयगीतेः पद-पात-तत्पराः।।५।।

गाईआल पिला गोठु बाहुड़ाइ
आणुथाए गाई बेणु बजाइ।
हाट काम सारि फेरन्ति बेपारी,
भञ्ज चउपदी-पद पकाइ।।

'यागेश्वरी'-पीठतले प्रदीपकं
दत्त्वा कुमारी-कुल एति कौतुकात्।

का वा मुदा केलि-कला रसैः हसेत्
का वा तु पुष्पं वकुलं नयेत्द्रुतम्।।६।।

यागेश्वरी पाशे दीपदेइ बासे
आसन्ति कौतुके कुमारीकुल।
किए करे कलि आग संगे खेलि
किए बा गोटाए बउलफुल।।

'वन्धे' कदा वा भगिनी-पुरोऽटति
भ्राता तु भारं विनिधाय पृष्ठतः।
सन्ध्या-समाच्छादित-कालमीक्ष्य च
शीघ्रं प्रयातुं कथयन् मुहुः गृहम्।।७।।

याउँली कान्धरे केबे बा बन्धरे
भउणी आगरे चालइ भाइ,
शाशूघरे निए सन्ध्या देखि कहे
चाण्डे गोड़ काढ़ि चालिबा पाइँ।।

सवालकक्षा नवयौवनोन्नता
झटित्यहो नैव च याति चञ्चला।
युवव्रजः वीक्ष्य सलील-चातुरीं
परस्परं हीङ्गित-दान-तत्पराः।।८।।

नव यउबनी काखे पिला घेनि
चालि न पारइ जघनभारे।
ता चाहिं चपल युबा सङ्गिदल
परिहासे एक आनकु ठारे।।

पुनाङ्गशाखासु दिवान्ध-पत्रिणः
कियद्दिशादेत्य च दोलनायिताः।
नदी-तटोद्धूत-समीर-सेवितैः
तरु-प्रकंपै तरलाऽस्ति कंपिता।।९।।

कंतेआडु उड़ि आसन्ति बादुड़ि
झुलन्ति पुनाङ्ग-फलित शाखे।

नदी चपे चपे पादप प्रङ्कपे
चलापाङ्गी चाहें चमकि पाशे।।

स्मरामि वासान्त-विमूर्त्त-यामिनिं
सुरातिथेरर्च्चन-गौरवोज्ज्वलाम्।
कथं च कारा-भवन-प्रवासिनो
वृथा तु भावो मनसि प्रजायते।।१०।।

घर कथा क्रमे पड़ियाए मने
अतिथि आदर देब-अर्चना।
कारागार कक्षे किंपाइँ ए बक्षे
आणिबि आउ से वृथा भावना।।

वसन्तवात! स्फुरदीष्ट-संचरैः
प्रदेहि घातं मम वेश्मनि क्षणम्।
वद दुतं दक्षिणवर्त्तिकां हृदि
सुशान्ति-पीयूषरसं तथा भर।।११।।

हे बसन्त वात! मो द्वारे आघात
करभला आउथरे सदये।
दक्षिण दिगर कह समाचार
सिञ्च शान्तिसुधा क्षणे हृदये।।

प्रियस्थली मे नितरां व्यथाकुला
तवायनं सन्तत-शोक-विह्वला।
मदर्थ-सन्देश-रस-प्रदायिनो
भवेदहो मन्मन एव लोलुपम्।।१२।।

मोर प्रिस्थली केते निउछालि
करिथिबे तब आसिबा बाटे।
देइथिबे परा केते कि सन्देश
शुणिबाकु मन अछि उच्चाटे।।

'मंजूषा' याः मुकुट-सुषमं द्राङ्महेन्द्रादिपुष्पं
गन्धोद्भूतं तव च नयनातिथ्यमाप्तं स्वरूपात्।

प्रेम्णा ते वाऽयन-पथि तरुः नर्त्तनानन्दरक्तः
शाखा पाणि-प्रसरण-विधौ स्वागतिं ज्ञापयन् वा ।। १३ ।।

करिथिब भेट मंञ्जूषा-मुकुट
महेन्द्र शइल सुबास फुल।
तब समागमे नाचिथिबे प्रेमे
दोइलाइ तरु-भुज-सङ्कुल।।

गंजामस्योपहरति मधुस्नातमेवं पुरस्तात्
रम्योद्यानं नयन-रसना-नासिका-स्वाद-धायि।
रम्भा-विल्वं पनस-सपुरीं लेम्बु-तालं रसालं
किं चावश्यं स्पृशसि तु विधे रक्षणाय प्रकामम्।। १४।।

रसना नयन नासा-रसायन
स्वादशोभा गन्धभरा आधार,
गञ्जाम-मण्डन 'सुरम्य उद्यान'
देइथिब केते कि उपहार।
आम्ब रम्भा बेत, लेम्बु नारिकेल
पनस, सपुरी, खजुरी ताज,
बिधिरक्षा पाइँ आसिथिब छुइँ
उद्यानर नाना फल रसाल।।

यद्वा वात! स्पृशसि तु ऋषे-कूल्यकां क्षीणतन्वीं
चम्पूगानं ललितमधुरं तोरगानां शृणोसि।
श्यामाङ्गीयं नु गिरि-सुषमा-स्फीत-वृक्षः प्रसन्ना
आश्लेषार्थं लसति चिलिका मुक्त-नीलाम्बु-केशी।। १५।।

कृशोदरी ऋषि- कूल्याकु परशि
आसिथिब येबे हे पबमान,
तीरबासीङ्कर रागिणि-मधुर
शुणिथिब चम्पू ललित-गान।
आलिङ्गन आशे तब पथ पाशे
चिलका आबेगे थिब अनाइ,
मुक्त नीलकेशी श्याम-शोभा-राशि
गिरि-शिरि-स्फीत-वक्ष मेलाइ।।

तस्याश्चारु-प्रवर-चिवुके लोल-हिल्लोलतालैः
चुम्बस्येवं मलय! यदि च स्फीत-लास्यं शुभांग्याः।
सर्वाङ्गं वा विपिन-पुलिने स्निग्ध-राग प्रवाहः
नौ-विभ्रान्ति-असर-पलकं वीक्ष्यते 'सोलरी' यम्।। १६।।

चञ्चन हिल्लोले चारु गण्ड स्थले
चुम्बिथिब येबे गाढ़े समीर,
सुन्दरी-सर्बाङ्गे उटिथिब रङ्गे
अपूर्व उल्लास कम्पाइ नीर।
पुलिन-कानने स्निग्ध-सनसने
खेलियाइथिब प्रेमलहरी,
हलियाइथिब केते केते नाब
देखुथिबे खण्डदूरे सोलरी।।

गण्डालिर्वा विविध-रुचिधृक् सारसो वा मरालः
तस्या वक्षस्यपि सुविलसेत् नीलमेघे वकालिः।
मीनाक्षीयं विचल-चिलिका प्रेक्षते वा यदा सा
ब्रीड़ानम्रा द्विगुणितगतिः शैलघात प्रपन्ना।। १७।।

माछरङ्का हंस खण्डालि, सारस
नाना जाति, खग-खचित मालि
चिलिका-बक्षरे दोलिथिव यथा
नील मेघे-धाड़ि धाड़ि बकालि।
फेड़ि मीननेत्र ओलटाइ गात्र
चाहिँला बेलकु चिलिका पुण,
शैलप्रतिघाते सरमे त्वरिते
चालिला बढाइ गति द्विगुण।।

श्रीक्षेत्रं वा भ्रम-हत-गतिः सिन्धुतीरप्रदेशे
आयास्येवं परम शुचि-धृक् पुण्य नीलाचले त्वम्।
स्वच्छन्दं वा चरसि सिकता-प्रान्तरे गन्धराज!
क्षेत्राधीशं नमसि रभसं दक्षिण-द्वारमाप्य।। १८।।

आसिथिब उड़ि भ्रमे पथ हुड़ि
सिन्धु सइकते श्रीक्षेत्रधाम,

पुण्य नीलाचले महोदधि जले
स्नाने होइथिब शुचि आराम।
सञ्चरि स्वच्छन्दे तुङ्ग बालिकुदे
ताल, लङ्काआम्ब छाया पन्तारे,
नीलाचलपति-पयरे प्रणति
करिथिब पशि दक्षिण द्वारे।।

मूर्द्ध न्यवं परभ-तुलसी-स्पर्शतः मोदचित्तः
प्रेम्णा भक्त्या स्पृशसि च सकृत् केतनं नीलचक्रे।
पुण्यप्राण! प्रवद वहते! श्रीपुरी-वार्त्तिकां मे
श्रोक्षेत्रेशः मनसि किमहो भावयेद् भावधायी।। १९।।

श्रीपदतुलसी शिररे परशि
लभिथिव महामोद अन्तरे
नीलचक्रचूले प्रेम-भक्तिभोले
देइथिव नेत उड़ाइ थरे।
पुण्य गन्धबह! कर अनुग्रह
कहि प्रिय पुरी सुसमाचार,
कन्दरनिबासी प्रभु ब्रह्मराशि
करुछन्ति एबे केउँ बिचार।।

गम्भीरायाः सुमधुरतरं ताड़नं प्रेषितं वा
आयुः क्षीणं भवति नियतं कालमीयद् ह्यपेक्षे?
आश्वास्यायं चिरशुभमयीं वार्त्तिकां भाषते वा?
सन्था लोकाः कथमपि कदा मुक्तिवार्त्ता गदन्ति?।। २०।।

गम्भीरारु किबा श्रीमुख-आदेश
पठाइअछन्ति देब मो पाइँ,
हे मलय बायु! क्षीण हुए आयु
रहिथिबि केते काल अनाइँ?
नीलाचलबासी मते कि आश्वासि
कहिछन्ति किछि शुभ बारता?
साधारण-सन्थ सेबक-महन्त
पकान्ति कि केबे स्वराज कथा।

श्रीक्षेत्रात्त्वं प्रसर-मलयोत्तीर्णदिग् वोत्तराशां
मार्गे तावद् ह्यपनयसि वै सत्यवादी-निकुञ्जे।
मञ्जुस्वानैः पठति च पिकः स्वागतिं दर्शनात्ते
मुग्धप्रेम्णा वकुल-मुकुलः दोलितः संचकास्ति।। २१ ।।

सारि दरशन क्षेत्र-प्रदक्षिण
करिथिब पुणि उत्तर-गति,
अटकाइथिबे पथरे टिकिए
सत्यबादी कुंजे तरुब्रतती।
सुमधुर ताने तब आबाहने
गाइथिब पिक स्वागतगीति,
वकुल तमाल देइथिबे ताल
पूरि उठिथिब परम प्रीति।।

गोपीनाथ-प्रिय-सुमुरली-रन्ध्रदेशे सुतानं
संरच्याशु त्वरित-सरणैः दोलयन् राधिकाङ्गम्।
युग्मामूर्त्तिः हसति रभसं लोलितं ह्यङ्गपुष्पं
मेघांगे वा नटति रुचिरं वक्र-मायूर-पुच्छम्।। २२ ।।

देउले प्रवेशि गोपोनाथ वंशी-
रन्ध्रे रचिथिब अस्फुट स्वन,
राधिका-अञ्चल उड़ाइ चञ्चल
छन्न करिथिब बेनिङ्क मन।
हसि उठिथिब युगल मूरति
खसि पड़िथिब श्रीअङ्गु फुल,
नबघन शिरे आहा कि रुचिरे
हलिथिब बाङ्क मयूरचूल।।

चम्पा-नागेश्वर-सुवकुलाः सेवती-जातिमुख्याः
गन्धव्यूहातिरचनपराः सौरभं संकीरन्तः।
गोपीप्राणाः विहरति मुदा गुप्त-लीला-विहारी
किंवा वण्यं तदपि मधुरं स्थानकं लोभनीयम्।। २३ ।।

बउल सेबती, मरुआ मालती,
चम्पा नागेश्वर जाति दअणा

चहटइ बास तब चउ पाश
करिथिबे गन्धव्यूह रचना।
बरजबिहारी गोपीमनोहारी
गुपते करन्ति यहिँ विहार
कि उपमा तारे सेहि सुषमारे
सेहि स्थान पटन्तर ताहार।।

कुञ्जं कुञ्जं प्रसरति सदा माधवश्री-विलासः
दैवंधाम प्रियतमपुरो लोकसे किं वसन्त?
अन्तेवासि-प्रिय-परिजनाः सोदरात्मीय-लोकाः
किंवा सर्वे नियत-सुखिनः षन्नचित्ताः न सन्ति?।। २४।।

वसन्तमाधुरी कुंजे कुंजे पूरि
पडुथिब यहिँ उछुलि सते,
देवदत्त धाम मो प्रिय आश्रम
पड़िछि कि तव नयनपथे?
मो सखा सोदर, प्रिय परिकर
अन्तेबासी बन्धु पड़ोशीगण
छन्ति त कुशले विरह-विकले
बिबश-बिबण्णं नुहेँ वदन।।

संचारन्ते यदपि वहते! वेत्ति कुंजं मदर्थं
गन्धोद्भारं मृदुमधुमयं प्रेरयत्याशु कान्तम्।
गन्धोद्भिन्नः सपदि चलितः वोत्तराशामवाप्य
मार्गश्रान्तिं ह्यपनयसि वा लिङ्गराजाधिपीठे।। २५।।

सत्यबादी कुंज-छुरिअना पुंज
जाणिथिले एथि तव संचार,
अवश्य मो पाइँ थिबे पठिआइ
मृदु मधुमय गन्धसम्भार।
गन्धभारे भरा आसिथिब परा
धीरे धीरे सिधा उत्तरदिके,
लङ्घि बिलग्राम कल कि विश्राम
लिङ्गराज देव देउलशिखे।।

सर्वग्रासी हरति सुकला-कौशलं काल एव
भूतेः शेषं मथित-हृदयः लौकयन्नुत्कलस्य।
रम्याः लोभ्याः कलित-मधुराः मन्दिराः भूमिलग्नाः
स्तूपाकारैरुपल-ततयो भान्ति वै गन्धराज।। २६।।

सर्वग्रासी काल प्राचीन उत्कल
कला-कउशल करे गरास,
बैभव-कङ्काल विलोकि अनिल
पाइथिब प्राणे गभीर प्रास।
केते चमत्कार मनोज्ञ मन्दिर
मिशिचि माटिरे पड़िछि पदा,
खण्ड खण्ड शिला खसि काहा देहुँ
उभा होइअछि पथरगदा।।

लावण्यान्ता ह्युपल-प्रतिमा कुत्र वा भग्नदेहा
मार्गे लग्ना विपिन-पुलिने वाऽपि पाद-प्रपन्ना।
क्वैवं प्राप्या निरुपम-रुचिः स्निग्ध-मूर्त्ति निकाशम्
क्षेत्राद् लभ्या ललित-सुषमा स्फूर्त्तिधात्री चकास्ति।। २७।।

शिल्पसिद्धि सीमा पाषाण-प्रतिमा
भाङ्गिअछि मुख तुटिछि कर,
पड़िअछि बाटे किबा बणपाटे
होइअछि काहिँ तुठपथर।
हलमुने खेते बाहारन्ति केते
खोदित अखण्ड अपूर्ब मूर्त्ति,
तुटिनाहिँ तिले लाबण्य-सुषमा
प्रकाशे सर्बांगे जीबन्त स्फूर्त्ति।।

क्षिप्ता गुप्तं किमपि निपुणैः शिल्पिभिः सद्य सृष्टा
किंवा मेना त्यजति विजने कणवजां कान्तिदप्तां।
मृत्स्तूपं वा जनयति हृदि द्राङ्नृप-प्राचीराभां
वल्ली-व्राताहत-सुषमाः कूप-वापी-प्रतिष्ठाः।। २८।।

लागे दक्षशिल्पी मने कि बिकल्पि
सद्य गढि रखिगला गोपने,

कि अवा मेनका चालिगला एका
शिशु शकुन्तला फिङ्गि बिजने।
नृपति नबर पतन प्राचीर
संचार देखाए मृत्तिकास्तूप,
लतागुल्मराशि गलाणि गरासि
केते सुगठित तडाग कूप।।

शक्तिभ्रष्टाः विपुल-पतिताः शर्वलिङ्गाः प्रकामं
ऐश्वर्य्याभा लसति नितरां बैभवं जीर्णशीर्णाम्।
ध्वस्तैश्वर्य्ये विलसति सदा लिङ्गराजाधिपीठः
योगारूढः प्रवरचरितः कल्पयोगि-प्रकल्पः।। २९।।

शक्तिछाडि अङ्ग केते शिबलिङ्ग
पड़िछन्ति काहिँ ता परिचय?
रहिछि केबल ऐश्वय्यर छाया
कि बिभव आहा कि विपर्यय।
विध्वस्त ऐश्वर्य मध्ये धरि धैर्ये
उभा लिङ्गराज तुङ्ग मन्दिर,
महाशममाने यथा बीरासने
योगारूढ कल्पयोगी शरीर।।

शैवलाक्तः विकृत-विमुखः दृश्यते शीर्णकायः
गम्भीरं वा भवविमुखतः वीक्ष्यते त्यक्तमोहः।
उग्रोदारं परिणतगतिं मन्दिरं शर्वकल्पं
भक्त्या वीक्ष्य प्रणतितितिभिः पादपूजावलग्नः।। ३०।।

शैबाल आबृत्त बिबर्ण बिकृत
दिशइ बिराट उन्नत काया,
गम्भीर उदासे चाहे चउपाशे
तुटाइछि कि से ए भवमाया।
से उरु उदार पुराण स्थबिर
सदाशिबकल्प शिबमन्दिर,
बिपुल आकृति बिलोकि प्रणति
करिथिब पूजा पादे समीर।।

वैषाद्याद्वा प्रभवति सखे! कालपातः न चाऽत्र
शीर्णैः दृश्यैः किमिति हृदयं दीर्ण्णमेवं भवेन्न।
शम्भूश्रद्धोपनतहृदयैरुत्तराशामवाप्य
स्तोकं गत्वा विलसतितरां मार्गकं खण्डशैलम्।। ३१।।

बेशि बेल तहिँ न थिब तरहि
किए से रहिब हृदय बहि,
से बिषादमय भग्न दृश्यचय
देखि काहा छाति पारिब सहि ?
शम्भूसुकल्याण घेनि समीरण
बहिथिब पुणि गति उत्तरे।
दि'पहण्ड याइ थिब बा न थिब
भेटिथिब खण्डगिरि पथरे।।

नो दृष्टो वेतिह-परिचितः खण्डशैलः प्रमाणं
गम्भीरं चोत्कल-कृतिचयं गाति यो देववाण्या।
भावोन्मादैः प्रथमसमये सौष्ठवालग्नचित्तः
चिन्तामग्नः चरण-पतितो लोकयन् मुग्धदृष्ट्या।। ३२।।

देखिनाहिँ केते दिनुँ खण्डगिरि
इतिहास यार अंके अङ्कित,
अमर अक्षरे नीरव गम्भीरे
गाए ये उत्कल गौरबगीत।
पड़े एबे मने प्रथम यौवने
सुषमा-पिपासा-भाव-उन्मादे,
खण्डगिरि शिरि देखि नेत्र मारि
चिन्ता निमगने वसिलि पादे।।

कालस्त्रोतो विकलित-मनोवेदनः चिन्तयामि
काव्ये यस्य रचनमतुलं काव्यकारैः न गीतं।
लोकश्रुत्या मधुरसुषमा विस्मृता यस्य काले
देशे वंधो! विगत-विभवा खारवेलस्य कीर्त्तिः।। ३३।।

कल्पनार पोते काल-प्रतिस्त्रोते
भासि देखिलि मुँ उज्ज्वल छवि,

इतिहास या'र न करे प्रचार
चित्रि नाहान्ति या' काव्यरे कबि।
कालर प्रभावे जनस्मृतिपटु
रूपरेख यार लिभिछि आजि,
कलिङ्गर सेहि अतीत विभब
ऐर खारबेल कीरतिराजि।।

शौर्य्यं वाद्यं श्रुतिपथगतं कुत्र वा युद्धसज्जा
गोप्यं मन्त्रं किमपि जयदा वार्त्तिका दूतगम्या।
तत्त्वार्थैर्वा श्रमण-पतिनः कुत्र वै सन्निमग्नाः
निर्घोषैर्वा प्रसरति मुदा कुत्र धर्मप्रचारः।। ३४।।

बाजे बीरबाजा काहिँ रणसज्जा
काहिँ बा लागिछि गुप्त मन्त्रणा,
दूरदेशु दूत बिजयबारता
घेनि आसि करे छामुरे जणा।
श्रमण सन्न्यासी दले दले बसि
चालिअछि काहिँ तत्त्वविचार,
गम्भीर निघोषे लोक उपदेशे
काहिँ बा अहिंसाधर्म प्रचार।।

शिल्पिवर्य्याः गिरितनुभिदा गह्वरं वा खनन्ति
दूतो गुप्तं कथयतितरां राज्यसद्देशसारं।
चित्तं व्यस्तं गिरितनुगतं कल्पनावीक्षितेन
दृश्यं स्याद्वा सपदि जरया जर्जरोऽयं चकास्ति।। ३५।।

खण्डगिरि अङ्गे शिल्पी शतशत
खोलन्ति निभृत गुम्फा निरते,
काहिँ गुप्तचर राज्य समाचार
एकान्ते जणाए नृप पुरते।
कल्पनार नेत्रे एहिपरि केते
दिशे चित्र खण्डगिरि शरीरे,
बिनष्ट सर्वस्व वृद्ध खण्डगिरि
विरक्त पराय उभा गम्भीरे।।

कालस्त्रोतोगमितमहिमा ह्युत्कल-स्फीतभूतिः
दीप्तं तेजः सपदि तनयाः तस्या वा विस्मरन्ति।
गाथां तस्य प्रवहति गिरिः स्फीत वक्षः प्रपन्नः
साक्षं दत्ते मलय! महिषी-वेश्म वै वीत-सौख्यम्।। ३६।।

महाकालनीरे बुद्‌बुद पराये
याइअछि मिशि कलिङ्गभूति,
कलिङ्गसन्तान भुलिछन्ति एबे
कलिङ्गर नाम गौरबस्मृति।
तथापि से गाथा रखिअछि गिरि
कालपराभबे देखाइ हिआ,
अति नारखार राणीहंसपुर
साक्ष्य देबा लागि अद्यापि ठिआ।।

सर्वं तावद् ह्युपललसितं मन्दिरं प्राङ्गणञ्च
वल्लोवृक्ष-ग्रसन मलिनं श्वापदाकीर्ण-गात्रं।
धर्मप्राणाः वहु-वचनिका मद्‌भुतामावदन्ति
प्रत्यक्षं वा स्मयजनकरो पादुकात्र प्रमाणम्।। ३७।।

चूलुँ मूलयाएँ शोभे शिलाकाये
प्रासाद प्राङ्गण गुम्फा देउल,
तरुलतादल रोधिछन्ति पथ
निवसन्ति यहुँ श्वापदकुल।
पदप्रान्तबासी साधु धर्मबेशी
कहन्ति अद्भुत बहु काहाणी,
देखान्ति श्रोताङ्कु प्रत्यक्ष प्रमाण
केते जीर्णास्मृति कठाउ आणि।।

सिद्धाः सन्ति प्रतिगिरिदरी गर्भके ह्यन्धकारे
गीतं येषां मधुरललितं श्रूयते वार्द्धयामे।
तेजोजालैः पथिकवदनात् संशयं ये वदन्ति
चित्रं नैतद्विपुलभुवने बिम्बिता चाऽऽत्मवृत्तिः।। ३८।।

तापस साधक अद्यापि अनेक
निबिड़ अन्धार गुहागरभे,

लुचि रहिछन्ति गभीर निशीथे
शुणायाए ताङ्क सङ्गीत नभे।
शुणिछि मुँ निजे कहन्ति से तेजे
पथिकबदने देखि संशय,
नुहे ता बिचित्र बाह्य विश्वेमात्र
प्रतिफले नर निज हृदयं।

आतिथ्याद्वा कृतगिरिपदाद्वन्दनः साग्रहं हि
स्वच्छन्दं वा विलसति वने गह्वरे मुक्तवेगः।
त्वद्गीतैर्वे स्वरमयगिरा कन्दरं गौरवान्तं
संगीतं वा मधुरललितं गाति वासन्तकान्त!।। ३९।।

अतिथि आदरे अति आग्रहरे
करिथब खण्डगिरि वन्दन,
वन उपत्यका गुहा गर्भे एका
स्वच्छन्दे संचरि थिब पवन।
तव आगमन सनपन स्वन
शुणि गिरि गुम्फा दरी-कन्दर,
गाइथिबे सीत गौरव-सङ्गीत
तुम स्वर सङ्गे मिलाइ खर।।

पूर्व-स्मृत्या द्विगुणितमहो दुःखकं भाति ह्यत्सु
सन्तापाद्वा विकल-कविता सान्त्वयत्येव चित्तम्।
किंवा दृष्टः मधुरवह ते! शुद्ध-साधु-प्रकाशः
येषां गीतेरमृत-सुझरः पीयते खण्डशैलैः।।४०।।

पूर्व सुख स्मृति-दुःख मने आसे
बढ़ाए विषाद द्विगुणा प्राणे,
तथापि उषत विषाद सङ्गीत
सन्तापे सन्तत सान्त्वना आणे।
कह समीरण कल कि दर्शन
शुद्ध साधु आत्मा गुप्त संचार,
खण्डगिरि चूले बहइ निरोले
या अमर सुधा-संङ्गीत-धार।।

काराद्वारं ह्युपसर सखे! श्रावय प्रीतिगीतिं
हृत्तन्त्री मे नदतु नितरां मन्मनः तद्गतं स्यात्।
किं वा दृष्टं मलय! निगद व्याजवृत्तिं विहाय
निर्विघ्नात्मा भवति सुखितः देश-सन्देशमाप्य।। ४१।।

ए मो काराद्वारे लागियाअ बारे
से दूर सङ्गीत शुभु मो काने,
कंपिउठु मोर हृद बीणा तार
मो अन्तर्ध्वनि मिशु से ताने।
कि देखिल आउ हे वसन्त वायु
कह बेगे कर नाहिँ छलना,
तुम्भे कि न जाण निर्वासित प्राण
स्वदेश सन्देश पाए सान्त्वना

उन्मुक्तायां वियति रचयन् "खण्डशैलस्य" रीतिं
मार्गे रुद्धः कथमपि महा-निम्नगाभिः स्वभावात्।
वेग व्याज-प्रगुणितगतिः ह्यादृतिं नो त्यजेस्त्वं
प्रेम्णा पाशैः क्षणमपि जनः कर्मठश्चेद् विलम्बी।। ४२।।

खण्डगिरि परे उन्मुक्त अम्बरे
करिथिव नव गति रचना,
बाटरे अटक कलकि कटक
महानदी नीलनीरबसना।
उद्वेग बाहाना करिथिब सिना
उपेक्षि न थिब ता समादर,
ये येड़े कर्मठ करे क्षणे मठ
हेलाबेले-प्रेम पाशुँ अन्तर।।

वक्षः स्फीतं ननु विचलितो वीचिहारस्तु तस्याः
तीरे शष्फाः स्मित-सुविनताः वीक्ष्य चाऽङ्गे विकारम्।
लोकेथा त्वं ह्युपगतशुचा सर्वथा 'वारवाटीं'
शूर-व्रात-प्रवारवसुधा शौर्य्य-हीनाऽद्य भाति।। ४३।।

फुलि उठिथिब महानदी-बक्ष
कंपि उठिथिब लहरीहार,

पठाखड़िपन्ति थिबे मथा पोति
मृदुहासे देखि अङ्गविकार।
देखिथिव तहिँ बारबाटी दशा
कि बेदना थिब मरमे बाधि,
उत्कलर वीर- बिहार-प्रांगण
आजि से उत्कल-शौर्य्य समाधि।।

कालो यातो नवतलगृहे भूप-यात्राऽवकाशे
राज्ञाः तावत् स्पृशति पवनं स्वेद-सिक्तञ्च भालम्।
विन्दुव्रातं लपन-भारितं नेत्रमार्गावलीढं
सिंचत्शीत-प्रसर-सरणैः मौक्तिकं तत् जहार।। ४४।।

थिला दिन येबे नबतल हर्म्य
युद्धयात्री राजा मेलाणि काले,
आणि नदीनीर सिञ्चिला समीर
स्वेदबिन्दु सिक्त महिषी भाले।
स्नेहसुधा बिन्धु येते मुखइन्दु
मण्डिला प्रसरि नेत्र युगले,
बिंचि सुशीतले हरिला कौशले
न पकाइ मुक्ता फलक तले।।

जित्वा युद्धं गजपतिरहो ह्यागतः जैत्रघोषैः
अर्घ्यस्ताल्या नृपतिमहिषी वन्दते स्मालिसंघैः।
भेर्य्यस्तूर्य्यः मलया नदिताः कंपितं केतनं च
जैत्रोद्घोषं नयसि विदिशं त्वं नु वासन्तरम्य!।। ४५।।

येबे रणे जिति पुरे गजपति
बाहुड़िले हेला जय घोषणा,
आलिगणे मिलि घेनि अर्घ्यथालि
कले बन्दापना बीर अंगना।
वाजिला महुरी शङ्ख, भेरी, तुरी
उड़िला अम्बरे जय केतन,
से बिजय घोष नेला दशदिश
कम्पाइल केतु तुम्भे पवन।।

वन्दापना-दीप्त-प्रदीप-नर्त्तनैः
वामाङ्गवासः प्रविकंपनैस्तथा।
सम्मोदिता भव्य वराङ्गनाततिः
त्वद्धृष्टतायै व्यपदेशरोषिणी।।४६।।

बन्दापना दीप नचाइल पुणि
उड़ाइल बामा मथा ओढ़णा,
तव धृष्टपण्णे पुलकित प्राणे
देले व्याजगालि बरवरणा।

सौभाग्यरंगे खलु तत्र वात! वा
दिष्ट्या सुरम्यं ह्यभिनीतमादरम्।
हा! वारवाटीमधुना विलोकसे
स्वप्नं नु सत्यं किमहो निवोध मे।।४७।।

बारबाटो अंगे से सौभाग्यरंगे
करिथिल अभिनय पवन,
आजि त देखिछ सेहि बारबाटी
देखिल सत्य कि अबा स्वपन।।

शौर्य्यं वीर्य्यं नवतलगृहं जैत्रवाद्यं ध्वजा च
शौर्य्योदात्त-स्वर-कवितया दीप्तभासः प्रजा वा।
पूर्वं दृश्यं स्पृशति नयनं "वारवाटी गड़े" किं?
नादे नादे हृदयकमलं कंपते किं वसन्त?।।४८।।

न'तल प्रासाद से सौर्य्य संपद
बिजय बाजणा बिजयध्वजा,
बीर कवितार शौर्य्य समादर
उत्कलर बीर बिक्रमी प्रजा।
वारबाटी गड़े नेत्र पथे पड़े
आजि कि से पूर्ब दृश्य पटल?
प्रतिबिम्ब शोभे प्रतिनादे कंपे
आउ कि सरित हृद कमल।।

वासो भाति स्मृतिविजड़ितं नष्ट-कर्पूर-भारं
तद्वा दिष्ट्याऽनल-कवलितं कोऽपि पांशु सहेत्?

मृत्स्तूपं वा मधुरवह ते! रक्ष-रिक्तां स्थलीं च
दर्शं दर्शं विगलितहृदा मानयेः गौरवं तत्।।४९।।

करपूर उड़ि कना थिले पड़ि
कना रखिथाए कर्पूर-स्मृति,
कना याइँ नाश रहिले पाउँश
किएसे धरिब देखि ता धृति?
उच्च माटिगदा रुक्ष रिक्त पदा
प्राचीन जातिर शक्तिमशान,
निरेखि मलय! सदय हृदय
होइ करिथिब शोके सम्मान।।

श्याम शष्पं स्पृशसि वहते! मृत्तिका-स्तूप-संस्थं
साश्रुल्पावैः कलयसि सखे! कालचक्रं करालम्।
रेणुव्रातः पतति महतो नाशधाम्नि यदा तत्
भक्त्या धूलि-प्रसर-भुवनं प्रेष्ठ-शिक्षां ददाति।।५०।।

से मृत्तिकास्तूप परे श्याम शष्फ
चुम्बिथिब अश्रुपूर्ण नयने,
कालग्रास नाश उत्कल पौरुष
कल्पिथिब तहिँ धराशयने।
महत निधने से महत स्थाने
पड़िथिले क्षुद्र धूलिकणिका,
भकति आदर करे ये ताहार
से दिए महत हृदय शिक्षा।।

ततो निमेषाद् विचरन् चतुर्दिशं
प्रवेक्ष्यसि स्पर्द्धित-शासनञ्चले।
वनाग्निना ततपुरुष-प्रवाहकैः
प्रतापयन् कानन-शैल-गह्वरम्।।५१।।

तहिँ मुहूर्त्तके अन्धारी मुलके
पशिथिब चउदिगे संचरि,
दाबानल सह परुष प्रवाह
तपिथिब बन शइल दरी।।

प्रजा तु यत्रातिभयेन 'भोज्यकं'
प्रदाय कालं नयति स्फुटं सखे!
न जीवने चास्ति धनेऽधिकारकः
कथाऽधिकारोऽपि तथा विड़म्बितः।।५२।।

ये राइजे प्रजा निति बलिभोजा
देइ अतिभये काटन्ति दिन,
कथा कहिबार नाहि अधिकार
नुहे धनप्राण निज अधीन।।

यस्मिन् वंशे कथमपि न वा दृश्यते क्षीणपुण्यात्
सौभाग्यं तत् प्रमद-विधुराः राजलोकास्तथाऽपि।
ग्रीष्मे शैले ज्वलति हुतभुक् वर्षकीं लोकपूर्य्यां
स्थानं चान्यत् सरति तु पशुः क्वैव शक्तिः प्रजानाम्।।५३।।

यहिँ राजवंशे क्षीणा पुण्यबशे
दिने नाहिँ काहिँ भाग्य लक्षण,
तथापि प्रपञ्च मदमत्त सर्व
न देखन्ति थरे फेड़ि ईक्षण।
निदाघे शइले दाबानल जले
प्रजापुरे जले बरष सारा,
छाड़ि पशु बन याए अन्य स्थान
प्रजा बापुड़ार काहिँ से चारा।।

स्वच्छन्दं वा प्रसरति गिरेः पादयोः स्वच्छधारा
हीरा-हार-भ्रममनुरणन् 'शुभ्रतोया' प्रवाहः।
नित्यं गान्तः पिकशुकखगाः चक्रवाकाः मरालाः
नानापुष्पैः मधुरविपिनं यत्र रागं तनोति।।५४।।

प्रसरे स्वच्छन्दे यहिँ गिरिपदे
निरन्तर स्वच्छ-निर्झरधार,
शुभ्रतोया नदी बहे निरबधि
बनकण्ठे यथा हीरकहार।
पिक-चक्रबाक हंस-कारण्डक
शुकसारी यहिँ गाआन्ति निति,

नाना फल फुल कानन मंजुल
जनमाए प्राणे पबित्र प्रीति।।

सरसि दोलित-शुभ्र-सरोरुहे
भ्रमर एव सुगुञ्जति मञ्जुलम्।
विहरतीह च कृष्णमृगव्रजः
सुतटिनी-तट-कानन-उत्सुकात्।।५५।।

शुभ्र शतदल सरे ढलढल
मंजु गुंजे अलि अस्फुट स्वने।
यहिँ कृष्णसार करन्ति बिहार
स्वच्छन्दे तटिनी तीर कानने।।

नित्या साध्वी सुरतरुगता मालती माधवी च
सद्भार्य्यावत् पथिक-हृदयं स्निग्धछायाप्रदानैः।
शस्योद्भारैः विहसति मही श्यामला तोषयन्ती
माधुर्य्यं वा सरलतरलं दिव्यराग-प्रसन्नम्।।५६।।

मालती माधबी सर्वदा साधबी
देवदारु-शाल-भुज-आश्रये,
सुगृहिणी सम दिअन्ति आराम
स्निग्ध छायादाने पान्थ-हृदये।
शस्य-आभरणे यहिँ अनुक्षणे
हसे सदा मही स्निग्ध श्यामला,
मानव माधुरी सरल चातुरी
प्रकृतिसहज छाञ्चरे ढला।।

विचित्रचित्रः कमलालयः सदा
निसर्ग-कास-द्युतिरेव मोहिनी।
पवित्रितं यत्सकलं कलान्वितं
प्रभावमुक्तं ननु शासकस्य वा।।५७।।

शुभ्र शोभामय कमला-आलय
प्रकृति-प्रकाश अति बिचित्र।
शासक स्वभाव बिना यहिँ सर्व
स्वरग-सुन्दर-भावे पवित्र।।

वनाद्वनान्ते खलु कन्दरे सखे!
सलीलगत्या वहसि स्वभावतः।
कदा च तप्तस्तु सुशीतलः कदा
कदा तु रौद्रातप-जर्जरो भवन्।। ५८।।

बनु बनान्तरे कन्दरु कन्दरे
अबाधे विहरिथिव से देशे।
काहिँ गुलुगुलि काहिँ वा शीतुलि
काहिँ बहिथिव हिङ्गुला बेशे।।

चक्रावर्त्तैः गुरु-परिगतैः धूलि-पत्राणि नीत्वा
व्योम्नि प्रेम्णा चरसि वहते! ह्युत्तराशामवाप्य।
दृष्टं किंवा जनगणसुखं दुःखकं तत्प्रदेशे
तेषां चित्ते प्रतिनवनवं चेतनं लक्ष्यसे किम्।। ५९।।

पत्र कुटाकाठि धूलि नालि माटि
चक्र आवर्त्तने उडाइ नभे,
उत्तर मुखरे आपणा सुखरे
चाहिँ थिब काहिँ क्रीडा सरभे।
अन्धारी मुलके प्रजा सुख दुःखे
कि देखि आसिछ कह पबन,
सहि नाना दण्ड दिअन्ति कि चण्ड
आसिअछि किबा नवचेतन।।

स्वक्षत्रे यः जनयति कृषि-द्रव्यकं दुःखदीर्णः
दारासुतैः सह वत! कदा तुष्ट-चित्तः भुनक्ति?
को राजा नो गणयति सखे! पुत्रवल्लोकजातं
राज्य-प्राणां निखिलसुखदां लोकते न प्रजां तु।। ६०।।

सहि खरावर्षा दुःखे पड़ि चषा
आपणा खेतरे करे ये चाष,
नोहि भयभीत घेनि दारासुत
खाए कि स्वच्छन्दे अन्नगरास।
केहि राजा जणे विचारे कि क्षणे
परजाए मोर पुअ समान,

परजाङ्क हित मो जीवन-ब्रत
परजा-सुखे मो सुखसम्मान।।

विना प्रजाशक्तिमिहास्ति नो गतिः
नृपस्य वा श्वेन-कपोत-भावकः।
प्रजा-जलोद्विन्दुभिरेव शोभते
सुराज्यसिन्धुर्मृप एव धारकः।।६१।।

विना प्रजाशक्ति राजार कि गति
राजा-प्रजा नुहे श्वेन-कपोत,
प्रजा जलबिन्दु मिलि राज्य-सिन्धु
राजा से सलिले केवल स्तोत।।

किमेव काराभवनप्रवासिनं
घृणाविचारैः निकषा न यासि माम्।
त्वमेव विश्वस्य विकाश-जीवनं
विभेदबुद्धिस्तव विस्मयाकरः।।६२।।

बन्दी बोलि मते किवा घृणा-नेत्रे
देख कि हे तेणु पाशे न आस।
भेदभाव तब लागे असम्भव
तुम्भे चराचर विश्व विश्वास।।

समाजघातैर्ननु जर्जरश्च यः
निसर्ग-सौन्दर्य्यसुखात् स किं च्युतः।
जले फले पुष्पचये दिवाकरे
निशाकरे व्योम्नि तथाधिकारकः।।६३।।

समाज निष्ठुर करे या'कु दूर
से नुहैं प्रकृतिप्रेमुँ अन्तर।
गगने पवने चन्द्रमा तपने
जले फले फुले ता अधिकार।।

नरं प्रति स्पर्द्धित-भेद-भावनं
नरस्य निःसर्ग-कृतौ समानता।
वसन्तवात! क्षणमेव शीतलैः
सुगंधरागैः स्पृश तप्त-मानसम्।।६४।।

नरप्रति पर करे अबि-वार
प्रकृति सकले देखे समान।
हे मलयानिल! सुगन्ध शीतल
प्रबाहे परश मो दग्ध प्राण।।

भजामि ते गौरवमेव शाश्वतं
त्वमेव विश्वस्य च जीवनं सुहृत्।
स्पृशाऽशु काराभवनं महोत्तम!
अनातुरं मुक्त-वसन्त-बोधक!।। ६५।।

करुछि कीर्त्तन सदा तब गुण
निखिल जगत जीव जीवन।
अबहेले बेले एथि काराविले
छुइँयाअ मते मुक्त पवन।।

पवित्रधामानि चरन्निहागतः
प्रसादभारैर्भर भालदेशकम्।
व्यथावसादः लयमेतु निर्भरं
प्रमादमोहश्च हृदस्तथा मम।। ६६।।

आसिअछ भ्रमि केते पुष्प धामे
लगाइदिअ मो शिरे प्रसाद।
से पुण्य परशे घुच्चु अवसाद
अपसरु हृदु मोह प्रमाद।।

सुभाषितानि

स्वदेशभूमौ ननु लीयतां तनुः
स्वदेशलोकाः मम यान्तु पृष्ठतः।
स्वराज्य-मार्गे यदि गर्त्तमस्ति वा
मदस्थि-मांसे परिपूर्णमस्तु तत्।। ६७।।

मिशु मोर देह ऐ देश माटिरे
देशवासी चालि याआन्तु पिठिरे।
देशर स्वराज्यपथे येते गाड़
पुरु तहिँ पड़ि मोर मांस हाड़।।

कुपौरुषं कातरतामलीमसं
रणेन वीरः म्रियते च मारयेत्।
न वीरभालेऽस्ति नु पृष्ठभङ्गता
न वा म्रियते स्फुट-भीति-शङ्कितैः।। ६८।।

कातरता सिना कापुरुषपण
वीर मारे अवा मरे करि रण।
पछघुञ्चा नाहिँ वीरर जातके
न मरे से केबे पराण-आतङ्क।।

प्रजार्थसृष्टिः विहिता स्वयम्भुवा
प्रजार्थवृष्टिर्निहिता शचीश्वरैः।
प्रजार्थमेवं रविचन्द्रतारका
प्रजा-शिवार्थं तटिनी-प्रवाहकः।। ६९।।

प्रजा लागि करे प्रजापति सृष्टि
प्रजा लागि इन्द्र करे जलवृष्टि।
प्रजा लागि उदे रवि-शशि-तारा
प्रजा लागि बहे शतनदीधारा।।

प्रजार्थमेतत् ननु राज्यशासनं
युगेयुगे शास्त्रकथेदृशी ध्रुवम्।
सनातनं भारत-राजधर्मकं
प्रजावनं रंजन-रक्षणन्वितम्।। ७०।।

प्रजा लागि राज्य प्रसार शासन
युगे युगे एहा शास्त्रर कथन।
मरतर राज-धर्म सनातन
परजा रक्षण पालन रञ्जन।।

स्वराज्यमार्गे प्रचलत् नयक्रमः
स वै दुराचार-विपाक-वर्जितः।
न कोऽप्यनाहार-शुचं भजिष्यति
धनि-प्रहारैर्न च दुर्बलस्तथा।। ७१।।

स्वराज्ये ए नीति होइव प्रचार
न रहिब आउ दुःख, दुराचार।
न सहिब कष्ट केहि अनाहारे
न मरिबे दुःखी धनीङ्क प्रहारे।।

Index